Paralegal Internships:
Finding, Managing, and Transitioning Your Career

Paralegal Internships:
Finding, Managing, and Transitioning Your Career

RUTH-ELLEN POST J.D.

Rivier College

WEST LEGAL STUDIES

an International Thomson Publishing company I(T)P®

Albany • Bonn • Boston • Cincinnati • Detroit • London • Madrid
Melbourne • Mexico City • Minneapolis/St. Paul • New York • Pacific Grove
Paris • San Francisco • Singapore • Tokyo • Toronto • Washington

Cover Design: Susan Mathews, Stillwater Studio
Cover Illustration: Matt McElligott

Delmar Staff

Publisher: Susan Simpfenderfer
Acquisitions Editor: Joan Gill
Marketing Manager: Katherine M.S. Hans
Editorial Assistant: Lisa H. Flatley

Production Manager: Wendy Troeger
Developmental Editor: Rhonda Dearborn
Production Editor: Laurie A. Boyce

COPYRIGHT © 1999
By West Publishing
an imprint of Delmar Publishers
a division of International Thomson Publishing

The ITP logo is a trademark under license.

Printed in the United States of America

For more information, contact:

Delmar Publishers
3 Columbia Circle , Box 15015
Albany, New York 12212-5015

International Thomson Publishing Europe
Berkshire House
168-173 High Holborn
London, WC1V 7AA
United Kingdom

Nelson ITP, Australia
102 Dodds Street
South Melbourne,
Victoria, 3205 Australia

Nelson Canada
1120 Birchmont Road
Scarborough, Ontario
M1K 5G4, Canada

International Thomson Publishing France
Tour Maine-Montparnasse
33 Avenue du Maine
75755 Paris Cedex 15, France

International Thomson Editores
Seneca 53
Colonia Polanco
11560 Mexico D. F. Mexico

International Thomson Publishing GmbH
Königswinterer Strasße 418
53227 Bonn
Germany

International Thomson Publishing Asia
60 Albert Street
#15-01 Albert Complex
Singapore 189969

International Thomson Publishing Japan
Hirakawa-cho Kyowa Building, 3F
2-2-1 Hirakawa-cho, Chiyoda-ku,
Tokyo 102, Japan

ITE Spain/ Paraninfo
Calle Magallanes, 25
28015-Madrid, Espana

1 2 3 4 5 6 7 8 9 10   XXX   03 02 01 00 99

Library of Congress Cataloging-in-Publication Data

Post, Ruth-Ellen.
      Paralegal internships : finding, managing, and transitioning your career / Ruth-Ellen Post.
         p.   cm.
      Includes bibliographical references and index.
      ISBN 0-7668-0394-5
      1. Legal assistants—Vocational guidance—United States. I. Title.
KF320.L4P67   1999
340'.023'73—dc21

98-42898
CIP

Contents

PART II

Finding the Right Setting   85

PART III

Mastering the Job 155

PART IV

Staging the Transition   203

Quick Tips

Point of Ethics

The Student's Perspective

Preface

GUIDING PHILOSOPHY

Paralegal Internships: Finding, Managing, and Transitioning Your Career builds on the premise that internships are most productive when students play an active role in their design and implementation. By empowering students to take responsibility for the success of their internships, this book helps students (1) ensure that the experience has genuine academic value, and (2) effectively use the internship as a springboard toward permanent employment.

FLEXIBILITY OF USE

This book is designed to allow maximum flexibility in its use. It can accommodate a wide range of paralegal program types and internship structures including two-year and four-year degree programs, nondegree certificate programs, internships that are closely monitored, and those that also provides detailed guidance for students who implement internship entirely on their own.

ORGANIZED BY FUNCTIONAL SEQUENCE

The book is divided into four parts, each part containing f responding to a major stage of internship development. Th I, "Finding the Right Setting," focus on defining what from an internship, provide an informational survey of p options, and include detailed instructions for obtaining pendently. Some schools will benefit by having stude months prior to the beginning of a scheduled internsh

Part II, "Beginning the Job," orients students to 1 ronments. Part III, "Mastering the Job," provides gui students on managing their time, their assignment relationships. Part IV, "Staging the Transition," sh ify the academic value of their experience and strengthen and solidify their employment search.

SPECIAL INSTRUCTIONAL FEATURES

Certain features appear throughout this book. Quick Tips provide added insights and reinforce key points in the text. The Student's Perspective offers firsthand observations from the student's viewpoint. Tables and Action Forms give students a concrete basis for factual understanding and enhanced planning. Exercises follow each chapter for use in an internship class or seminar or for students to complete on their own.

ETHICS AND PROFESSIONAL RESPONSIBILITY

A series of Subsections entitled Point of Ethics covers the full range of ethics issues that paralegal interns most often encounter. These subsections are specially marked for easy identification. For a sound, situational understanding of the principles involved, each Point of Ethics subsection is presented in the context of the internship activity in which it arises. Point of Ethics subsections may be supplemented by frequent reference to the National Association of Legal Assistants (NALA) and National Federation of Paralegal Associations (NFPA) Codes of Ethics and Professional Responsibility in Appendix 3.

ABOUT THE AUTHOR

An experienced attorney licensed to practice in three states and a tenured professor, the author has directed the internship program of an ABA-approved paralegal program for ten years and has been named in *Who's Who Among America's Teachers*. She served on the Board of Directors of the American Association for Paralegal Education and as chair of that organization's education committee for five years. Former chair of her state bar association's Task Force on Paralegals and member of the state bar Committee on the Unauthorized Practice of Law, she was responsible for completion of her state bar's first publication for lawyers on paralegal utilization. In 1997, the paralegal association of her state named her "Attorney of the Year" for her contributions to the paralegal profession.

Acknowledgments

The author would like to give special thanks and acknowledgment to the following for their great helpfulness: to Elizabeth Hannan for the opportunity to write this text; to Patty Bryant for her unflagging encouragement and advice; to Eleanor Dailey, Legal Administrator at Boynton, Waldron, Doleac, Woodman & Scott, P.A., for her many practical insights; to Elaine Rapp and Judith Lavoie for their meticulous proofreading; to Cassie McInnis and Rebecca Post Corliss for their visual artistry; to Rivier College for the sabbatical that made it possible to complete this text; and to Dale Corliss—my computer guru, gentlest critic, and partner through all of life's endeavors.

Introduction: Taking Charge of Your Own Experience

I am grateful for this experience. I'm walking away with research skills and drafting skills I never thought I had. Most of all, I now have confidence that I can succeed in this position, and I am no longer intimidated by the thought. Paralegalism is no longer just textbooks and reports. It's real.

—Anne Swenson Lane, 1990 Paralegal Graduate

Whether it is called a practicum, an internship, an externship, or some other name, the off-campus work experience is much more than just a requirement to be endured for graduation. It can be the most rewarding and valuable component of your entire education—if you manage it effectively. That means doing two things. First, you must prepare for your internship, carefully laying the groundwork for the best possible experience. Then, after your internship begins, you need to keep playing an active role in making the experience a truly useful one.

Compare, for example, the experiences of three paralegals: Joyce, Chris, and Alicia. Alicia graduated a few years ago after completing a senior-year internship option that her school created just that year. Joyce and Chris graduated more recently, following an internship in which students were encouraged to participate actively in creating valuable, practical experience.

Alicia

"It was a new program so I had no idea what to expect and neither, apparently, did my law office supervisor. I did receptionist work, ran the copier, and performed odd errands. I felt like a glorified 'go-fer' most of the time but I didn't feel it was my place to complain about it. They were the ones in charge—not me—and they always seemed too busy to be interrupted. They were nice people and somehow I got a good grade out if it. But I didn't feel as though I learned very much. It's sad to say, but I mostly felt as though it was a waste of time."

Joyce

"I deliberately chose to work with a lawyer who expects a lot from paralegals and keeps them challenged. I made sure she understood I needed as much litigation experience as possible and, fortunately, she was willing to give me all the responsibility I could handle. On the job, I checked around and found several people who were willing to help me out with instructions and advice: other paralegals, secretaries, and two other lawyers who were really helpful. I can hardly believe all I learned in just a few short months—it was incredible! When my internship ended, they gave me an unexpected bonus for my work, which apparently paid off for the firm. Also, my supervisor offered me a part-time paralegal position starting immediately, with every indication that it will soon become a full-time job as this busy office grows. You could say that this internship clinched my career."

Chris

"I wasn't sure, really, whether the paralegal profession was right for me. I knew that I wanted to go on to graduate school at some point to get a master's degree in public policy or some subject that would help me develop a career in politics. So I looked for an internship office where I could develop good paralegal skills while also exploring my other academic and political interests. I also wanted an environment that would be supportive of a so-called minority student like myself. I found all of that in Attorney Rodriguez's unbelievably busy, neighborhood law practice.

"He turned me loose to research some pretty sophisticated case law and medical data for an important appeal. It was hard work. I learned that litigation can sometimes bring significant changes in the law but that it doesn't necessarily bring the best solution for everybody, all of the time. And, man, I sure learned a lot about research! I'll continue working for Attorney Rodriguez after graduation, helping him with his law practice and also with his campaign for state senator—which should be a great experience. He's helping me sort out my grad school options, too. My internship really has been one of the best things that ever happened to me careerwise and also personally."

Joyce's and Chris's success, and Alicia's disappointment, cannot be dismissed as just a matter of luck. Chris and Joyce did not count on luck. They took definite steps to help create the positive experiences they had. To a large extent, they took charge of their own internships.

The purpose of this book is to show you what you can do, starting right now, to make your internship experience as valuable to you as Joyce's and Chris's internships were for them.

Part I

Finding the Right Setting

Chapter 1

What Are Your Learning Objectives?

How did Joyce, in the Introduction, know what work setting was best for her? How did Chris go about choosing among the options he had? The answer is this: they thought carefully about what kind of experience would be most beneficial to them at this critical turning point in their careers. They started by making definite decisions about what they needed to learn.

No two students are alike in this respect. Joyce loved the excitement of litigation and knew she needed to sharpen her litigation support skills to succeed in that field. Chris wanted to explore the paralegal profession as well as a possible career in politics, so he needed to be in a setting where both these options could be developed. In other words, both Chris and Joyce began with specific goals in mind. These goals then became the framework of their entire internship experience and the driving force behind the success they enjoyed.

Defining your learning objectives begins with knowing yourself. It ends with identifying what complements you—your strengths, your interests, and your personal vision of the future. It is the crucial first step toward taking control of your internship experience.

YOUR PROGRAM'S OBJECTIVES

Personal goals have to be defined within the context of your paralegal program's broader internship objectives. A program's internship objectives vary considerably from one school to the next. Some have a predetermined list of minimum professional competencies that all students must achieve. Some allow students to choose their own internship settings, whereas others offer internships by assignment only. Venturing beyond conventional law office work may or may not be permitted. Compensation for internship work may be disallowed in some schools and allowed in others, at least in certain circumstances.

QUICK TIP 1.1

At most schools, you can try a *noncredit* internship any time. It may be strictly a do-it-yourself arrangement with little or no oversight from your school, but it offers a great introduction to the professional environment and a head start toward a more substantial

Internship guidelines contain countless variations, but some generalizations can be made. They are usually designed to be consistent with two things: the particular goals of your paralegal program and the larger educational objectives of your school. You need to know what those objectives are and follow them with care. Your director is your best source of information on your school's internship objectives.

Generally, schools can structure a paralegal internship in three ways. The learning and career objectives you can pursue—and the academic requirements you must meet—depend largely on how your school defines paralegal internships. Consequently, your first step is to answer these questions:

1. Are you pursuing a do-it-yourself, *noncredit* internship?
2. Alternatively, are you seeking *academic credit* for your internship?
3. If this is a credit-bearing internship, is it structured as *legal specialty courses* as defined by the American Bar Association?

Being aware of these differences will help you plan your internship experience in the light of your program's objectives.

Noncredit Internships

Informal, noncredit internships are exciting because of the great flexibility they offer. Usually, students can arrange such internships on their own at any point during their schooling—even during the first term of their studies. Free of the standards necessary to earn college credit, students can "test the waters" in whatever career setting they choose. Reporting requirements and academic assignments are minimal or nonexistent, and grades are not usually involved.

Information about noncredit internship opportunities may be available through your paralegal program or through another office at your school, such as a career counseling office or an office coordinating student-volunteer positions. Often, students find noncredit internships completely on their own. Part I of this book shows you how to do that.

A noncredit internship can be as simple or as complex as you and your office supervisor make it. Ideally, it will be structured to give you many of the same paralegal learning opportunities described earlier. It may give you a chance to experiment with new and different career options—political activism, human services, or special research, for example. Best of all, it also allows you to start building a résumé.

Noncredit internships are especially useful to students who are unsure of their career choice. For a student just beginning paralegal studies, a noncredit internship offers a valuable introduction to the law office environment without restrictions on the kind of work that must be done there. Performing even simple clerical chores may be fine in a noncredit internship, allowing the student to experience, early on, the office culture and see how paralegals work.

In the Introduction, Alicia described her senior-year internship as inadequate for transition to permanent paralegal employment. At an earlier stage in her training, however, the same "receptionist" experience might have facilitated a more substantial internship later on. Her insider's view of the law office environment and her new professional contacts might have eventually paved the way to genuine paralegal assignments—worthy of academic credit and more impressive to future employers.

Internships for Academic Credit

If you are earning academic credit for your internship, you are likely to be held to academic standards that are similar, in many ways, to your other courses. This is because academic courses themselves must meet certain standards, particularly in degree-granting programs. Like you, schools are also subject to guidelines and requirements. These requirements tend to be more stringent whenever academic credit is granted.

As in other courses, you may be graded on your internship performance. You may have to meet a quota of internship hours and document their completion. Your school may require certain on-the-job work requirements and periodic reports or other assignments. Your internship may include classroom sessions. Completing all requirements well and on time is as important here as it is in any other paralegal course.

Although internships for academic credit might seem restrictive at times, they also bring significant advantages to the student-intern. Stricter standards reduce the risk of wasted internship time and help insure the educational value of the experience.

The Internship as "Legal Specialty Course"

Not all paralegal programs opt for American Bar Association (ABA) approval. But among the schools that have become ABA-approved, an additional set of requirements may exist. If your school structures paralegal internships to be what the ABA defines as a "legal specialty course," then certain things must be happening. Paraphrasing the applicable ABA guideline, an internship probably meets the definition of "legal specialty course" if it does the following:

- Includes instruction in a specific area of law, procedure, or legal process
- Is structured specifically for paralegals (not, for example, mainly intended for criminal justice students or business majors)
- Emphasizes paralegal skills, forms, documents, procedures, legal principles, and theories
- Is pertinent to paralegals' on-the-job performance[1]
- Promotes development of work-related paralegal competencies—not just knowledge of theoretical law[2]

To many students and educators, this situation describes the ideal paralegal internship anyway, regardless of ABA guidelines. It emphasizes career-oriented, truly educational objectives.

If these requirements apply to your internship, you can expect to work hard, be held to rigorous standards, and learn a great deal. In some ways, you may have the best of all possible worlds.

 ## WHAT BASIC JOB SKILLS NEED DEVELOPING?

Previous experience is your best guide to identifying general job skills and work habits that need further development. Students with an extensive work history will probably know which, if any, of the following skills still need attention. Students with little or no work experience should consider which of the following skills have perhaps been mastered in the classroom setting. Any items that have not been mastered should be added to your list of learning objectives.

Basic job skills include the following:

- Being present when expected, except in times of genuine illness or emergency
- Notifying your boss when you cannot be present

- Making sure you understand assignments correctly, asking for clarification when any doubt exists
- Estimating the amount of time that will be needed to complete an assignment
- Planning early, to insure completion before the due date
- Consistently meeting your deadlines
- Alerting your boss or instructor to serious difficulties
- Knowing how and where to get help when it is needed
- Often working beyond the minimum requirements
- Learning to anticipate the boss's or instructor's expectations
- Volunteering for unassigned tasks
- Establishing a cordial, personal relationship with your instructors or boss
- Establishing friendships with colleagues and coworkers
- Adapting to a new and different environment

Few students have mastered all of these skills. Make a list of the skills and habits you still need to develop and review that list often during the early days of your internship. Work at making those items a part of your own behavior on the job.

WHAT PARALEGAL SKILLS NEED DEVELOPING?

The various paralegal skills that students can acquire would fill whole chapters. Your paralegal course textbooks, paralegal associations' materials, and other references describe general paralegal skills and tasks. Many of these materials also describe tasks performed in various specialty areas.[3] Prospective interns should consult these sources for a broad overview, knowing that no intern can learn every skill listed.

As you glance through available lists, use the following guidelines to identify the paralegal skills that you most need to develop:

1. Determine what kind of job you most want after graduation
2. Use previous course experience as a guide
3. Use previous work experience as a guide

Where Do You Want To Be After Graduation?

Your internship should provide a springboard toward permanent employment. Having a clear picture of the kind of employment you want makes it easier to choose an appropriate setting and meaningful learning objectives.

Joyce was fortunate in that respect. She already knew what she wanted to be: a litigation paralegal for a private law firm. This awareness made it possible for Joyce to narrow her focus. All she had to do was identify the skills needed by litigation paralegals to know what she needed to learn and practice in her internship. Similarly, students interested in real estate work, family law, or administrative advocacy, to name a few examples, can identify from available lists a definite "skills" base for developing during their internships.

Naturally, not all paralegal students begin their internships with such definite career goals. A career focus that takes time to develop often endures longer than one that is chosen hastily.

Before settling on their initial career goals, both Joyce and Chris spoke to several working paralegals, including graduates of their program and members of the local paralegal association. They asked these professionals what a typical workday was like, what they liked most about their jobs, and what they enjoyed least. These conversations gave Joyce and Chris a fairly good preview of large offices, small offices, different law practice specializations, and related fields. What they learned from these discussions helped both of them develop a clearer picture of where they, themselves, would eventually prefer to be.

Be sure to convey your employment goals to your director or career advisor and to the internship supervisors with whom you interview. Ask for their assistance in identifying internship tasks and on-the-job learning opportunities appropriate to your goals. After those tasks and learning opportunities have been identified, do not lose sight of them. Make a checklist for verifying what you have accomplished during your internship and what remains to be tried. You will later incorporate those accomplishments into your résumé.

Previous Course Experience as a Guide

As you consider the possibilities, look back at the paralegal courses you have taken with two questions in mind. First, which subjects did you enjoy most and want to learn more about? Your internship offers the chance to expand your experience in those subjects. Draw up a list of the tasks you want to experience, and bring that list to your interviews with prospective supervisors. Ask each internship supervisor whether you will have an opportunity to work on those tasks.

Second, with which important subjects did you have difficulty? Most legal work requires some familiarity with basic litigation procedures and fundamental research skills. If these or other key courses were a problem, you may still have an opportunity to catch up on those skills. Using the "list" technique just described, try to confirm the chance to fill these educational gaps during your internship.

"Of all the paralegal courses I have taken, real estate law was my worst subject," Anita lamented. "I never felt I really had a grasp of it. However, much of Attorney McDowell's work centers on real estate. This internship has given me a far better understanding of how to solve title questions, make sense of mortgage documents, and apply real estate concepts in general. This was my last chance to learn these things before graduating, and I'm really glad I did."

Previous Work Experience as a Guide

Sometimes, previous jobs provide useful clues about the kind of paralegal position a student should pursue. A pleasant experience in a corporate setting, for example, may suggest that a law-related office in the same setting would also be a good place for a paralegal internship. The same can be said for prior experience in a governmental agency or in a nonprofit association. Special knowledge about such organizations and familiarity with how they operate may make the internship supervisor all the more eager to have you on board.

Also, firsthand knowledge about a certain industry is valuable if that industry is represented among the law office's major clients. Information in the *Martindale-Hubbell Law Directory* on the business clients of law firms in your area might reveal useful links to your prior business experience.

Samuel, for example, came to the paralegal program with several years of experience in the mortgage department of a bank. His experience made him a valuable intern to law offices practicing in real estate and banking matters. Chignon, on the other hand, had spent two years as a computer technician before beginning her paralegal studies. Her technical experience opened doors for her with a local patents attorney serving clients in the computer industry.

What about younger students whose job histories may be limited? Prior work as a sales clerk or waiting on tables may not seem immediately useful

> ## QUICK TIP 1.2
> Getting a "fix" on the future is hard for younger students. They may need more time—and much more fact gathering—than their older peers. If you lack a significant work history, gathering insights from other paralegals will make you much more confident about the choices you face.

> ### THE STUDENT'S PERSPECTIVE 1.1: CHRIS
> ## Where Do I Want To Be After Graduation?
>
> Chris's vision of the future was not yet entirely clear, so he wanted to keep his options open. He decided to intern for a small neighborhood general practice where he would be free to choose among a wide variety of assignments and develop broad, diversified experience. His fascination with politics led him to choose a lawyer-supervisor who shared that interest and was preparing to run for political office. Chris knew he would be able to observe that process and gain some political knowledge and skills.
>
> After a few weeks on the job, a major research project gave him the chance to acquire the kind of advanced research and writing skills he would need in graduate school, so he stayed with that project. As his internship progressed, Chris improvised occasionally, jumping at new opportunities as they arose.
>
> Now, as a paralegal graduate, his career focus is still in its formational stage. That is fine with him. He is confident that the perfect career will become clear to him soon enough, after he has acquired additional knowledge and experience.

in a law-related environment. Nevertheless, all previous employment reveals something about your work habits and preferences. It may give you important clues about what kind of setting will work best for you.

For example, did your job require you to work quickly under pressure, making rapid decisions about customers' problems? Were your responsibilities mostly people-oriented or did you work alone, quietly? How you were able to handle these and other job requirements may give you useful ideas about the kind of internship environment you should seek.

WRITING AND COMMUNICATIONS SKILLS

Most law office employers report good writing skills and effective communications as absolute requirements for all paralegals. That is because, in legal work, words are the tools of the trade. Becoming proficient at their use must be a key learning objective for every student.

Writing: A Top Priority

Your internship provides a wonderful opportunity to learn the language of the law in a setting where you are constantly surrounded by it. Use this opportunity to its fullest. Plan to observe how letters, memoranda, and other office documents are written. You will need to note what formats are used, how sensitive matters are handled, how difficult concepts are made understandable to clients, and what sets writing apart as "professional." Include these skills among your learning objectives.

Be sure your writing is up to the appropriate college level before you begin an internship. Submit a sample to a writing instructor and get help if there are problems. Many colleges offer remedial writing instruction at little or no additional cost. After graduation, such valuable assistance may never again be so readily available.

Professional Communications Skills

In the internship office, students lacking prior business experience will need to observe how phone calls are handled and how clients and others are greeted. Younger students will notice, too, that slang is used less often and the "umm's" frequently heard among classmates are rarely heard in the office. You may need to imitate the more professional speech patterns used in your new setting. Include these communications factors among your personal learning objectives.

Dina recognized this need very quickly. "I really don't like speaking over the phone. During my first week at the office, I had to call several contractors for information, so I had to start sounding 'polished and professional' fast! Now that my internship is ending, I still don't enjoy phone work very much but I know how to handle it effectively."

Students working in law offices for the first time usually pick up a good deal of legal jargon. Using it among other professionals in the office often saves time, smooths communications, and makes the intern a part of the law office culture. With clients and others not trained in the law, however, legal jargon frequently has the opposite effect: it intimidates. It prevents good understanding of principles and procedures. Knowing when to use—and when to avoid—legal jargon should also be among every intern's learning objectives.

Becoming Computer-Competent

The overwhelming majority of law offices use computers extensively. To succeed as paralegals, students need to learn everything they can about burgeoning office technologies. Students who do not will be left behind. Even if you have learned the basics in a computer course, take every opportunity to learn still more during your internship.

Among your learning objectives, consider including experience in some of the following:

- Word processing and document assembly
- Database management
- Storage and retrieval of litigation documents
- Using spreadsheets
- E-mail and interoffice network systems
- Internet research
- Voice recognition systems
- CD-ROM legal research
- On-line computer-assisted legal research
- Portable document imaging
- On-line retrieval of government documents[4]
- Timekeeping and billing software
- Specialized legal transactional software
- Electronic filing of court documents

Justice Sandra Day O'Connor of the United States Supreme Court foresees the filing of court documents on computer disk and perhaps even telecommuting to court.[5] In many federal and state jurisdictions, courts have begun implementing electronic filing systems.[6] Increasingly, paralegal graduates with experience in such systems will have an advantage over other job candidates.

In every internship interview, ask about the office's computer systems. What opportunities will you have to develop career-related computer skills? Look for a good match between the skills you need for maximizing your career options and the learning opportunities available at each office.

QUICK TIP 1.3

In doubt about your specific career direction? Go for the most varied experience possible. A small or solo law practice often gives you a well-rounded, versatile background for selective development later in your career.

BEGINNING AS GENERALIST OR SPECIALIST?

For our purposes, *generalist* refers to a paralegal whose knowledge and skills are versatile enough to support several different areas of law practice—in a small, general practice firm. Such work may include, for example, litigation in the local county courts, divorce work, residential real estate transactions, simple wills and estates, and work with closely held corporations and small businesses.

The number of attorneys who can accurately call themselves *general practitioners* is dwindling. Most limit themselves to three or fewer areas of practice, accepting work outside of those areas only occasionally. General practitioners tend to be in small, neighborhood offices and in rural areas.[7]

Specialist, for our purposes, means someone whose knowledge is highly developed in one area of legal work but not necessarily in others. Although most lawyers are not legally permitted to call themselves specialists,[8] most work almost as if they were—particularly in larger firms. The paralegals who work for them become similarly specialized. Examples might include a patents paralegal in a corporate legal department or a litigation support paralegal in the environmental litigation division of a large law firm.

Becoming Well-Rounded in a General Practice

The students who benefit most from a highly varied, generalist internship are those who are not sure about what legal work suits them best. Many paralegal interns find themselves in this situation. In a small, general practice firm, students are likely to experience several different areas of legal work. In a large firm, on the other hand, such diversified experience happens only if the intern is allowed to accept assignments from several different departments, which can be difficult to arrange.

After completing a well-varied internship experience, students have a more concrete basis for making future career choices. Wonderful personal discoveries are often made along the way. Liz, for example, enjoyed all her legal specialty courses equally well and could not decide on a specialty area, so she interned with a small general practice. On the job, she discovered that some tasks were much more interesting than others. "I never dreamed that real estate could be so exciting," she later reported, "but it is! Now I know what I want to do after graduation!"

Barbara, on the other hand, interned with a small general practice because this was precisely the career she preferred. Barbara knew she performed best with highly varied, rapidly changing work. Focusing on the same subject every day would not be satisfying to her. She also remembered from summer jobs that she was most comfortable in an informal, loosely structured environment. She found all of that in the smaller offices she contacted.

Interning in a small, general practice firm sometimes limits your initial job opportunities to similarly small firms. Also, salaries at small firms tend to be lower than at larger firms and opportunities for promotion may not exist. Factor these considerations into your long-range plans, which might include a second foray into the job market a few years later for a more specialized (and perhaps higher-salaried) position at a larger firm.

In short, a small general practice is the best setting if

THE STUDENT'S PERSPECTIVE 1.2: RENÉ
Choosing a Specialist or Generalist Focus

As René began selecting an internship office, she remembered a conversation she overheard at a paralegal association meeting. A specialist in foreclosure work was worried about where his career was headed. "I can't believe how things have changed, or how fast," she heard him say. "Until this year, the demand for people skilled in real estate foreclosures was so great, I could have had my pick of high-paying jobs. But now, my boss is talking about cutting back on my hours! I'm glad the local economy is improving, but I'm worried about what this does to my career. It's been years since I did anything else."

René was sure she would love environmental law and was considering an internship with an environmental law activist group. But now she wondered: would she eventually end up like the paralegal she overheard at the meeting? She decided to talk to as many people as she could about this.

An older lawyer helped René look at what he called "the big picture." "Economics is what drives a lot of our careers," the attorney admitted. "For example, bankruptcy work kept many of us busy in the past, but now that's dropping off. As a result, some offices have had to make major changes. My feeling is that most areas of legal work have their peak times and their lean times—none of us is immune to that phenomenon. The key is to remain as versatile as you can."

Armed with that advice, René went ahead and took the environmental law internship. But she also kept careful track of the general litigation skills she was developing in her internship work—just in case she might need to highlight those on a résumé some day.

- You are not sure what kind of legal work you will enjoy most
- You want to experience several different practice areas
- You like highly varied work, "switching gears" easily from one subject to another
- You are uncomfortable in highly structured organizations
- You prefer somewhat less formal working relationships
- You do not mind playing many different law office roles
- Highest possible salary is not your immediate goal
- Access to higher promotion levels is not critical at this stage in your career

Seeking a Specialty Focus

Becoming an expert in personal injury litigation support, estate planning, or blue-sky regulations (to name a few examples) can lead to well-paid participation in a high-powered team of legal professionals in a prestigious firm. It can open the door to settings in which supervisory paralegal positions, and other opportunities for promotion, can be pursued. With experience and hard work, top paralegal specialists sometimes find themselves being simultaneously sought by more than one firm.

Students often wonder what disadvantages could possibly exist in such an upbeat scenario, but there are a few. For example, the fast pace is not for everyone. The burnout rate is high in fields where work becomes repetitive. Also, limiting yourself to a highly specialized area can sharply limit your career options later on. If you ever become disenchanted with your specialty, finding similarly paying work in a different practice area can be difficult. These factors make it important to seek out opportunities for involvement in other subject areas at all stages of your career.

Interning as a specialist in a larger firm is ideal if

- You have a strong preference for a certain field of practice
- You prefer a well-structured environment
- You seek a larger, more prestigious office
- Higher salary is more important to you than career flexibility at this stage
- You want access to promotional opportunities as soon as possible
- You are comfortable handling the same kind of work, or same subject matter, on a daily basis
- Your research shows that this specialization has a reasonably solid future

PARALEGAL, PRELAW, OR BOTH?

Most paralegal students plan to become career paralegals, and it is for them that the entire paralegal program is usually designed. However, a sizable minority has law school on their minds as well. Whether viewed as a distant prospect or as an immediate goal, law school candidacy introduces special considerations for the paralegal intern.

Law school requires an enormous commitment of time (at least three additional years of very demanding work) and can strain financial resources to their limits. Before making such a big commitment, students should learn as much as possible about what it is really like to practice law. To the extent that your school's internship guidelines allow, the law-school-bound students should include this objective among their personal internship goals.

Additional learning objectives for future law school candidates might include

- Meeting lawyers in different areas of practice
- Asking them about how they spend their workdays
- Observing court proceedings
- "Shadowing" a practicing attorney for a few days
- Finding paralegals who considered law school and decided against it, and learning why
- Meeting lawyers who began as paralegals and learning how that career progression was helpful

Maria, for example, planned to begin her law school applications a few months after graduation while working as a paralegal. During her internship, she watched the lawyers just as closely as she watched the paralegals and had discussions with both about their respective professions.

Particularly revealing was what she observed about a new associate, hired just out of law school. The associate was assigned lengthy research tasks and spent most of his time alone in the law library. Unlike the office's paralegals, most of whom had frequent client contact, the young associate rarely saw clients. This observation gave Maria second thoughts about rushing into law school.

Upon graduation, she accepted a position as a paralegal in the corporate department of a medium-sized law firm and she is very happy with her decision. "Law school remains in the back of my mind," she admits, "but I'm not rushing into it."

EXERCISES

1. Verify all internship requirements with your program director. Be sure you understand the answers to the following questions:
   a. Is academic credit granted for your internship? If so, how many credits?
   b. How many hours of internship work are required? Will your work schedule be flexible or fully set in advance?
   c. Will you be given a list of prearranged placement options or must you seek placement on your own?
   d. How much lead time will you have to arrange placement?
   e. What reports will you have to submit?
   f. What records will you have to keep?
   g. What are the responsibilities of your office supervisor to you and to your program?
   h. Will the internship include a classroom component? If so, verify the class schedule.
   i. Who will be evaluating you and what criteria will be used?
   j. Does your program have requirements for the following? If so, what are they?
      (1) The kind of work interns are *permitted* to do.
      (2) The kind of work interns are *required* to do.
   k. Does your paralegal program specify certain learning objectives for paralegal interns? If so, what are they?
   l. Is lawyer supervision required or are non-law-office positions a permitted option?
2. Consider whether you want to pursue an internship in a general practice area or in an office that provides specialized experience, and then do the following things. First, list three reasons for your decision. Second, list whatever drawbacks there may be. Then discuss these pros and cons with at least three professionals from the following categories: working paralegals, lawyers, your program director, paralegal instructors, and a placement specialist on your campus. Add new viewpoints to your list. When your list of pros and cons is complete, reevaluate it. Has your decision been strengthened or changed?
3. For students thinking about law school: meet with two or three attorneys, individually. Ask each of them why they went to law school and whether they would do it again today. Ask what skills were needed to do well in law school. Add those to the list of skills you want to learn in your internship.
4. Review the list of basic job skills appearing in this chapter. Identify the things on that list that were most difficult for you in prior job situations. Add those items to your learning objectives for your internship.
5. List the paralegal courses you have taken. Next to each course, list the skills or practice assignments that you found difficult or did not completely understand. Add the most important of these items to your learning objectives.
6. Find the best sample of your written work that you have on hand. Take it to a writing instructor for evaluation, asking him or her to identify writing skills needing improvement. Consult your writing instructor or your program director regarding the availability of writing workshops, tutoring, or coaching for improvement in those areas. Also, add "improved writing skills" or "improved drafting skills" to your list of learning objectives, noting the type of written work most needing attention.
7. Speak to a paralegal who does the kind of work you plan to do during your internship. What kind of computer skills does this paralegal use in his or her

work? Do you have those skills? If not, add them to your list of learning objectives. Begin working on those objectives before your internship starts.

8. From the lists you have compiled as a result of the preceding seven exercises, create one cohesive list of learning objectives for your internship.

Preserve this list. Items on this list will eventually become a part of your learning contract with your office supervisor, as explained in Chapter 5. You will also need to check these items periodically (weekly or biweekly) during your internship to monitor the achievement of your goals, as explained in Chapter 15.

ENDNOTES

1. See *Guidelines for the Approval of Legal Assistant Education Programs* (American Bar Association Standing Committee on Legal Assistants, 1997), Rule G-303, Section D.
2. Ibid., Rule G-301, Sections A and C.
3. For a detailed description of numerous practice areas, see National Federation of Paralegal Associations, *Paralegal Roles and Responsibilities* (Kansas City, MO: Author, 1998). (A 1996 version is also available.) Also see William Statsky, "Paralegal Specialties: A Dictionary of Functions," in *Introduction to Paralegalism*, 5th ed. (St. Paul: West, 1997), 47–75.
4. For a more complete survey, see Job Klemens, "Legal Technology Offers Double-Edged Efficiency: Tips to Ensure a Smoother Transition," *Law Practice Management* 20 (March 1994): 40–43.
5. See Sandra Day O'Connor, "The Role of Technology in the Legal Profession," *Law Practice Management* (March 1994): *20.*
6. For example, electronic filing is replacing faxed filings in Arapahoe County, Colorado. See Judith Baxter, "Colorado's 18th Judicial District Launches Electronic Filing," *National Paralegal Reporter* (Winter 1997): 36.
7. A more complete discussion may be found in the 1992 Report of the ABA Task Force on Law Schools and the Profession, entitled *Legal Education and Professional Development—An Educational Continuum* (often referred to as the "MacCrate Report") by Robert MacCrate et al. (American Bar Association, 1992): 38.
8. Traditionally, only three legal specialties were recognized: patents, trademarks, and admiralty. In 1990, the ABA created Model Standards for Specialization in twenty-four specialties for states to consider. As a result, a sizable minority of states have adopted plans for the recognition and regulation of additional areas of specialization for attorneys. Consult your state bar association for up-to-date information on attorney specialization in your jurisdiction.

Chapter 2

Choose Your Destination

Now that you have decided on the learning objectives that are most important to you, the next step is to examine the wide variety of internship settings that are available in your community. Naturally, different offices and different areas of specialization will emphasize different skills.

What follows are descriptions of the many paralegal and law-related options that are available in many areas of the country. Information is provided under six major categories. The first section describes conventional law office options including large and medium-sized firms, small firms, sole practitioners, and publicly funded law offices. Opportunities in the corporate sector are outlined in the second section. For students whose programs permit internships in law-related but non-law-office settings, the third and fourth sections relate opportunities in allied fields and the burgeoning market for paralegal training in the government sector. Working with an independent paralegal and working in mediation are described in the fifth and sixth sections. The chapter concludes with a few words of advice for the student whose career direction is undecided.

After completing this chapter, you should be able to identify two or three office categories that appear to meet your learning objectives and career goals.

 ## CONVENTIONAL LAW OFFICE OPTIONS

For decades, most paralegal students have performed their internships in private law firms. Law offices are "private" if they are owned and managed by the attorney-partners or attorney-shareholders and financially supported by clients' fees. Though other internship options are also becoming very attractive, this remains the internship setting that most students prefer, and with good reason. *This is where almost three quarters of surveyed paralegals report being employed.*[1]

The Large and Medium-Sized Law Firm

For our purposes, we define *medium-sized firms* as those having eleven to thirty lawyers and *large firms* as those with thirty to fifty lawyers. About 14 percent of American lawyers in private practice work in large and medium-sized firms as defined here.[2] Another 14.6 percent of American lawyers in private practice work in firms of over fifty attorneys.[3] In major metropolitan centers, such as New York or Los Angeles, students can find law firms with three to five *hundred* lawyers— what some call *mega-law firms*.

Large and medium-sized firms tend to have formal, often complex organizational structures, as would be expected in any sizable business. The larger the firm, the more intricate its organizational makeup tends to be. Legal work is divided among various departments or divisions within the firm, such as for corporate work, personal injury litigation, criminal defense, family law, and so on. Typically, the attorneys and paralegals in each department work exclusively in their assigned area of law. Because their work is so sharply departmentalized, these firms frequently want paralegals with specialized expertise and extensive experience within each specialization.

Lasting changes in the way law is practiced often originate with larger firms. In time, small offices usually follow the lead of the larger ones. So it is not surprising that the movement toward effective use of paralegals was led primarily by larger law firms. It was in that setting that the principles of paralegal utilization were often developed and, to some extent, perfected. The advantage for paralegals in large law firms is clear: challenging work in a well-defined, respected role.

However, a disadvantage may also be emerging. *Perhaps because they led the way in paralegal hiring for so long, paralegal opportunities in large law firms are no longer increasing significantly.* Many large firms have reached the attorney/paralegal ratio with which they are comfortable and now hire mainly to replace departing staff, who usually are highly experienced. Consequently, entry-level paralegals are hired less frequently by these firms.

Even where the local economy is growing, big firms are often expanding their technology—not their staff.[4] Consequently, they are very selective about

THE STUDENT'S PERSPECTIVE 2.1: DEBORAH
Aiming for the Top

Knowing how selective big firms can be, Deborah felt some apprehension when she sought an internship at the largest firm in her city. "I had been following the classified ads for the last year and a half and every time this firm advertised, it was for someone with five years' experience in some narrow, esoteric field I hardly recognized. I wanted desperately to intern for a big-time firm like this but didn't think I had much of a chance.

"I managed to get a meeting with the paralegal manager there, who was impressed with my earlier experience in the state environmental protection office and my high grade point average in paralegal studies. The law firm's ads, she said, didn't assume the kind of advanced paralegal training I had or my prior work experience, which was valuable to their environmental litigation department. I was thrilled when she agreed to take me on as a student-intern 'to see how it goes,' as she said.

"And it's going really well. I'm hoping that, when the internship ends, they'll keep me on as a paid document clerk in the environmental law department. And it's upward and onward from there!"

whom they hire. Most students would be wise to target this setting as their second job, a few years after graduation. That way, they will be better qualified for the "experienced-only" slots that large firms most often want to fill.

Some large and medium-sized firms have begun structuring their entry-level hiring around in-house internship programs of their own creation. This arrangement streamlines the hiring process and provides greater control over entry-level selection and training. Students who can identify offices that work this way can sometimes combine their school's internship program with one already in place at such a firm, gaining a big advantage over other entry-level candidates.

Large law offices are known for having perhaps the highest expectations for hourly billing. The larger the firm, the greater the pressure may be to meet a stated or unstated quota of billable hours, often from fourteen hundred to sixteen hundred per year.

A more favorable factor is the ranking system that larger firms often use to classify and promote paralegal staff. It generally works like this: at the lowest end of the ranking system is the first tier of entry-level paralegals, who may be known as "document clerks." In time, top performers in this group may be promoted to a second tier of experienced, more highly paid paralegals. Some offices have a third tier of senior paralegals. In addition, there may be a paralegal manager whose job it is to hire, train, and manage the office's paralegal staff. This hierarchy creates exciting opportunities for promotion, which small offices, with fewer paralegals, can rarely offer.

In a large or medium-sized firm, students will often find

- A high degree of specialization among lawyers and paralegals
- Well-defined tasks and clear job expectations
- High hourly billing quotas for paralegal employees
- A tradition of respect for paralegals as professionals
- Reluctance to hire the inexperienced
- Very high expectations for paralegal competence
- Strict educational requirements (a four-year degree may be the absolute minimum)
- Top compensation levels and a wide range of benefits
- High levels of formality in conduct and appearance
- Significant opportunities for promotion
- In-house programs for continuing paralegal education
- In-house internship programs in some firms

The Small Law Firm

Small firms may be thought of as those that employ from two to ten lawyers. About 25 percent of America's lawyers in private practice work in law offices of this size.[5] The major characteristic of this segment of law offices is their great diversity—and the fact that they should be individually researched by anyone who hopes to approach them effectively (as should all offices).

Some small law offices are "boutique" firms catering to clients in a certain industry, such as entertainment or the arts. Some are high-volume "legal clinic" offices offering fairly standardized legal services (such as uncontested divorces, bankruptcy, and auto accident cases) for middle- and working-class clients at lower costs than other firms. Many follow the classic "large firm" model of law practice but on a smaller scale and often with greater flexibility in management and assignment policies.

These offices also vary greatly in the manner and extent to which they use paralegals. Some, such as the clinic-type firm, delegate heavily to paralegals and employ a proportionately larger number of them. Others have yet to catch the trend toward greater paralegal involvement. In fact, schools often report that many small and medium-sized firms do not yet understand the benefits of using paralegals effectively. Consequently, students sometimes encounter inexplicable resistance among firms in this group.

Relative latecomers to full paralegal utilization, this segment of law practice will probably produce much of the future growth in paralegal employment. Educating them to understand the value of paralegal work should be considered an investment in every paralegal's future.

Usha, for example, was among those who found that the resistance of a smaller firm *can* be overcome. "At first, it seemed that they didn't even want to talk to me. So I did some homework. I found out what kind of work they did, and I submitted a written proposal listing the tasks I could perform for them while learning. They went for it! Now I'm interning there and I'm still pointing out things I can do, many of which they never thought of."

Usha continues, "Sometimes their lack of awareness has turned around to my advantage. I have so many opportunities to surprise them and really shine in their eyes."

Students considering an internship in small firms will find

- An exciting, highly varied, and often untapped market for entry-level employment
- A need to research each firm as to the kind of work it does and whether it has had experience with paralegals
- A common need to demonstrate what they can do
- A need for sensitivity toward a natural reluctance to change long-standing staffing practices
- The need to be flexible and adaptable
- Unpredictable variations in the following:
  - Degree of acceptance of the paralegal profession
  - How the paralegal's role is defined
  - Preferred qualifications
  - Level of intellectual challenge
  - Extent and nature of specialization
  - Salary levels

The resistance of small law offices can either be viewed as an obstacle or as a major opportunity. Among small firms, resistance to taking their first intern usually comes from nothing more than a lack of experience with paralegals. In other words, the problem is not the result of what they know—it is the result of what they do not know. It is a matter of ignorance. Compared to some things, ignorance is easy to correct!

Overcome resistance to paralegal utilization by gently but confidently educating offices about what you can do for them. Supply them with short, credible book passages or articles from bar publications[6] that your program director may have on hand. The American Bar Association is an excellent publications source whose credibility few lawyers will doubt. For example, *Leveraging with Legal Assistants*, edited by Arthur G. Greene (1993), contains many useful articles on the advantages of paralegal utilization. Also, *Working with Legal Assistants: A Team Approach for Lawyers and Legal Assistants*, edited by Paul G. Ulrich and Robert S. Mucklestone (1980), provides tried-and-true checklists of paralegal tasks for specific areas of law practice. And finally, small and solo practices will find Susan Kliggerman's article, "The Paralegal Working with the Solo Practitioner" very persuasive. It appears in *Flying Solo*, edited by Joel P. Bennett (1994).

In addition, a growing number of state bar associations have committees or task forces devoted to paralegal issues, many of which have produced articles and guidelines educating bar members about effective paralegal utilization. Informative booklets have been published by numerous state bar associations. Check with your state bar about the availability of such publications.

A list of the tasks you can perform[7] may persuade potential internship supervisors. A list of offices that have accepted interns in the past brings great credibility to an internship proposal when a resistant employer recognizes on your list the names of respected professional colleagues and peers.

The resistance of the small law firm is a challenge, but it also presents significant opportunities. If you meet that resistance with helpfulness rather than indignation, it can translate into future jobs for yourself and others.

The Sole Practitioner

The sole practitioner or "solo" office is also an unpredictable group in its paralegal utilization. Schools in some areas report that solo offices offer some of their most prized internship opportunities. Other schools indicate resistance among sole practitioners to the use of paralegals and interns. Where such resistance exists, students should try the persuasive strategies outlined in the preceding section on small law firms.

Attorneys in this category *are* worth pursuing. For beginning paralegals, this group of attorneys represents the largest segment of potential employers, constituting about 46 percent of all lawyers in private practice in the United States.[8] In other words, *solo practices constitute the largest single segment of American law offices.* Savvy entry-level paralegals see this market as a huge half-empty glass, just waiting to be filled. This category may have greater potential than any other for future growth in paralegal employment.

In addition, the solo law office is often where entry-level paralegals can get the most varied experience possible. Working for a sole practitioner typically brings exposure to several different practice areas. Also, it enables students to experience different law office roles and see firsthand the business aspects of a law office and what makes it work.

Also, students often describe the solo law practice as a very egalitarian work setting, where job descriptions overlap and every employee has occasion to do almost everything. An opportunity to see many sides of the business of law practice, it requires great versatility and willingness to adapt to constantly changing needs. The student who enjoys variety can flourish and learn a great deal in this setting.

Another advantage exists here for paralegals who value close, personal community ties. Solo practitioners (and members of small firms, too) who practice and live in the same rural or neighborhood setting rely heavily on their reputation in the community. They work hard to maintain solid relationships with clients and townspeople both in and out of the office. Their livelihood depends on it. The satisfaction these relationships bring may be greater than in some large firms where associates and paralegals sometimes toil for months for clients they never see.

In a small or solo practice firm, students generally find

- A greater willingness to train
- Varied experience, working in diverse subject areas on many different assignments in one office
- Frequent shifting of law office roles and combining of job titles (such as paralegal/secretary)
- An opportunity to learn virtually all aspects of law office operations

QUICK TIP 2.2

About 46 percent of practicing lawyers are sole practitioners—the largest single group of potential law office employers. Another 25 percent of private practitioners are in small firms of two to ten lawyers. As these groups start to use paralegals more fully, a serious new hiring trend may be

> ## THE STUDENT'S PERSPECTIVE 2.2: KILEEN
> ## Interning for the Sole Practitioner
>
> When Kileen listed her career goals, she had a big question mark at the top of her list. "I love the law and this profession, but I didn't have a clue about where in this profession I wanted to go." So she took her program director's advice and interviewed with several sole practitioners. "Attorney Pozluzny said that what she needed most was someone who was flexible—and that's exactly what this internship was! I did real estate work, wills, divorces, county court litigation—everything, it seemed.
>
> "Not only that, but at one time or another, I experienced every kind of staff work that can be done in a law office—some receptionist's work, some bookkeeping, and a good deal of paralegal work. Sometimes I'd sit down with Attorney Pozluzny and we'd do some "attorney work" together, like brainstorming strategies for an unusual collections case. Everyone there has to be versatile—even the boss drafted documents at the computer, made copies, and answered the phone at times. I loved it. I want to work for a sole practitioner after graduation."

- Conflicting demands on their time and frequent interruptions
- Stronger ties to the local community
- More frequent and more personal relationships with clients
- No opportunities for promotion unless they go to another firm
- Generally, lower salaries and fewer benefits
- Less-than-ideal equipment and work space
- A more flexible work schedule
- A somewhat less formal atmosphere than in larger firms

The Publicly Funded Law Office

Found in every state, publicly funded law offices generally come under two categories. One is the *public defender,* which provides free legal representation to criminal defendants whose income is below certain levels. The other is *legal assistance* or *legal services*, which also serves indigent clients but in civil—not criminal—matters. As taxpayer-funded offices, legal assistance offices are funded, in large part, by the federal Legal Services Corporation (LSC) and usually carry the name of your state, such as Massachusetts Legal Assistance Corporation. Only about 1 percent of practicing lawyers work in these settings,[9] but the proportion of paralegal and similarly trained non-lawyer personnel tends to be somewhat higher here than in many private law firms.

Legal assistance offices should not be confused with legal aid societies, which are private, charitable organizations providing free legal services in a few metropolitan areas where donations are sufficient to support them. (There were about 250 such societies in the early 1960s; now they have been almost completely replaced by federally funded legal assistance offices.[10]) Sometimes a Legal Aid Society receives additional funding under a contract with the local municipality. For example, the city of New York has long contracted with the Legal Aid Society of New York to handle a majority of the city's indigent criminal defense cases. Where not limited by the terms of municipal contracts, a Legal Aid Society will pursue whatever particular legal objectives its sponsoring membership prefers.

THE STUDENT'S PERSPECTIVE 2.3: ANDY

Getting into the Public Defender's Office— Ahead of Time

Andy was only in the criminal law course for two weeks when he knew this subject offered the excitement he wanted. "Criminal Law was exhilarating, challenging, and it became my passion. The instructor was a public defender, and I thought: Ah-ha, that's my ticket in!

"I didn't want to wait until my senior year to intern there; I wanted to start as soon as possible. After getting an A for the course, I telephoned the instructor and what great news! It turned out that this public defender's office had its own internship and training program. It was competitive, though. Not everyone who applied was accepted.

"To make a long story short, I got the internship, and some of the best experience of my life. I was given hours of instruction on investigation techniques, interviewing witnesses, summarizing statements, following rules of evidence, and ethics—all from the public defender's point of view. I'm now doing many of those things on my own as a paid employee. I can hardly believe how far I've come since those first weeks in criminal law class."

Legal assistance offices also should not be confused with the free legal aid clinics operated by some law schools, where law students gain practical experience serving the poor or pursuing special legal projects. The latter normally have few, if any, opportunities for paralegal internships.

Both the public defender and the legal assistance offices are supported by a combination of federal and state tax money. Professionals in either of these settings will tell you that their work tends to be underfunded, understaffed, and fast-moving, and that they can use all the intelligent, well-trained help they can get. In fact, recent funding cuts have actually redounded to paralegals' advantage. Many of these offices are now turning to paralegals (rather than attorneys) for a greater share of the workload.[11]

Carlotta, for example, was initially discouraged when she called the local legal assistance office about an internship. Told that they simply did not have time to train a student, she tried a different approach. She sent a collection of her best drafting assignments, including litigation documents and a research memorandum on constitutional law. Her strategy worked. They agreed to give her a try as an intern. "With what I'm learning here, I'm going to be able to hit the ground running in any one of a dozen law offices in town," she now says confidently. "This place is a proving ground for the steadfast!"

Students who intern in these offices will find

- Coworkers who are dedicated to making the legal system work for everyone
- Unpretentious realism rather than prestige
- Proficiency in a second language a plus
- A more relaxed appearance and conduct in the office than in many private law offices
- Furnishings, equipment, and systems that might not be as innovative as they are elsewhere
- Competence is still an absolute "must"
- Active involvement with clients
- Opportunities to be very resourceful
- Opportunities to think and work quickly

Is There a Law Office "Personality"?

Every law office seems to have a character of its own. It is shaped by the expectations of its clientele, the management style of those in charge, the resources it has available, and its location. For example, law firms serving large institutions—such as banks and corporations—often convey the image of power and prestige their clients seek. This image will be apparent in employees' more formal conduct, attire, and physical surroundings. Offices serving everyday, middle-class clients tend to create a professional but comfortable environment and may also be more cost conscious. Firms having an authoritarian management style will have a strict hierarchy to follow for getting things done. And offices in large metropolitan areas may maintain a faster pace and more sophisticated appearance than those in rural areas.

Students need to think about these differences so they can plan an internship that is comfortable for them as individuals. To better understand the personality of any office, students should answer the following questions:

- What kind of clients does this office serve, and what expectations do those clients have of a law office and its staff?
- What image does this office try to convey?
- What management style prevails in this office?
- Is cost-consciousness a high priority?
- Is this office in the city, the suburbs, or a rural area?

THE BUSINESS OR CORPORATION PARALEGAL

According to the 1997 Paralegal and Compensations Benefit Report of the National Federation of Paralegal Associations (NFPA), for-profit corporations are the second largest paralegal-employer group in all regions of the country. Only employment in private law firms was greater. In six out of twelve regions, the percentage of paralegals employed in for-profit corporations was around 20 percent. Another survey puts the percentage at 19 percent nationwide.[12] These figures follow a decade-long trend toward greater paralegal presence in the corporate setting.

Assisting Corporate Counsel

Due to the rising cost of hiring outside counsel, corporations are performing more of their legal work themselves (see Table 2.1). According to the 1994 President of the American Corporate Counsel Association, "You are going to see more and more companies handling litigation in house—not just managing litigation, but actually handling it."[13] Consequently, corporate legal departments (often headed by a vice president and general counsel) are hiring paralegals at unprecedented rates. Corporate paralegals assist with such activities as

- Real estate leases, purchases, and sales
- Labor regulations
- Employee benefits
- Contracts administration
- Franchising
- Trademark and copyright matters
- Environmental compliance
- Securities transactions

Table 2.1

In-House Clout—*Companies with the largest in-house legal departments*

Company	Value
State Farm Mutual Auto. Ins.	485
General Electric	457
Liberty Mutual Insurance	433
AT&T	379
Travelers Corp.	375
IBM	330
Prudential Ins. Co. of America	318
Chevron	208
General Motors	202
Bank America	177

Source: Corporate Legal Times/McGladrey & Pullen 1994 survey

- Annual meetings and annual reports
- In-house litigation support

Students who research their target companies thoroughly and present a detailed internship proposal will often be well-received and used fully. The contacts that can be made and the experience that is gained can lead to positions in various departments of the corporation. It can also be useful for future employment in a law office that serves corporate clients.

Other Law-Related Corporate Work

Law-related work is also performed in corporate offices other than the legal department by employees whose job title may not be "paralegal" but who nevertheless benefit greatly from paralegal training. Three examples follow.

- The *personnel (or human resources) office* may need someone to work in employee benefits and compliance with Equal Employment Opportunity Commission (EEOC) rules in hiring and promotion.
- A separate *office of contracts administration* may need someone familiar with contracts law, commercial law, and the Uniform Commercial Code in preparing proposals, following through on negotiations, and developing costs and budget information.
- An office on *government compliance* may need someone skilled in understanding regulatory law and carrying out reporting procedures.

Law-related work in the corporate setting is by no means limited to the legal department. Students interested in the corporate sector must check the functions of numerous corporate offices where a great deal of law-related work is often being done.

 **ALLIED FIELDS**

Allied fields include businesses, industries, and other enterprises that are highly regulated or that provide major law-related services. They include real estate businesses, insurance offices, banks, and many nonprofit activist or service organizations. *You will rarely find the word* paralegal *as a job title in these fields, but that does not signal a lack of opportunities.* On the contrary, the nature of their business often requires staff who are educated in legal principles and procedures.

Increasingly, paralegal graduates are finding rewarding careers outside of the law office in these law-related fields. Not all schools permit students to intern in non-law-office settings, however. If one of these allied fields appeals to you, be sure to check with your program director before applying for an internship there.

The Real Estate Industry

Every time real estate is bought, sold, developed, mortgaged, managed, or leased, a myriad of legal procedures must be followed. Real estate sales offices, residential and commercial development companies, mortgage companies, and firms managing rental properties are examples of settings where a paralegal background is often useful. Many of these offices have begun to see the benefits of having on their staff someone with paralegal training. In states where title companies have legitimately replaced private practitioners in searching titles and preparing title abstracts, additional employment and internship opportunities exist and valuable skills can be learned. A resourceful student with an interest in real estate can often uncover—or even create—interesting internship opportunities in these areas.

The Insurance Industry

A highly regulated field whose professionals frequently interact with lawyers, the insurance industry has long offered alternate careers for paralegals. Claims representatives and adjusters, for example, benefit enormously from paralegal education in litigation procedures, torts, and personal injury law. Insurance sales personnel gain from the paralegal's familiarity with estate planning principles, including the laws of inheritance, taxation, and property.

Positions in the insurance industry often require specialized on-the-job training in addition to a college degree. Interning for an insurance company may lead to a trainee position faster and more surely than approaching an office after graduation, without that connection. You can help smooth the way by mentioning, in your internship proposal, that a certain trainee position is your goal.

The Banking Industry

The banking business, of course, consists of more than tellers and check handlers. Commercial banks, savings banks, trust companies, mortgage companies, credit unions, and savings and loans provide many law-related services for which paralegal training is a definite asset. Lending offices and mortgage departments require personnel who are knowledgeable about laws and procedures surrounding personal and real property. Many banks also have trust departments—usually headed or staffed by lawyers—serving as fiduciaries and managers for large trusts. Trust departments often help customers with their estate planning needs as well. Such operations require a thorough understanding of property law, estate planning, taxes, and the law of agency.

Smaller, local banks are normally easier to approach about a possible internship than larger ones. Start by finding out who heads the department in which you want to intern and be well prepared with a list of related courses and sample assignments.

Nonprofit Organizations

In *The 100 Best Jobs for the 1990s and Beyond*, Carol Kleiman quotes the Foundation Center, a publisher specializing in information about nonprofit organizations, as follows:

> [T]here are more than 1 million nonprofit agencies in the United States concerned with health, education, social welfare, religion, unions, arts, culture, community activism, social and fraternal organizations and foundations. One of the fastest-growing sectors of the service economy, with more than 8 million employees in 1991, nonprofit agencies are projected to continue to grow into the next century.[14]

Students who are activists at heart can put their paralegal training to valuable use in environmental protection groups, consumer protection organizations, health and counseling associations, senior citizen centers, labor unions, teachers' unions, and organizations promoting the legal and political rights of different segments of the population. In addition, nonprofit *lawyer-referral programs* and *pro bono lawyers' networks*—both of which may be sponsored by your state or local bar association—frequently welcome paralegal assistance. While gaining experience in screening complaints and referring cases, you can greatly expand your network of professional contacts in providing such services.

A program called CASA trains volunteers to act as *Court-Appointed Special Advocates* in states where this program is legally authorized. CASA offers the chance to engage in actual courtroom advocacy on behalf of a child or incapacitated adult. And growing numbers of prosecutors' offices offer victims' assistance programs in which interns can gain valuable insights into the operations of the local criminal justice system.

Jeannine, for example, interned with the Rape and Assault Crisis Center in her city. She assisted clients in obtaining protective orders, helped prepare them to testify in court, and generally accompanied them throughout the court process. "I got an incredible bird's-eye view of the entire legal system. I now know how it works and also how it doesn't work. I met some lawyers and prosecutors I will admire forever—and a few I would love to work with some day."

Nonprofit organizations typically depend on dues, donations, and grants for their existence, so resources are likely to be limited and internships in such settings are almost always unpaid. After graduation, however, a paid career in one of these settings is sometimes possible. For many, it is a personal dream come true.

OPPORTUNITIES IN GOVERNMENT

Wherever there is government, there is law—in abundance. And wherever there is law, there will always be a need for employees with law-related skills and training. Perhaps that is why the federal government is the largest

QUICK TIP 2.3

For opportunities in government, you have to look beyond job titles. Check actual job *descriptions* for internship slots where paralegal training is highly relevant—regardless

employer in the United States, with a civilian workforce of about three million, working in roughly two hundred different jobs. As a group, state governments cannot be far behind. Nationally syndicated business columnist Carol Kleiman reports:

> After more than a decade of budget cutbacks in personnel, reductions in force, massive switching of full-time jobs to part-time ones and the use of temporary workers, local, state and federal government jobs will be in a hiring mode by the 21st century. Job opportunities are expected to grow by 9.7 percent. Hiring by governmental bodies—not including schools, universities or hospitals—is projected to account for 811,000 new jobs, according to the Department of Labor.[15]

Though many government jobs call for law-related skills and training, the job title of "paralegal" may not appear in any listing you check. If you hope for experience in this arena, you must focus on the job descriptions you find—not on job titles.

In the federal government, hiring is a highly structured process, usually involving written tests administered through thirty-nine different federal offices of personnel management. This highly structured process sometimes makes it difficult for federal agencies to conform to the scheduling needs of any particular school.

Internships with state and local agencies, on the other hand, can be much easier to arrange due to the greater flexibility that often exists at that level. Thoughtful and well-prepared inquiries about internship opportunities in state governmental offices can be surprisingly productive.

Federal and state government offices frequently parallel each other. For example, state and federal governments each have their own general prosecutorial offices: the Department of Justice and the United States Attorney's Office on the federal level and the Attorney General's Office on the state level. Also, state governments often maintain their own environmental offices and civil rights offices, both of which are usually small-scale versions of their federal counterparts. Additional examples of parallel agencies at the state level abound.

Because of their overlapping subject matter and similar procedures, internship experience at the state level can be useful in later seeking employment at the federal level. So if interning in a state office fails to bring permanent employment, it at least enhances candidacy for employment in a corresponding federal office, where salaries may be considerably higher.

Government Agencies

Existing on both state and federal levels, regulatory agencies may have opportunities for investigative work, monitoring compliance among businesses and other groups, enforcing agency regulations, rule making, and perhaps even adjudication in out-of-court administrative hearings. All of these functions require legal understanding.

Whether state or federal, government agencies tend to fall within one of two categories: regulatory agencies and service agencies. Below are just a few of the countless examples for each category.

Regulatory Agencies	Service Agencies
• Environmental Regulation	• Legislative Services
• Education	• Child Welfare
• Taxation	• Economic Development
• Prison and Corrections	• Public Health

- Public Utilities
- Civil Rights
- Labor
- Workers' Compensation
- Occupational Licensing

- Human Services
- Elder Affairs
- Community Services
- Cultural Affairs
- Drug Counseling

As a rule, internships in government agencies do not lend themselves to future law office employment. These internships should only be pursued by students with career goals that are clearly related to the subject matter the agency addresses. Career changers with a work history in one of these regulatory or service fields may find that their paralegal training now makes them doubly useful in that setting.

Municipal Offices

From Colorado Springs, Colorado, to Hudson, New Hampshire, city governments are discovering how valuable paralegals can be. These offices often screen potential employees by trying them first as interns. Under pressure to keep budgets down, one city attorney reports, "I want to hire more paralegals, not attorneys."[16]   In city and town offices, paralegals might work with

- Municipal court pretrial procedures and prosecutions
- Corporate (city or town government) issues
- Building or planning departments
- Zoning and subdivision boards
- Property tax issues
- Eminent domain issues and the sale or acquisition of municipal land
- Researching and drafting ordinances

In local government offices, paralegal interns can be given heavy responsibilities and learn extremely valuable skills that transfer easily to many law office settings—particularly those dealing with municipal regulation.

Law Enforcement

In schools where the paralegal program has long been linked to a criminal justice program, law enforcement internships are nothing new. Other schools are only beginning to see some appropriate connections between these two related fields, and a few may still need to be persuaded on this point. Virtually all schools, however, are quite willing to place interns in the office of a local, state, or federal prosecutor.

Although police work normally requires additional specialized training and special tests, paralegal skills can be extremely useful in the office or community-service aspects of police work. In these settings, students can develop analytical ability; communications skills; and familiarity with legal principles, terminology, research, and procedures. Schools report useful internship experiences in the following areas:

- State Attorney General's Office
- County Prosecutor's Office
- Regional Office of the United States Attorney
- Regional Office of the United States Department of Justice
- County sheriffs' departments
- State or local police department headquarters

- Parole offices
- Corrections facilities

Bob, a paralegal senior with a military background, won a paid position with the Immigration and Naturalization Service (INS) doing detective work and conducted his internship in this capacity. "With my paralegal training, I was able to do things none of the other detectives knew how to do. I had to teach them! I uncovered a money-laundering scheme by tracing a chain of title at the registry of deeds. I knew my way around courthouse records like nobody else. In my detective work at the INS, I drew on every paralegal course I ever had—even divorce law. You'll never be able to tell me that paralegal training has nothing to do with law enforcement."

Before accepting an internship position with police, sheriffs' departments, or parole offices, students should check the office's prior experience with paralegals and with interns generally. Be sure your law enforcement internship gives you the chance to handle challenging and productive law-related assignments—not just to observe others at work.

Court Offices

The court clerk and his or her staff act as an administrative buffer between the judges of the court and the attorneys who bring cases before them. In the municipal, district, superior, and appellate courts of your state, the clerk's office ensures that deadlines are met and that appropriate steps are taken when deadlines are missed. It organizes and maintains court documents and schedules court proceedings.

Students vying for a future in litigation can get a detailed, behind-the-scenes view of the process while working in this setting. As interns, students gain familiarity with all kinds of litigation documents, get a clear picture of procedural strategies available to litigants, and may have frequent contact with attorneys appearing before the court. The networking opportunities here are sometimes among the best an intern can find. The skills and knowledge a student can acquire in this setting translate well to future law office employment—and also to continued employment as courthouse personnel when an opening becomes available.

Do not overlook the federal courts in your locale. The offices of some bankruptcy courts, for example, have actively sought paralegal interns for years. United States District Courts cannot be far behind. The trend toward paralegal utilization in the courts seems slowly but finally to be catching hold on the federal, as well as the state, level.

Legislative Offices

Students located in or near their state capital may enjoy the excitement of working directly with elected lawmakers in researching the law, gathering data, and helping to create new legislation. Some find internships in the offices of individual state senators and representatives where they also help respond to citizens' complaints and requests. Others pursue challenging assignments with the state's Office of Legislative Services or *Office of Legislative Research* (the name varies) providing general research and drafting support. In a few states, such offices have begun soliciting highly competent interns on a regular basis. Often these internship slots are competitive.

Interning with a state *senator* or *congressional representative* is also possible, even for students located far from Washington, D.C. All United States legislators maintain at least one office in their home state and many have several local offices. These home offices mostly serve the local constituency—responding to inquiries, acting on complaints, and assisting voters in their dealings with federal offices and agencies.

The names and locations of senators and representatives on both the state and national level can be found in the Lawyer's Directory for your state or at the reference desk of your local public library. Your school's library will also have this information.

Students interning with individual legislators gain great organizational and problem-solving abilities and rapidly heighten their communications skills. Some also find the influence of a well-known legislator useful in future job hunting. Those pursuing mainly research and bill-drafting assignments build impressive skills for use in law school some day or in some specialized paralegal positions. And those with definite political ambitions can hardly find a better place to start.

The Military Setting

Larger army bases around the country maintain what might be described as a sort of "legal services" office for local army personnel. One of several divisions of the Judge Advocate General (or JAG office), *JAG Legal Assistance* is staffed by lawyers, paralegals, and secretaries who help soldiers and their families with noncriminal legal matters, both on and off base. Other divisions of the JAG office handle criminal cases, tort claims, trial defense, administrative law, and military offenses. In all areas but those dealing with sensitive government and military matters, civilian interns are welcome and security clearance is not required. Major navy and air force bases maintain similar facilities for their personnel.

Students who volunteer internship service to JAG Legal Assistance will gain well-rounded experience similar to many general practice law firms. Like local legal assistance offices, JAG Legal Assistance often welcomes trained, qualified help. They use paralegals extensively and their paralegal/attorney ratio tends to be more favorable than in many private law firms. An internship with the JAG office is normally arranged through the post's Volunteer Services office. It is always an unpaid position.

Extensive legal work is also done in the offices of the United States Army Corps of Engineers, which, like many JAG offices, accepts well-trained civilian paralegal interns. The office of *Counsel of the Army Corps of Engineers Regulatory Division,* for example, does not normally work with classified documents so security clearance is not necessary here either. Often, these offices work closely with nearby colleges and law schools to draw on some of their best interns on a regular basis.

Students attracted to the growing fields of environmental and administrative law can find challenging opportunities in this setting. To see whether an office of the United States Army Corps of Engineers is located near you, check the white pages of the telephone directory for your metropolitan area (or the blue section for federal government listings, in some directories) under "United States."

WORKING WITH AN INDEPENDENT PARALEGAL

There are two kinds of independent paralegals. *Freelance paralegals* are those who work for law firms, but as independent contractors—not as regular employees. Working out of their own offices, freelancers accept assignments for hourly or per diem wages from numerous attorneys. Their relationship with law offices is in some ways similar to that of a temporary employee.

Although the sufficiency of attorney supervision over freelance paralegals was questioned in a few states and the unauthorized practice of law by free-lancers was sometimes feared, this breed of paralegal has now become a respected member of the legal community in virtually every state.[17] Many law offices rely on them heavily.

Extensive experience can be gained and many law office contacts can be made while interning with a well-known, reputable freelance paralegal. Students who want to become freelancers themselves can also get a realistic, firsthand view of how such a business is run and what it takes to succeed on your own.

Independent paralegal practitioners or *legal technicians,* on the other hand, sell their services directly to the public, with no attorney involvement. Also known as *document preparers* in some areas, they offer an alternative to the conventional law office, serving clients who many believe might otherwise receive no legal assistance. However, they usually operate in violation of state statutes and case law on the unauthorized practice of law. The courts of Florida, Texas, and Oregon, for example, have prosecuted nonlawyers who assisted clients in immigration matters.[18]

Not all states have reacted so negatively. Perhaps because of the public's acceptance of legal technicians in certain regions, some states have largely refrained from prosecuting such violations. The legislatures of a few states, such as California, have gone even further, proposing regulatory schemes for authorizing legal technicians. As of early 1998, however, none of these proposals has become law.

The delivery of legal services directly to the public by independent, unsu-pervised nonlawyer practitioners remains an extremely volatile issue. *In most jurisdictions, working with a legal technician or nonlawyer document preparer puts your career at serious risk.* Until legal technicians or document preparers become a legally authorized occupation, students are wise to avoid intern-ing with such offices.

MEDIATION AND ALTERNATE DISPUTE RESOLUTION

As you may have learned in some paralegal courses, alternate dispute reso-lution (ADR) refers to the various methods available to settle disputes out of court. One such method is mediation, in which the parties agree to take their argument to a neutral third party for a thorough exploration of the facts and a proposed resolution. Unlike arbitration, mediation is not always con-ducted by lawyers or retired judges, and it is not binding. The parties can still hire attorneys and go to court if they wish. Most often, they do not.

Because the costs of litigation are so high, ADR in general and mediation in particular are often replacing the courtroom as faster, cheaper, and per-haps saner ways to resolve differences. Across the country, courts are strongly supporting this trend, sometimes even mandating it. Because not all programs require their mediators to be lawyers, this field is often open to paralegal participation.

For example, many district and municipal courts are creating mediation offices for landlord-tenant conflicts, consumer complaints, and neighbor-hood disputes. Churches and nonprofit humanitarian organizations some-times offer such services as well. And in a growing number of family courts, marital mediation by trained (and usually certified) nonlawyer mediators offers a nonadversarial approach to property and custody disagreements as well as a rewarding job alternative for well-trained paralegals.

Interning with a marital mediator or a nonprofit or court-affiliated mediation program may not provide the most direct route to law office employment. However, it will sharpen your skills in fact gathering, investigation, communications, record keeping, and problem solving. It will provide intense exposure to the particular areas of law involved and, sometimes, a chance to interact with law offices and court personnel.

The experience gained may lead to a career in the growing field of mediation services. It can also be of value as an employee to sole practitioners, small neighborhood law offices, and certain businesses.

 ## ADVICE FOR THE UNDECIDED

Paralegals Have Many Different Job Titles

Some people say that the paralegal profession has fewer opportunities now than in the past. Those who say this (and students who mistakenly believe it) may have lost sight of all the law is and does in today's world.

Until fairly recently, the term *paralegal* described one only thing: a professional employed in a law office. Today, the profession includes employment settings unheard of years ago, and this trend shows no signs of stopping. American law has become so pervasive that it affects virtually every form of human endeavor. There is hardly a business or undertaking anywhere in which legal expertise is not needed and a law-related career cannot be made.

For that reason, your internship opportunities are by no means limited to what is described in this chapter. Neither are your career prospects. The students who find career paths they love are the ones with their eyes constantly on the horizon and enough imagination to envision the ever-expanding possibilities.

Your First Job Is Not Your Last

Most people change careers at least three times during their lives.[19] Within each career, most people change jobs several times as well. Economic conditions are constantly changing. Technologies and the demands of the workplace are constantly evolving. Adaptability is the key to survival in the midst of constant change. Keep that perspective in mind as you decide what kind of internship to pursue.

For most students, the sanest approach is to view their internship as the first step in a complex, long-term game plan. Your ultimate career goal may be still three or four steps away. Look for an internship that will get you to step one first. Someone with an eye on a litigation-support slot at a large, prestigious firm, for example, might focus first on becoming qualified for work in a small or solo firm. The big firm could still be three years away or more.

Students with even small doubts about their career goals are smart to seek the most varied experience possible. They need a wide base of experience from which later career decisions can be made. And no one should ever be afraid to imagine, dream, and go beyond textbook definitions. The world is going beyond those definitions even as they are written.

QUICK TIP 2.4

Interns who are not in a law office setting may inadvertently be asked to "play lawyer." A non-lawyer supervisor may not fully understand the unauthorized practice of law, so it is up to you to explain. Make it clear you are not a "junior lawyer" and do not give legal advice.

POINT OF ETHICS
Risks for Non-Law-Office Interns

In working or interning for offices other than private or public law firms, students need to be alert to a major risk factor. The internship supervisor in a non-law-office setting may not be a lawyer and may not have had formal legal training on any level. Consequently, he or she may have no idea what constitutes the unauthorized practice of law.

Students seeking internships with such offices must be careful to communicate their legal limits in that regard. Explain that part of your expertise lies in knowing *when* a lawyer is needed and that you can alert your supervisor to such situations. You cannot, however, advise clients or coworkers regarding their legal rights and responsibilities. Only a lawyer is permitted to give such advice unless a statute, court rule, or agency rule authorizes others to do so in certain situations.[20]

Make it clear that you are no substitute for a law-school-trained, licensed attorney. Throughout your internship, remain constantly alert to situations that could carry you over that line. Know when to stop and tell your supervisor that a lawyer's advice is needed. When in doubt, check with your school's program director.

EXERCISES

1. **The Internship-Options Notebook**

   The following exercises will guide you in preparing a notebook of internship information on which your internship decision will eventually be based. You are gathering information about local options among as many different office categories as possible. This exercise will also give you practice—and greater confidence—in contacting prospective offices later.

   As you follow these steps, keep careful notes on each interview or telephone call made and of all correspondence received. Be sure that names, addresses, and telephone numbers are included for each contact, along with the date of contact. Keep your notes in numbered sections, corresponding to each exercise you followed.

   a. **Law Offices** Beginning with the yellow pages of the telephone book (under "Lawyers" or "Attorneys at Law") and then checking the descriptions in the *Martindale-Hubbell Law Directory*, try to identify two local law offices meeting the definition given in this chapter for each of the following nine categories. If you find so many offices that it becomes overwhelming, narrow your selection to the kind of legal work described and the convenience of its location. Alternatively, these categories can be distributed among several students and the results shared with all participants.

   (1) Large law firm
   (2) Medium-sized law firm
   (3) Small law firm
   (4) Sole practitioner
   (5) Legal clinic
   (6) Boutique firm
   (7) Public defender

(8) Legal assistance

(9) Bar association lawyer's referral service

b. **Paralegal Information** Contact at least one office from each category, and ask for the opportunity to speak briefly with a paralegal at that office. You can explain that you are a paralegal student, that this is part of a career-planning assignment, that you know their time is limited, and that you will be brief. Be prepared for the possibility that some offices—smaller ones in particular—may not have a paralegal on staff.

When you contact each paralegal, ask to arrange a ten- or fifteen-minute informational discussion at his or her convenience. The discussion could take place during a personal meeting or during a telephone appointment. In your informational discussions, ask what they consider to be the advantages and disadvantages of their office type—small, medium, or large law firm; corporate legal department; nonprofit organization; and so forth. Also ask about the office type of their previous job and how it compared with the present one. And finally, ask whether their office has ever had a paralegal intern and what responsibilities were (or might be, in the future) given to such an intern.

c. **Legislators** Find out the names and office locations of your state representative, state senator, United States representative, and United States senator. (Instructions are provided earlier in this chapter.) Contact the offices of one state legislator and one federal legislator, and ask what responsibilities a qualified volunteer or intern might be given.

d. **Nonprofit Organizations** Make a list of the nonprofit service or activist organizations you know of—nationally and in your local community. Check the telephone directory for the phone number and address of those having offices in your area. Contact at least three of these organizations and ask what law-related projects or assignments might be given to a paralegal-trained volunteer.

e. **Court Offices** Using the Lawyer's Directory for your state (available at your school's library or from your Program Director or Placement Office), make a list of courts in your area, the names of the court clerk for each, and his or her address and telephone number. Call and ask to speak to someone about whether a paralegal-trained volunteer from your school might be useful to that office and for what kinds of responsibilities.

f. **Local Government Offices** Using the white pages of the telephone directory (under the name of your city or town), copy the names, addresses, and telephone numbers of all law-related town and city offices, such as the planning department, corporate or city counsel, city attorney, and police headquarters. Contact each with the same question given in the preceding exercise.

g. **Law-Related Businesses** Using the telephone directory, make a list of several of the following, with their addresses and telephone numbers. Contact several of them to ask the same question given in Exercise e.

(1) Title company

(2) Claims department of an insurance company

(3) Trust department of a bank

(4) Mortgage department of a bank

(5) Real estate development company

h. **State Agencies** Using the white pages of the telephone directory and the Lawyer's Directory or Lawyer's Diary for your state, make a list of at least five state agencies that do law-related work in which you might be interested. Contact each with the same question given in Exercise e.

    i. **Corporations** Contact the chamber of commerce (or business association) in your area for a listing of businesses in your area, and ask them to identify their largest members/employers. (Friends and relatives, your church or synagogue, and organizations such as the Rotary Club or the Lions Club are also good sources of information about businesses in your region.) Call several of these businesses, ask for the legal department, and pose the same question given in Exercise e. If their legal department is located at offices in another region, ask for the personnel department, and pose the same question. Other offices you might ask for are contracts administration and environmental compliance.

    j. **Previous Employers** Make a list of employers you have worked for earlier in your career. Contact them again, this time to identify offices in which law-related work is done. Such offices exist, for example, in hospitals, restaurant chains, and many businesses. Once such offices are identified, pose the same question given in Exercise e.

2. This exercise helps you become skillful at identifying work settings for which paralegal training is appropriate even though the word *paralegal* may not be listed in connection with that job. Buy or borrow a copy of a major newspaper in your region—preferably the Sunday edition. Turn to the Help Wanted classified section. As you read each advertisement in the professional section, list each nonlawyer job that requires legal training or experience similar to yours.

3. Together with other students or your paralegal club, schedule an Interns Alumni Night and invite last year's or last semester's interns to make ten-minute presentations about the offices in which they worked. Give each alumnus a list of five topics to cover briefly, such as
   a. Office type
   b. Their most prevalent work assignments
   c. The physical surroundings
   d. The job opportunities it created
   e. The drawbacks experienced, if any

ENDNOTES

1. Jeff Barge and Gina Farrell Gladwell, "Hot Job of the '90s?," *Legal Assistant Today* (January/February 1996): 27.
2. Robert MacCrate et al., *Legal Education and Professional Development—An Educational Continuum* (Chicago: American Bar Association Section of Legal Education and Admissions to the Bar, 1992), 33.
3. Ibid.
4. Ellen Joan Pollock, "Top Law Firms Emerge from Doldrums," *Wall Street Journal*, 30 June 1994, sec. B, p. 1, 5.
5. MacCrate, *Legal Education and Professional Development*, 33.
6. Paralegal association publications are certainly as credible and sometimes even more informative than those of bar associations. However, lawyers who are unfamiliar with the paralegal profession may be more open to material written by other lawyers—at least in the beginning.
7. The textbook for your introductory paralegal course may have lists of paralegal tasks for various practice areas. If not, such lists are provided for several areas of law practice in *West's Paralegal Today*, supra. Also, "Paralegal Responsibilities" (1996), a detailed, 62-page list of paralegal

tasks for twenty-six practice areas, is available from the National Federation of Paralegal Associations, Inc., headquartered in Kansas City, Missouri.

8. MacCrate, *Legal Education and Professional Development*, 33.

9. Ibid.

10. Robert J. Janosik, ed., *Encyclopedia of the American Judicial System*, vol. 2 (New York: Scribner's, 1987), 646.

11. Mark Curriden, "LSC Budget Cuts May Spell Opportunities for Paralegals," *Legal Assistant Today* (September/October 1995): 21.

12. Barge and Gladwell, "Hot Job," 27.

13. Wade Lambert, "Firms' Legal Costs Rose to 18% in '93 Despite Efforts to Curb Expenses," *Wall Street Journal*, 6 July 1994, sec. B, p. 8.

14. Carol Kleiman, *The 100 Best Jobs for the 1990s and Beyond* (New York: Berkeley Books, 1992), 41.

15. Ibid., 39–40, quoting from Department of Labor, "Projections 2000," *Occupational Outlook Quarterly* (Washington, DC: U.S. Department of Labor, Fall 1987).

16. "Municipal Governments and Paralegals Make a Great Team," *DPI* (Denver Paralegal Institute) *Discovery 6* (June 1994): 1.

17. In 1990, New Jersey shocked the paralegal profession with a ruling that freelance paralegals were insufficiently supervised by the lawyers for whom they worked and therefore engaged in the unauthorized practice of law. See Opinion No.24 of the Committee on the Unauthorized Practice of Law, 126 N.J.L.J. 309 (November, 1990). Upon appeal and extensive argument by various paralegal associations, the New Jersey Supreme Court reversed this ruling; see In re Opinion of the Committee on the Unauthorized Practice of Law, 128 N.J. 114, A.2d 962 (Sup.Ct. 1992). Freelance paralegals are now permitted in New Jersey as in virtually all states.

18. Herbert M. Rosenthal et al., in Appendix to "Non-Lawyer Practice in the United States: Summary of the Factual Record Before the American Bar Association Commission on Non-Lawyer Practice" (April 1994) (Discussion Draft): A, IM-1.

19. Richard Nelson Bolles, *The 1994 What Color Is Your Parachute?* (Berkeley: Ten Speed Press, 1994), 156.

20. For additional guidance, see the Codes of Ethics and Professional Responsibility of the National Association of Legal Assistants (NALA) and of the National Federation of Paralegal Associations (NFPA) in Appendix 3.

Chapter 3

Paid or Unpaid: Resolving Compensation Issues

Before you can resolve the question of whether to seek payment for your internship work, you must first determine your school's policy on this issue.

In some programs, internships are not treated as an academic endeavor. Programs following a cooperative education or work-study model, for example, may view student placement in law-related work merely as an early employment step for which compensation is expected. Work-study or cooperative education students may not earn academic credit for the experience and probably are not paying full tuition for it. On-the-job learning is left to the supervisor and student to arrange (or not), and academic monitoring may be minimal or nonexistent.

The cooperative or paid work experience provides valuable links to the professional community. However, neither the school nor the student may have much to say about the kind of work the student will perform. It can also be difficult in such arrangements to measure—much less predict—what skills will be learned on the job and in what depth.

Among schools that do treat internships as an academic endeavor, charge tuition, and grant academic credit for internships, the attitude toward compensation still varies. In many of these schools, the answer is clear and final: internships are regarded as a purely educational experience, and payment should not be accepted for internship work. Schools have good reasons for this policy, but it does force hard choices for students who may be supporting themselves and perhaps a family as well. Several strategies for these students are suggested in this chapter.

In other schools granting academic credit for internships, payment is sometimes regarded as optional—a matter to be resolved privately by the student and the office supervisor. Even in these schools, students face tough decisions that can have long-term consequences.

WANTING PAYMENT IS UNDERSTANDABLE

Being a student and being cash-poor have gone hand in hand for as long as anyone can remember. Today's students are paying the highest tuition rates in education history and often borrow heavily to get through school. Many wonder whether their car will still be roadworthy at the end of their program. Most put off buying things they desperately want. Students wait a long time—perhaps four years—for the chance to earn money as a paralegal. It is no wonder that so many see their internship as "payback" time.

Besides these worries, students who have made a living at other careers sometimes chafe at the notion of providing free labor. "I expect to be doing valuable work," complained a former elementary school teacher. "Why should I make a 'donation' of my time and skill? Why shouldn't the office that benefits from my work pay for it?"

These feelings are entirely legitimate. However, they only reflect immediate, short-term concerns. Students need to weigh these concerns carefully against the long-term career gains that may be had—or lost—depending on how this issue is resolved.

THE "PRICE" OF BEING PAID

Everything has a price. Students who seek only paid internships often encounter problems as a result of that decision. *"Employee" status frequently stands in the way of personal, educational, and career goals.* Sometimes it defeats the entire purpose of the internship.

The "cost" of being a paid intern can take the following forms:

- Less freedom to request assignments you want
- Greater likelihood of repetitive tasks or clerical work
- Fewer opportunities to experiment
- Less tolerance for mistakes
- Inadequate instruction and feedback
- Greater pressure to produce
- Less freedom to ask questions or seek advice
- Little or no time for career-planning discussions
- Fewer occasions for pure learning
- Restricted professional contacts
- Limited power to shape your own experience

Beth, for example, opted for a pure learning experience. "I deliberately chose an unpaid position in a small law firm," she explains. "That way, I'd feel less pressure to know how to do everything. It would be okay to make occasional mistakes and to learn from them. Also, being unpaid allowed me to push for detailed feedback and input regarding my work. The attorneys were more willing to take time to do that because I wasn't costing them a salary. Sure, I could have used the extra money, but I'm really glad I did it this way."

THE STUDENT'S PERSPECTIVE 3.1: ELLIS
Your Money or Your . . . Education

For Ellis, the cost of being paid was higher than he expected. "I admit that being paid was a big priority for me. Unfortunately, I limited myself terribly because of it. Rather than checking several options, I took the only paid internship I could find. I'll never know what I missed. My recommendation is to check out at least three offices—paid, or not."

During his internship, Ellis encountered another problem. "After a while, it seemed like I was doing basically the same things over and over and not getting new experiences. But since they were paying me, I didn't think I had the right to complain. As an employee, I had to do what I was told."

Then a third problem emerged. "It was also hard to take someone aside and ask them questions. After all, I was getting paid to do a job—not to go around picking their brains. Someone actually said that to me. It was very discouraging."

Ellis summarized his experience this way: "If I had it to do over again, I would hold off on salary for the short time involved and instead use the internship for every learning experience I could wrangle out of it!"

STUDENTS WHO "CAN'T AFFORD" AN INTERNSHIP

When it comes to unpaid internships, career changers probably face the greatest conflict of all. Some are employed in other positions throughout their studies, often full time. They see no hours available in their full-time work schedules for toiling, without pay, in an office that might not even hire them. Typically, they believe their economic survival depends on remaining at the present job until a permanent, full-time paralegal position comes along.

Hidden in this thinking is a sometimes tragic Catch-22. Lacking good internship experience to cite in their résumés, these students may never get a chance at that permanent, full-time paralegal position. And the long-awaited career change, into which so much has been invested, may never become a reality.

Jackie, for example, came back to school almost a year after graduation. "I've got a problem," she confided to her director. "Remember how I couldn't 'afford' to do an internship last year? Well, I've sent out literally hundreds of letters and résumés. I've made more phone calls than I can count. I've responded to every ad, and I am getting nowhere. Not doing an internship was a serious mistake. Can you help me find some sort of volunteer law work, even though I'm not a student anymore? I'll work for free in any law office that will take me, just to get a foot—even a toe—into the door of this profession!"

Internships provide the best entry into many professions. A survey of internships in the business sector states: "Of firms with cooperative work-study arrangements or internships that were surveyed last year, 93% offered graduating participants permanent jobs."[1] The hiring rate for interns in law firms may not be quite that high, but many paralegal directors report that internships often lead to employment in the same firm. Indeed, some law firms use internships to test potential job candidates—even though the intern may not be aware of it. And many law firms see challenging, well-documented internships as providing much of the "prior experience" they require in a job candidate.

Often, the best internship offices are the ones that can least afford to pay an intern. The small and solo general practice firms—ideal for inexperienced students—usually cannot pay a student the going professional rate, but they need and welcome paralegal support. Nonprofit organizations rarely have money available to pay a trainee, yet the training could be very valuable to a future career. Most governmental offices are restricted in matters of payroll and hiring; if a paid, in-house internship program is not already in place, the chances of being paid as an intern in this setting are very slim. In short, *insisting on payment rules out a wealth of internship options.*

In the paralegal profession, in which employers increasingly want only "experienced" people, an unpaid internship may be the *only* entry point. No amount of course work provides equivalent, hands-on experience. For anyone intent on making a career in this field, a good internship should be thought of as the most important educational investment of all. It may be worth almost any sacrifice.

 ## SOME STRATEGIES TO CONSIDER

Financially, interning does not have to be an all-or-nothing proposition. With some creativity, compromises are often possible. Below are eight strategies for easing the hardship of an unpaid internship.

As you read about these strategies, keep in mind two overriding principles. First, check your school's internship policies to be sure you are not acting in conflict with them. Second, remind yourself regularly that you will "profit" greatly from your internship in ways other than immediate payment.

The "Trial Period" Technique

Once you have narrowed your sights to two or three potential offices, propose to each of them a period of unpaid time—perhaps the first one-third of your internship period—after which your performance would be reviewed. If your work has become genuinely productive for the firm, an hourly wage might be implemented at that point. Assure them that it will be entirely their decision.

Some offices will be more receptive to this proposal than others. It is best not to make this arrangement the sole basis for choosing one office over another, or to pursue it too aggressively if a prospective supervisor resists. It might be enough to put the idea in their minds, and let it go. They may remember it on their own after you have proved yourself.

The End-of-Internship Bonus

A gratifying form of compensation in many law offices, bonuses have been reported by numerous paralegal interns—many of whom never asked for one. A bonus might be in your future as well. Here is how to find out whether it is possible.

Toward the end of your meeting with a prospective supervisor, clarify your view of the internship as an extremely valuable educational experience for which payment is not expected. This statement makes it clear that you have the right priorities. Mention that you have heard, however, of paralegals and even interns who sometimes receive bonuses for highly productive work. You can add, without belaboring the point, that attending school does involve financial hardships.

Then ask, might a bonus be contemplated if your internship was productive for the office? Even if the answer is no, at least you have planted the thought. It might resurface on its own at the end of a mutually beneficial experience.

The Hourly Billing Approach

Introduce this suggestion by emphasizing your desire to start producing income for the office as soon as you can. Producing income, of course, is the objective of everyone there. Showing that you understand this reality makes you even more desirable as a candidate.

Then ask if your work might become billable. If the answer is that it will not, then you need to consider some other approach. But if your work might be billed hourly to clients at some point, then you would not be out of line in arguing that increased profits justifies some level of compensation in return.[2] Know that you are not likely to receive more than one-third of the amount of revenue generated by your work. This is partly due to overhead or the cost of having you aboard (space, equipment, and training time).

Hourly billing also brings tangible proof of your value to the office. You will be gently, but inexorably, easing your way into employee status. Even if a permanent job cannot be created for you, you will still be working toward an eye-catching addition to your résumé. "Billed fifty hours in a two-week period" gets employers' attention faster than any course title in existence!

The Long-Term "Proposal" Approach

Rather than seeking "front-end" financial rewards, you might forgo immediate compensation and work toward developing a long-term job proposal. This attitude frees you to accept the best internship opportunity available, regardless of its financial pluses or minuses. This approach postpones the financial discussion to a later stage in your internship—often with better results.

Students who choose this approach go through their internships constantly looking and listening for the office's most pressing needs. They will spot gaps that could be filled by an eager, entry-level paralegal like themselves.

They also try to get a sense of what similarly situated paralegals are paid. They ask questions of other paralegals, without prying for personal data, about prevailing salary ranges and usual hiring practices for the kind of work they have in mind. After weeks or even months of gathering information, they put their most relevant skills on paper and propose at least a part-time position.

Jill, for example, detected a great need for someone to coordinate and expand the office's computer functions. Toward the end of her internship, she submitted a three-page proposal detailing the improvements she could create, noting the skills she could bring to the effort, and estimating initial costs and long-term savings. The proposal included case-management functions that she would assume, using enhanced computer assistance. The result was an impressive job offer, which she readily accepted.

Combining Other On-Premises Work

This approach involves seeking nonparalegal work in an office where paralegal assignments are also possible. It works best where substantial lead time is available, allowing you to plan several months in advance.

> ## THE STUDENT'S PERSPECTIVE 3.2: CARMEN
> ## Planning Ahead for Financial Needs
>
> Carmen began thinking about her internship as she completed her first year at the community college. The internship was still several months away, but she spent the summer seeking whatever law-related employment she could find. She found a part-time clerical position processing claims for an insurance company. She established a good record and was respected for her hard work and problem-solving ability.
>
> As internship time approached, she inquired at the law firm that she knew handled the insurance company's litigation, pointing out the connection they shared. Not only was the law firm willing to take her on as an intern, they also were willing to work with the insurance company to accommodate Carmen's two work schedules.
>
> "I don't think I ever worked such long hours: 25 hours a week at the insurance company, 20 hours a week at the law firm, plus an evening course. I was going days, nights, weekends—you name it. But I got great internship experience, two terrific job references, several serious job leads, and all my bills are paid! It was worth every minute."

For example, some students seek clerical or receptionist work at a law office well before their internship, with the understanding that—if they prove themselves—they will eventually be given some more challenging, paralegal work. Others find that a legal department or other law-related work already exists elsewhere in the business or corporation that already employs them. When internship time comes, they continue the responsibilities of their regular job, also taking time out to try new (but often unpaid) paralegal tasks in the legal department or benefits office, for example.

Timekeeping becomes crucially important in these situations—not just to meet internship requirements, but to meet your regular employment obligations. Also, the combined-work approach may mean working evenings, weekends, or both, to make up any paid employment time that was missed. Nevertheless, this is an effective way to meet financial needs while also furthering your paralegal career—all at one location.

Adding Off-Premises Work

The age-old method of taking a job—any job—to pay the bills while interning without pay strikes some students as downright demeaning. Nevertheless, this strategy has helped newcomers break into the profession of their choice since the days of Benjamin Franklin.

It was not a new idea to Marshall, who interns by day and pumps gas at night, or Susan, who spends noninternship hours waiting on tables. "I know I'm not going to do this forever, and I'm working toward something that's really important to me," says Susan. "Does someone think this is something to be embarrassed about? I've got news for them," she laughs.

"I'm kind of proud of what I'm doing," Marshall declares. "I like the fact that I'm doing this on my own—paying my own way. My dad got through school by tending bar. He says I'm 'paying dues,' just like he did. I hate to admit it, but I think he's right." Aware of their circumstances, Marshall's and Susan's internship supervisors have great respect for their determination.

Modifying Present Employment

Students who insist that current employment rules out unpaid internships probably have not checked all the possibilities. Assuming a student only has evening classes (or no classes at all) during the internship, a 200-hour internship can be completed in five weeks, or a 160-hour internship in four. By combining vacation time, unused sick days, and other time-off opportunities, working students can sometimes take the needed time off without jeopardizing their regular jobs. Alternatively, some companies even allow a leave of absence for educational pursuits. Leave may be unpaid but it provides the needed time off while insuring job security—a luxury most students lack.

Another alternative is to temporarily switch from full-time to part-time work, as employees commonly do in response to new family demands, illness, approaching retirement, or simply personal preference. Why not do as much to launch a new career? Careful planning and getting your family's cooperation to cope with reduced income helps make the temporary change less traumatic.

Finding an Off-Hours Internship

Career changers with competing employment obligations are sometimes able to find an internship office that operates during evening and weekend hours when they are free to do internship work. Although most law offices operate mainly during daytime hours, legal clinics (see Chapter 2) and offices catering to middle-class clients are sometimes more flexible.

Nonprofit associations sometimes operate during off-hours. The offices of elected officials may need an intern for an evening and weekend schedule. Or, a student may find research work that can be done at the school's law library during evenings and weekends.

Off-hours internships are limited in number. Sometimes, they are also limited in the experience they can offer. They may also raise questions about adequate supervision and training. This option is not strongly recommended unless the student's professional focus is very specific, the off-hours internship matches that focus closely, and adequate supervision is insured.

GETTING PRIORITIES STRAIGHT

Unfortunately, many students face financial hardships just as their education reaches its most crucial turning point. In a more perfect world, we would find a way to pay all interns a genuine, living wage. But so far, no one has found a way to achieve that noble ideal. Interning almost always involves sacrifices—sometimes major ones.

The financial sacrifices that your internship requires are as worthwhile as the career change you are making. If this is the career you truly want to pursue, then this is the time when all students must make sacrifices. Successful paralegal graduates across the nation will tell you: Yes, it is worth the hardships!

EXERCISES

1. If you are thinking about waiving an optional internship, ask your program director for the names of graduates who waived their internship

and contact them. Find out what became of their careers after graduation. This information will provide a realistic glimpse into what may be your own future. Perhaps they found employment in a law-related field. Often, you will find that they did not.

2. Make two separate lists entitled "Benefits" and "Costs."

   a. In the Benefits column, list every possible advantage to pursuing an internship. This list will include, for example, experience in the specialization of your choice, law office contacts, other items from this chapter, and some personal benefits that may not have been mentioned here. In the Costs column, list the disadvantages, if any, that would exceed those of taking equivalent courses. This list may include, for example, additional personal time, travel, additional wardrobe, reduced income, and the like.

   b. Now assign a point value to each item on both lists: "critically important" merits a "4," "important" gets a "3," "useful but not really important" is a "2," and "1" is for items you would not miss for long. For every item having long-term value to your future, add two extra points.

   c. Add up the score for each column. Which is highest?

3. If financial hardship is a serious issue, take an inventory of your resources and available strategies. On the following chart, check the strategies that might be possible for you to pursue. After you have put a check mark next to all of your possibilities, rank each according to priority in time. In other words, which can and should be pursued now, and which should be investigated only after other possibilities have ruled themselves out? Then begin investigating each appropriate item as you have ranked them.

Strategy	Possible?	Time Priority	Date to Begin
Reschedule courses:			
Delay some			
Advance some			
Find additional part-time work			
Reduced hours (present job)			
Leave of absence (present job)			
Take a loan:			
Relatives			
Friends			
Bank			
School			
Seek partial internship compensation:			
Propose a trial period			
Ask about bonuses			
Negotiate billing rewards			
Employment/ internship combo			

4. Contact two or more personnel agencies, temporary employment agencies, or placement firms that deal with paralegals. Have them describe current job prospects in your area for graduates with no experience compared with job prospects for graduates with substantial internship experience. The same may be done with law office managers, legal administrators, and law office partners responsible for hiring.

5. Contact alumni of your program for advice about the financial aspects of their paralegal internships. What personal adjustments did they make in their lives to accommodate the demands of interning? In what ways were they rewarded for their work? Have them describe the intangible as well as the tangible rewards.

6. This is a role-playing exercise. One student plays the part of prospective internship supervisor (lawyer or paralegal). Another student plays the part of prospective student-intern. Assume that they have already agreed that this student can intern with this supervisor's office. Before concluding their agreement, the student-intern wants to inquire about partial compensation in the form of an end-of-the-internship bonus or an hourly wage after a satisfactory trial period. The student should begin this discussion, and both should proceed as if they were in a real meeting.

ENDNOTES

1. Diane Hales, "Finally, Some Good News for Young People," *Parade: The Sunday Newspaper Magazine*, 26 June 1994, p. 8.

2. There is a subtle but significant difference between fee splitting (strictly prohibited between lawyers and nonlawyers under Rule 5.4 of the ABA Model Code and under the Rules of Professional Conduct in most states) and normal compensation facilitated by the firm's overall profits. Never suggest that the fees you bill to clients should be split according to some fixed percentage. Merely ask for compensation out of the firm's general profits, to which your efforts have contributed.

Chapter 4

Lining Up the "Right" Office

TAKING ACTION

We now move from the initial thinking-and-planning stage to concrete action. Chapter 1 helped you clarify your learning and career objectives—outlining the script, if you will, for your upcoming internship. Chapter 2 surveyed a wide range of employment settings, enabling you to choose the category that best meets your goals. Chapter 3 charted several options for lessening the hardships of working for free. This chapter helps target the best possible office within the employment category that meets your goals. You will be guided through the specific steps needed for finding and then confirming the office in which you will work.

Not all schools arrange and confirm internship offices in exactly the same way. Some schools provide upcoming interns with a list of offices with which a tentative understanding may already have been reached. Other schools require students to locate and schedule their own internships, subject to the approval of the program director. And many use a combined approach, having ongoing internship arrangements with several offices and also guiding students toward finding new ones.

THE "PRACTICE" JOB SEARCH

No matter how your school approaches internships, the same basic steps are usually required of students: (1) research and identify the best offices for you, (2) contact several of those offices, (3) provide a résumé and interview with each of them, and (4) follow up to confirm placement.

If this sounds very much like job hunting, your intuition is correct. The steps needed to arrange an internship closely parallel the steps you will later

QUICK TIP 4.1

As you contact offices and arrange a position, think of this process as an "internship in job hunting." The experience you gain in the search process may be as important as the internship itself.

take to find permanent employment, but under far more relaxed circumstances. There are several reasons for this difference. For instance, the internship search is conducted from within the shelter of the academic environment. Your school's reputation stands behind you, bringing legitimacy and credibility to every step you take.

Another difference is that your livelihood does not depend on the outcome of a single law office interview, as it might for a graduate. If one internship application is not successful, there are always other possibilities. In addition, you can seek the advice and guidance of your program director or placement office whenever needed; for graduates who are no longer on campus, that can be difficult to arrange. And finally, internship supervisors know they are interviewing students, so they tend to judge them less critically than actual job candidates.

For students who have not yet experienced a professional job search, this is a chance to *start developing job-hunting skills and confidence in the security of the academic environment.* For career changers who have already had job-hunting experience in other fields, this process offers the opportunity to adapt those job-search skills to the expectations of the legal community. Smart students will see the internship search as the important learning experience it is.

To make the most of this learning opportunity, try to do the following:

- Start early. Allow up to two months for completing the four-step process at several offices (initial contact, résumé and cover letter, interview, and follow-up or confirmation).
- Experience three or more interviews before responding to any of them with a decision.
- Let each interviewer know that you are also interviewing at other offices if that is the case.
- Tell each interviewer when you will confirm internship placement. If they require an earlier response, note it on your calendar and respond at that time.
- Keep notes on each office you contact, using the Office Contacts Worksheet at the end of this chapter.
- Keep a Job-Finder's Skills Diary on communications techniques, job-hunting strategies, and interviewer expectations that you learn along the way. A form is provided at the end of this chapter.
- Preserve your skills diary for reviewing when you begin your *real* job search.

GETTING SUPPORT FROM YOUR PROGRAM

It is ironic but true that the more students look after themselves, the more helpful the program director or placement advisor is able to be. A student who takes some time to analyze personal learning objectives and identify several offices that seem consistent with those objectives can then get very specific advice about the value of particular offices. On the other hand, the student who just says, "Where should I go?" has not even provided a starting point on which guidance can be based.

Begin by mapping out a personal plan of action to ensure that you will meet your school's deadlines. For example, how many weeks or months will you need to secure internship placement, and how many to complete the required number of internship work-hours after you are placed? Your plan should follow the four numbered stages listed below. Use the Plan of Action form is available at the end of this chapter.

Students' levels of confidence and preparedness for this process vary widely. Many will proceed on their own without having to contact their director until internship placement is confirmed. Others need occasional advice along the way. Generally, students may need to consult the program director at any one of four stages in the internship-placement process:

1. Acquiring background on several internship positions
2. Preparing résumés and cover letters
3. Preparing for and conducting interviews
4. Evaluating three or more internship offices for final acceptance (if your school permits this)

When you do need to consult your school's internship director, bring all relevant information with you. If your question is about a certain office, for example, be prepared to provide the name, address, and phone number of the office involved along with whatever information you have about that office. If your question is about your résumé or cover letter, bring your best draft.

Think of your program director as the coach for an entire team of players. Relegated to the sidelines, your director cannot go out and play the game for you. Each player has to do that on his or her own. But your director is the expert on overall planning and strategy—a valuable resource who should be consulted whenever an unusual or difficult decision has to be made.

WORKING FROM YOUR SCHOOL'S LIST

In some schools, students are given a list of prospective offices by their program director. The offices on this list may be drawn from the following:

- Past internships that were successful
- New offices that recently requested an intern
- New offices that your program director has solicited for internship placement

If you are given a prearranged list of offices, you are fortunate. Part of your job has already been done for you. However, you still need to ask: are internships *limited* to offices on this list? In schools where a long list of reliable offices has been developed, the answer is sometimes yes. Past experience with known offices reduces the risk of unsuccessful internships. If, on the other hand, the answer is no, then you are free to pursue offices that do not appear on the list—subject to your program's guidelines and your director's approval.

Many schools let students pursue untried offices when the student's particular career interests would be better served in an employment setting not on the list. Some non-law-office settings such as government agencies, insurance companies, corporations, legislative offices, or nonprofit associations may be better suited to a student's personal career goals. Experimentation can also lead to increased opportunities for future interns. Mention these advantages to your program director if you need to negotiate greater freedom to search on your own.

Evaluating Offices on Your School's List

Evaluating *any* office—whether or not it is included on your school's list—requires returning to the objectives you established in Chapters 1, 2, and 3. First, identify the office type. Sometimes this information is evident on your school's list. If not, you can consult your program director, check the

QUICK TIP 4.2

Do not lead your program director or placement counselor down blind alleys. When you pose a question about your internship search, have background information available and a solution or two of your own to suggest. To get effective support, be sure you have done your "homework" first.

QUICK TIP 4.3

Does this office know how to use paralegals, and who in that office will take time to mentor you? Begin determining their prior experience with paralegals and interns before the interview. Pursue these issues further during each interview. And explore several offices

Martindale-Hubbell Law Directory, or telephone selected offices and ask the secretary who answers the phone to confirm the information you need.

The second consideration is your specific learning objectives. Students who want to develop litigation skills, for example, will target offices having strong litigation practices or perhaps seek a court clerk's office. Some learning objectives—such as developing writing skills, learning more about computer utilization, or acquiring skills in client contact—are best explored at the interview stage.

For some students, a third issue is the question of compensation. The rule to follow on this issue is the same one that smart job hunters use: do not inquire about compensation until you are sure the position is being offered to you. Do not even mention this issue until you are well into the interview stage and, even then, only *after* the internship has been fully discussed. Bringing up this issue prematurely almost always conveys the wrong priorities. It can be taken as a sign that money means more to you than your career or your education, and it can preclude you unnecessarily from valuable internship opportunities. So, wait until you have a very clear picture of what each internship offers before asking about payment.

The most important factor by which all prospective offices should be evaluated is this: Does this office offer a good "teaching" environment? Will it provide genuine opportunities to learn and grow professionally? Will there be adequate training in new tasks? Will you get periodic feedback on your performance? Will supervisors and coworkers be willing to take time to answer questions and teach you new skills? Or are you likely to be assigned to repetitive tasks with no opportunity to learn something new?

Offices that have accepted interns from your school in the past are easy to investigate in advance. You can ask your director what he or she observed during the last experience with a known office. See whether the last intern submitted an evaluation of the office. You might even ask to contact the former intern yourself.

Offices seeking an intern for the first time on their own initiative may or may not have motives consistent with yours. At the interview, you should inquire about their reasons for wanting an intern and their willingness to spend some "teaching" time with you. Their need for an intern's help may give you leverage for occasionally pursuing your own interests. Keep this in mind when discussing your internship goals with a new, untried office.

Internship opportunities that were newly solicited by your director (rather than created on the office's initiative) have the advantage of careful screening and up-to-date knowledge of your director's expectations. However, they remain untried offices. When interviewing with them, you still need to thoroughly discuss such issues as anticipated assignments and adequate supervision.

Courtesy to Other Students

Sometimes, an internship slot becomes quite competitive. You may never know what other students have interviewed for the same internship you are seeking, especially if many students are working from the same list of offices. The best attitude is the one assumed by job candidates everywhere: there probably were other candidates before you and there probably will be others after you—and no office is obligated to take you in. This attitude will bring thorough preparation and professionalism to your initial contacts, your interviews, and your follow-up communications. In the end, this attitude will make you a desirable candidate. It also prepares you well for the eventual rigors of job hunting.

As a student, you must also remember that you are not an independent agent pursuing purely personal interests. You are part of a student community—a representative of your school. Many besides yourself will be affected by how you conduct this internship search. Your actions and your words can affect the internship searches of your classmates and colleagues for years to come. Fairness, professionalism, and clear communications are crucial.

A few simple rules should be followed:

- Before leaving an interview, clarify your understanding about whether the internship is being offered to you. If it is not, then ask when a decision will be made and contact them again at that time. If the internship is being offered and you are not yet prepared to make a decision, say so. Agree on a date when you will respond with a definite answer.
- Never let two or more offices believe you are accepting an internship with them, hoping to choose between them later. You (as well as someone else) could lose *both* positions.
- Keep your director informed of your progress, including what offices you are contacting and which one is your final choice.
- Never circulate false or inaccurate reports about an internship office to discourage competition.
- Rely on your own good qualifications for competitive internship positions. Downgrading other students reflects negatively on your school—and also on yourself.
- When you confirm acceptance of an internship, *promptly* notify all the other offices you have contacted, so that they may consider other candidates.

 ## FINDING YOUR OWN INTERNSHIP

For a majority of students, independently finding an internship office is one of the most exciting challenges of their paralegal education. Sometimes it is a matter of necessity. In a rapidly growing program, for example, the school may not have created enough internships to guarantee a place for everyone. Some schools provide no leads at all, believing the internship search to be every student's personal responsibility.

Other times, it is a matter of students' preference. As the paralegal profession expands into more diverse settings, so do students' aspirations. Whatever your reason for seeking placement on your own, check with your program director before interviewing at an office that is new to your school to ensure its consistency with your program's objectives.

How to Find Internship Offices

The resources that are most helpful in finding offices depend on the kind of work setting you prefer. The following guidelines will help you locate prospective offices in the following categories: law offices, corporate business offices, nonprofit associations, and government offices.

Finding Law Offices For most students, the easiest place to start is the Lawyer's Directory for your state. Usually, lawyers are listed alphabetically and, in another nearby section, grouped by county or city. The latter

THE STUDENT'S PERSPECTIVE 4.1: SHAUNA
A Backfire of Failed Communications

"I never meant for this to happen," Shauna pleaded to her program director. "What can I do?" Her dream was to intern with the firm of Bertram and Zall in the litigation department. She thought it was all set—until a previous internship offer caught up with her.

A few days earlier, the director at her school had received a call from a sole practitioner, inquiring about Shauna's internship status. The sole practitioner had also interviewed Shauna and told her that she was perfect for his office. She had responded so favorably that he thought Shauna would be interning with him. Having turned away two other candidates in Shauna's favor and not having heard from her lately, he wondered what happened. The director apologized and told him that Shauna reportedly had accepted an internship elsewhere.

Confused and upset, the sole practitioner described the incident to local colleagues. Through the legal grapevine, the sole practitioner's unhappy story reached the supervisor at Bertram and Zall, who then developed reservations about Shauna's reliability. Soon afterward, Shauna received a call from Bertram and Zall and was told: "We've decided we would be better off with someone else." Of course, the sole practitioner would no longer have her either; he was too angry. Suddenly, Shauna was left with nowhere to intern.

"In my interview with the sole practitioner, he never said—in so many words—that I was definitely interning there," Shauna explained. "So I assumed it was, well, just sort of 'open.' Was that so bad?"

"Only if you allowed him to assume differently," the director cautioned. "Did you tell him about Bertram and Zall?"

"Well, I meant to," was the answer. "I called to tell him I had settled on another office, but he was in court that day. I meant to call again later but I was so busy, I forgot."

The consequences were serious for both Shauna and her school. Another internship was hastily arranged in the short time she had left, but it did not meet many of Shauna's litigation career goals. Meanwhile, the school lost Bertram and Zall, as well as the sole practitioner, as internship offices for future students.

At least Shauna learned a valuable lesson about job hunting: never mislead prospective employers—even inadvertently. Clear communications with all players is essential.

is the most handy reference for finding law offices located near you. In addition, the *yellow pages* of the telephone directory for your target city (look under "Lawyers" or "Attorneys") is a gold mine of information regarding the kind of work performed in the law offices that advertise there. Often, the yellow pages ads list the names of lawyer-partners and sometimes the names of well-established associates as well. More specific information, such as the professional background of individual lawyers and law firms, their major clients, and their primary areas of practice can be gleaned from the *Martindale-Hubbell Law Directory*. In fact, no law office should be contacted until this source (found in nearly every law library and also on the Internet) has been checked.

Finding Corporate Opportunities   One of the best sources of information on corporations in your area is *The Career Guide 1998: Dun's Employment Opportunities Directory,* which is published annually by Dun and Bradstreet, Inc., in Bethlehem, Pennsylvania. It can be found in many public libraries. It might also be available at the college library or placement office of larger schools that can afford its hefty subscription price. Your library may have other directories that are quite good, but the information in this one is among the most reliable and up-to-date you can find anywhere—short of contacting each corporation yourself.

In spite of its comprehensive coverage, *Dun's Employment Opportunities Directory* is surprisingly easy to use. It lists employers in several different ways: by state; by industry; by disciplines hired; and also according to location of branch offices, state by state. One section lists employers offering work-study and internship opportunities. Each of these sections is color-coded for easy identification. The "industry" section does include "legal" as one industry, and lists mostly insurance companies. Because this is a directory of business corporations, law offices are not included.

The larger, alphabetical listing in the front of the directory contains the longest, most detailed reports about each company. These lengthier, alphabetical descriptions should be checked for every company a student intends to contact so that he or she can be a knowledgeable applicant in phone calls, letters, and interviews.

One word of caution is needed about this reference book. Companies that have substantial legal departments and hire paralegals regularly do not, unfortunately, usually list "legal" (much less "paralegal") among the professionals hired—perhaps due to the publisher's method of gathering information. This oversight should not discourage students from inquiring about possible paralegal internships with corporate employers. The important question is where the company's legal department is located: at a facility near you or at corporate headquarters in another state.

For corporations having a legal department in your locale, standard information (such as office address, names of the principal officers) might also be obtained from the office of your *Secretary of State.* Sometimes the name of the corporation's legal counsel is also a part of the state's records.

Finding Nonprofit Associations   These admirable but often struggling organizations can be difficult to locate. For associations whose names you already know, the *white pages* of the telephone directory may be your best starting point. If you know that an association has offices in your state but you are not sure of the city in which it is based, the Secretary of State's office can often supply this information because nonprofit entities are ordinarily registered with the state in which they operate.

Another technique is to check the periodicals section of a large public library for specialty magazines, trade journals, and publications of special-interest groups. Often the association and the publisher are one and the same, so the address is easy to obtain in this way. In addition, these publications frequently contain display ads and news about an association's local and regional chapters and offices.

In addition, there is a four-volume directory of nonprofit associations, which—like *Dun's Employment Opportunities Directory*—is available at many libraries. Known as the *Encyclopedia of Associations '98* (published annually by Gale Research, Inc., in Detroit, Michigan), it bills itself as the only comprehensive source of detailed information on thousands of non-profit American membership organizations of national scope. It lists associations by subject matter such as environmental and agricultural; legal, government, public administration and military organizations under one heading; educational organizations under another; and cultural organizations under yet another heading, to name a few examples. A companion volume groups associations by region and a separate index volume lists organizations alphabetically.

The *Encyclopedia of Associations* can be difficult to use, perhaps partly due to the constantly changing nature of the associations it reports. Their addresses, phone numbers, and key personnel tend to change fairly often. Information is sometimes outdated by the time it is published, so patience and persistence may be required.

Finding Government Offices   The surest source of information about state, county, and municipal offices in your area—including court clerks' offices—is the Lawyer's Directory for your state. Usually, this directory contains separate listings for state administrative agencies, state courts, county offices, and municipal offices. In most states, the Lawyer's Directory also lists federal government agencies, United States District Court offices, Bankruptcy Court offices, and other local federal courts.

The white pages of the telephone directory also lists state offices. Check listings following the name of your state, county, and city or town, respectively. For federal agencies and military offices in your area, look under "United States." In addition, the office of your local state legislator or of your local congressional representative can supply information about the state or federal government offices you are considering.

Students looking for an internship in law enforcement might ask the reference librarian for a copy of the *National Directory of Law Enforcement*, published annually by the National Police Chiefs and Sheriffs Information Bureau in Stevens Point, Wisconsin. It lists chiefs of police, sheriffs, county and district prosecutors, state criminal investigation units, correctional agencies, numerous federal agencies, certain United States military units, and other offices.

In addition to the above resources, the World Wide Web may be another source of information on prospective officers for internships (see Table 4.1).

Whom Should I Approach First?

After selecting your target offices, the question arises: "Whom in this office should I speak to first?" When job hunting, successful candidates are usually those who zero in on the person who has power to make a hiring decision. In internship hunting, the same rule applies. For example, career counselors often warn job hunters to avoid personnel or human resources offices in large organizations because the normal function of these offices is to screen out candidates—not to hire them. Instead, many counselors recommend going directly to the person for whom you want to work. This strategy is usually effective for internships as well.

A major exception is when an in-house internship program already exists in your target office. In this situation, the personnel director or human resources manager may be the person who oversees the selection of student-interns. He or she may have even designed the in-house program and, as a result, may know more about it than anyone else in the office.

Table 4.1

Researching Offices on the World Wide Web

The Internet provides easy, cost-free access to many helpful resources. Be warned, however, that the Internet is perhaps the least reliable of all media. Many Web sites contain out-of-date information. Some are "under construction" and therefore incomplete. Nevertheless, Web sites often provide helpful leads that shorten your research significantly. Here are several locations to try.

States' Home Pages

Many states' home pages will lead you to a wealth of information about each state's courts, government offices, regulatory agencies, cities and towns, chambers of commerce, and sometimes major businesses as well. Some even list employment opportunities. Check the "menus" that are provided for a variety of leads.

Each state's Internet address follows the same pattern: *www.state.___.us*, with the postal abbreviation for each state typed into the space between "state." and "us." For example, the home page for Pennsylvania is *www.state.pa.us* and the one for Texas is *www.state.tx.us*.

United States Government Agencies

For information about United States federal government agencies, try *www.lib.lsu.edu/gov/fedgov.html*. For information about the United States Courts, try the United States Courts' home page at *www.uscourts.gov*.

State Bar Association Home Pages

Many state bar associations have home pages, sometimes with links to the home pages of major law firms. Try *www.___bar.org* with an appropriate abbreviation for your state typed into the space indicated. For example, the home page for Massachusetts Bar Association is *www.massbar.org*. Alternatively, try this site, which provides links to various bar associations and law firms: *www.clark.net/pub/cargui/legal.html*.

Lawyers and Law Firms

In addition, information about attorneys and law firms can often (but not always) be found at the following locations:

- *www.martindale.com* (the *Martindale-Hubbell Law Directory*)
- *www.westpub.com/htbin.wld* (*West's Legal Directory*)
- *www.yahoo.com/business_and_economy/companies/law/firms*
- *www.legal.net/attorney.viewlist.html*

Businesses and Nonprofit Organizations

For information about corporations, businesses, and major nonprofit organizations, a good place to start is the "Bigbook" at *www.bigbook.com*. Other routes include large, general search engines such as

- AltaVista at *http://altavista.digital.com*
- InfoSeek Net Search at *www.infoseek.com*
- Yahoo at *www.yahoo.com*

Table 4.2

Sample Telephone Inquiry

Receptionist: Good morning, Rodriguez and Steinman.

Student: Good morning. My name is Chris Dumont. I'm a paralegal student at South Dakota Paralegal College. I'd like to speak to Attorney Rodriguez, please.

Receptionist: I'm sorry, he's with a client. May I ask what this is regarding?

Student: It's not a legal matter. I'm just calling with a question regarding my paralegal program. It won't take but a minute or two. What would be a more convenient time to reach him?

Receptionist: Well, wait a moment, now. I think I see the client getting ready to leave. I'll see if Mr. Rodriguez is free. Please hold.

Attorney: Gerald Rodriguez.

Student: Mr. Rodriguez—hello. And thank you for taking my call. I'm Chris Dumont, a senior paralegal student at South Dakota Paralegal College. I was hoping we might just briefly discuss whether I could volunteer my paralegal training to your office to fulfill my college's internship requirement.

Attorney: Oh, right. I've heard about that. Smith, Ballen and James had an intern from your program last year. 'Sounds good in theory, Chris, but we're so busy here, we just don't have time to train and supervise an inexperienced paralegal. Sorry.

Student: I understand your concern—you have a busy law practice to run. What I think you'll find, though, is that we're far more experienced than many lawyers realize. May I send you copies of some of the drafting work I've done, so you can judge for yourself? I understand you do a lot of corporate work, wills, and litigation, for example. I'd be happy to send you sample documents I've prepared in each of those areas. I think you'll be pleasantly surprised.

Attorney: Sure, I'll take a look at your work. Supervision is still a big obstacle, though. You have to understand—I'm not even in the office half the time.

Student: What I would be doing, Mr. Rodriguez, is working to *reduce* your workload, not add to it. One of the things we've learned in our program is how to find our own answers to questions, and also to work with whoever's available—not just looking to one overworked attorney. I really don't think this is the big time gobbler you imagine it to be. Just the opposite—I'd be there to *help* you out.

Attorney: Tell you what—send me what you've got. I'll look it over, talk to my partner, and see what she thinks. When is this internship supposed to take place? I do have an appeal coming up and I really could use some help with that. Are you any good at research?

Student: September 15 until December 15, Mr. Rodriguez, and yes—I've had great comments on every research project I've done. We're required to put in at least 200 hours, but I'll be able to put in more hours than that if you need it. How about if I send a copy of our internship guidelines along with my work samples? They explain the whole set-up pretty well. After you've had a chance to look it all over, we can meet in person to see if I'm really someone you want in your office and to discuss any other details you might need cleared up.

Attorney: You're a very persuasive person, Chris. Sure, send it all. Then maybe we'll talk, okay?

Student: Great! I'll send it out right away. Thank you so much, Mr. Rodriguez. It's really been a pleasure talking to you.

When a certain contact person is named on your school's internship list, contact only that person by whatever method (letter or phone call) is specified. If no contact method is specified, begin with a brief telephone confirmation of internship availability (see Table 4.2); then follow up with your letter and résumé.

Follow these guidelines in determining whom to contact first:

- With *law offices* (including the public defender and legal assistance offices), your best bet is to telephone the lawyer or experienced paralegal for whom you want to work. If the approval of a legal administrator or personnel director is also needed, you will be told. You may then comply with whatever procedures the office requires, knowing that at least you have the "go-ahead" from the professional with whom you will work.

- There is one exception to the law offices rule just stated. If you have targeted an office that offers *an in-house internship program,* ask to speak to the person who directs that program.

- When seeking a *corporate internship,* ask to speak to the head of the department in which you want to work (such as legal department, employee benefits, contracts administration). If you do not know the individual's name, ask for him or her by department job title. This strategy also works with banks, insurance companies, and other corporate entities.

- Do not discuss internship details with the switchboard operator or whoever takes incoming calls. At most, briefly explain the nature of your call to this person.

- Getting past the switchboard operator or secretary at *governmental* and *court offices* can be difficult. If asked about the reason for your call, explain that you are a student who wants to volunteer paralegal services. If the operator is not cooperative, just get the name of the person you need and call back later.

- When seeking *military internships,* begin by contacting the Office of Volunteer Services at the base near you.

- With *nonprofit associations,* almost anyone who answers the phone will be delighted that someone wants to volunteer time and service. Whoever has the authority to decide about interns will probably get back to you promptly.

Getting to talk to the person you want often takes persistence and a bit of ingenuity. Occasionally, an overworked secretary or switchboard operator may provide inaccurate or incomplete information just to move on to the next call. If this happens, ignore it and try again an hour or two later.

How to Make the First Contact

Unless you are instructed otherwise, the initial contact is best made by telephone. Unsolicited letters and résumés are almost always a waste of time. If they are not addressed to the right person or if no one is expecting them, they might end up in the wastebasket. A telephone inquiry in advance helps create the right expectations in the right individuals and ensures that your follow-up letter and résumé will be read attentively by its recipient.

If your telephone inquiry is not successful, try paying the office a personal visit. Dress professionally and prepare for the visit as you would for an interview (see the Interview section, later in this chapter). Such a presentation will bring tremendous credibility to your inquiry. But be prepared to settle—graciously—for an appointment with the right person at a later time.

What Should I Say When I Reach Them?

The purpose of your initial telephone inquiry is to get two questions answered:

1. Would this office consider a paralegal internship at this time?
2. To whom do I address my letter and résumé for consideration?

The first question is the most important of the entire conversation. Save it for the person who is in a position to answer it with some authority, such as the attorney, paralegal, or department head for whom you hope to intern. This is also a question that should be followed quickly with pertinent information, before the listener has a chance to say no.

Anticipate the concerns that your listener is likely to have and try to address them even before they are raised. Have in front of you a copy of your program's internship guidelines, policies, or brochure for easy reference. Or have within easy view your own written list of key points. Try to address the office's most likely concerns even before they are expressed, such as:

- Is this to be a paid or unpaid internship? If unpaid, this is a key selling point that you should mention early in the conversation.
- How long would the internship last?
- How much supervision and instruction will be required—an hour or two per week, or (gasp!) per day?
- What kind of training do you already have?

If you quickly put your listener's mind at ease on these issues, you bring yourself closer to a "yes"—or at least a "maybe"—on your first and most important question: would they consider an internship at this time. The rest is easy.

Doubtful questions can be cut short by offering to send your school's written guidelines or brochure along with your résumé, so they can think about your proposal without feeling pressured. If they agree, you have already paved the way to step two: introducing your résumé and cover letter.

Here are a few additional techniques you can use to help overcome the doubts you may detect at the other end of the phone:

- Speak in a calm and professional manner.
- If the office supervisor seems to misinterpret your intentions, briefly mention the fact that you are *volunteering* your services (if that is the case) for a *temporary* position.
- Mention the name of your school and any outstanding features for which it is known (such as "ABA-approved" or "the largest" or "the first" in your area). Your school's reputation adds credibility and clout to your inquiry.
- Name-dropping sometimes helps. If a former intern or someone in the legal community suggested this office, say so and mention that person by name. You can also provide the name and phone number of your program director.
- Early in the conversation, offer to send samples of your work. Or, as a test of your usefulness to the office, offer to research a legal issue of the supervisor's choosing for his or her review. (One paralegal program requires this of all internship candidates.[1])
- If you are cut short or if your call is misdirected, try again the following workday.

Fielding Unusual Questions

Be well-acquainted with your program's internship policies and guidelines so you can respond competently to routine questions about scheduling, reporting, evaluations, and so on. (Always have these details handy as you call.) Having established clear learning objectives for yourself, you are also prepared to discuss internship tasks and assignments. But in spite of the best preparation, a question will sometimes be raised that you cannot—or should not—answer on your own.

Often these are questions that suggest some departure from normal procedure. For example, you might be told that interns must attend in-house training sessions prior to the internship or that this office only uses its own forms, criteria, and timetable for evaluations. In such situations, your best approach is a noncommittal one that buys you time to consult your director. A good, all-purpose response is: "That might work fine, but I won't know for sure until I check with my program director. How soon do you need to know if this is okay?" Then contact your director immediately about it.

Other times, it is not a question but a statement that causes you concern. Broad, discouraging remarks often signal a misunderstanding of what an internship involves. "We don't have time for training and supervising" is a common example. Does this statement mean they do not have time for *constant* supervising (which no one expects anyway) or that they do not even have time for a few short conversations each week (which is probably closer to your own expectations)?

When such doubts are expressed, rapid clarification is needed and you should lead the way. Define what you understand to be adequate supervising. You might also offer to have your director call them for further clarification on that point.

WRITTEN COMMUNICATIONS THAT OPEN DOORS

In most successful internship searches, the cover letter and résumé do not precede the initial telephone (or in-person) inquiry—they follow it. This sequence is different from the procedure used by some job seekers who blanket the legal community with résumés and then make follow-up calls, usually without success.[2] The send-résumé-then-telephone technique is a high-cost recipe for rejection and frustration. In many offices, the only résumés that are read seriously are those received from experienced candidates, and only when there is a currently advertised opening.

Most offices will not consider a student intern unless the idea was introduced to them first, in a way that made it sound useful. If your target office never heard of you or your school's internship program, then your unexpected letter and résumé are likely to be discarded. But if you handled your telephone inquiries well, you probably succeeded in introducing the idea effectively in several offices. Your résumé will then be read attentively by someone who matters to you.

The Purpose of a Cover Letter and Résumé

A good letter and résumé accomplish three things. First, the letter tells prospective supervisors why you want to intern with *them*, as opposed to the many other offices you could have contacted. Second, your résumé highlights the training and qualifications that make you useful to their work. And third, your letter and résumé continue to convey absolute professionalism—this time in written form.

Your Cover Letter: Why *This* Office?

Nothing gets others' attention faster than genuine interest in who they are and what they do. Conveying such interest is a main objective of the internship-seeker's cover letter.

If you did your assignments in the preceding chapters, you already know why you are interested in the offices you have targeted. These offices have a high probability of meeting your personal learning objectives and career goals. You have researched the work they do, and it is the same work that you would like to pursue as a career. You may even have learned something about the educational and professional backgrounds of key individuals in this office and found something that you admired. If you have done these things, then each cover letter has almost written itself.

Cover letters should be no more than one page long. They should have a formal business format (see Table 4.3 for an example). The body of the letter usually conforms to the following outline:

Table 4.3

Internship Inquiry Letter

2345 Education Road
Paralegal City, North Dakota 02000

August 10, 1998

Gerald Rodriguez, Esquire
Rodriguez & Steinman, P.A.
54321 Career Way
Opportunity City, North Dakota 02222

RE: Paralegal Internship

Dear Attorney Rodriguez:

Thank you for taking the time to speak with me yesterday about the possibility of interning with your office. I am genuinely excited about the prospect of working with a firm like yours.

One of my goals is to acquire a well-rounded experience, and your busy general practice presents a wonderful opportunity to do that. I am especially enthusiastic about your need for research for an upcoming appeal. Challenging research is something I have always enjoyed, and I welcome the chance to bring my research skills to the highest possible level. Your involvement in local politics is also fascinating to me. I've often dreamed of running for office myself someday. So it would be a pleasure to use my paralegal skills to assist you with your campaign, should the need arise.

You may remember that North Dakota Paralegal College requires its interns to begin work on September 15 and to complete at least 200 internship hours by December 15. A copy of my program's internship guidelines is enclosed, along with a copy of my résumé and three work samples. The name and telephone number of my program director also appears on the guidelines.

I will telephone your office at the end of next week to see whether you would like to schedule an interview. Please feel free to call me in the meantime with any questions you may have. I can be reached at (701) 555-9340. I truly look forward to meeting you.

Sincerely,

Chris Dumont

Enclosures (5)

1. *Introduction:* Begin with a short introduction reminding the reader of the recent telephone (or in-person) conversation about a possible internship. This paragraph should be short—only one or two sentences in length—and convey a cordial tone.
2. *Rationale:* A longer paragraph follows, stating two or three reasons for wanting to intern with this firm. Describe learning objectives that are consistent with work performed in this office. Mention other features that attracted you to this office, such as its reputation or its computer facilities. Avoid citing features that are not work related (such as convenient location or anticipated compensation).
3. *Internship essentials:* This short paragraph explains essential details of the internship such as the date it begins and the number of internship hours needed. Also refer here to your enclosures, which are (1) your résumé; (2) a copy of your program's internship brochure, guidelines, or policy statement, if one is available; and (3) possibly some work samples. If no brochure or any equivalent is available, you can enclose an information sheet of your own, following the instructions in Action Form 4.4 at the end of this chapter.
4. *Closing:* End with an upbeat sentence stating when you will contact them again. Make sure your letter creates a bridge to an appropriate next step.

Each office is unique and each offers different career and learning opportunities. For that reason, it is to your advantage to tailor your cover letters to each office. Let each letter speak honestly but specifically of the recipient-office as if it were the only internship letter you were sending. Such personalization creates maximum impact on those you most want to reach.

Your Résumé: Emphasize the Relevant

Countless job-hunting guides and résumé "how-to" books are on the market, providing extensive and detailed instructions on creating a résumé. Generally, all such guides describe two ways of presenting your background and experience in a résumé: chronologically and functionally.

The oldest method is the chronological résumé. Under the customary headings (mainly education and work experience), information is listed in reverse chronological order, beginning with the most recent experience at the top of each list, and then working backward through time.

From an employer's point of view, the chronological résumé has only one advantage: it accounts for the applicant's entire professional history. Any gaps in the applicant's employment history (such as for child-rearing, hospitalization, or—heaven forbid—jail sentences) become easy to spot. An explanation can then be requested. In other words, the chronological résumé becomes a basis for screening out candidates but rarely any reason for hiring them.

The chronological résumé has far more disadvantages than advantages. Chronologically listed job titles tell little or nothing about what applicants actually did in their jobs, what achievements were attained, and what skills were developed. For applicants with a limited job history and also for many career changers, the lack of achievement-based information in their résumés can cripple their job search.

Now imagine a résumé listing not job titles but skills and functions that law offices value, noting several personal achievements under each. For example, under "Organizational Experience," a student might write as one entry, the following:

> *Responsible for properly storing, displaying, documenting, and maintaining records for 2,500 leased items without error over a three-month period.*

Does this sound more like someone who would be a definite asset to a busy law office? Of course it does, even though it is a description of a video store clerk—a position that is not even remotely related to law. That is how the functional or achievements-oriented résumé works. It highlights tasks and accomplishments experienced in previous jobs that would be of value in a paralegal internship, even though these tasks were not performed in a law-related setting.

The functional or achievements-style résumé can also include references to nonpaying jobs. Students who have done significant volunteer work should list the relevant skills and accomplishments they have experienced in that effort. Outstanding course work can also be included. When course work accounts for the only drafting, research, or other law office tasks that the student has ever performed, it is all the more important to mention specific examples in your résumé.

Tables 4.4 and 4.5 give you examples of each type of résumé—chronological (to be avoided unless you have fairly substantial law office experience) and functional or achievements-based (better for highlighting relevant accomplishments and skills). To satisfy the few offices that still expect to see a chronological job history, you can add a brief chronology at the bottom of the résumé, or note at the end of your achievements-style résumé that a full job history will be provided on request. If you decide on the latter approach, be sure that you have such a chronological history ready.

A word of caution about functional or achievements-style résumés: do not become too imaginative in describing skills or accomplishments. If a description of a summer job in the complaints department at Macy's reads like a job description for president and CEO of the company, all credibility is lost. At the same time, avoid being too ambiguous about the nature of previous employment. Provide enough specifics so that earlier jobs are not mysterious.

Look for examples of difficult achievements and useful skills—every student has several. Describe them in meaningful detail, and keep the descriptions within the realm of verifiable reality. For an intern's functional or achievements-style résumé, specific items can be listed under some of the following categories:

- Computer skills (every student should include this)
- Organizational ability
- Drafting experience
- Research experience
- Analytical skills
- Writing experience
- Litigation experience (or experience in criminal law, probate, environmental law, etc.)
- Administrative or managerial experience
- Technical expertise (such as nursing, engineering, accounting, bookkeeping, or others, if relevant)
- Experience with clients or customer relations
- Problem-solving ability
- Publications

Résumé guides and job-hunting manuals typically recommend limiting your résumé to one page and, in many offices, a one-page résumé is what employers expect. For young candidates with limited work experience, the one-page rule is probably easy to follow. For mature career changers, this may be a difficult restriction.

As you consider each résumé item, ask yourself: how might this skill or achievement be useful in this particular internship setting? Are you listing

Table 4.4

Chronological-Style Résumé

CHRIS DUMONT
2345 Education Road
Paralegal City, North Dakota 02000
(701) 555-9340

Education	North Dakota Paralegal College (ABA-approved; Paralegal Certificate to be completed in December, 1998)
	North Dakota University (B.A., History, 1997)
	Voorhees County Community College (A.A., Political Science, 1995)
Honors	Dean's List, Spring and Fall Semesters, 1996-1997
	"Who's Who in American College and Universities," 1997
	Legal Writing Award, 1996
Employment History	*Substitute History Teacher* (September 1997 to present) City Township Middle School City Township, North Dakota
	Head Counselor and Staff Coordinator (Summer, 1997) Mount Kuaola Summer Camp Mount Kuaola, South Dakota
	Night Clerk (1995–1996) Grand Hotel Opportunity City, North Dakota
	Library Assistant (1994–1995) Voorhees County Community College City Township, North Dakota
	Camp Counselor (Summers, 1994 and 1995) Mount Kuaola Summer Camp Mount Kuaola, South Dakota
	Assistant Manager (1994-1995) Johann's Deli Paralegal City, North Dakota
	Wait Staff (1993-1994) Johann's Deli Paralegal City, North Dakota
Activities	Member, North Dakota Paralegal Association Student Coordinator, Paralegal Speakers' Bureau, 1997 Volunteer Advisor, Voorhees County Elderly Services Bureau, 1998 Campaign Volunteer for State Senator Bob Gordon, 1997 Volunteer Sports Trainer, Coos Community Youth Program, 1994-1995
Computer Skills	Proficient in WESTLAW, LEXIS, WordPerfect, Windows, DOS, and Excel
Drafting Experience	Wills, trusts, deeds, real estate closing documents, corporate formation, partnership agreements, case briefs and all phases of civil litigation including complaints, answers, motions, interrogatories and other discovery documents, memoranda of law, and digesting of depositions.

REFERENCES AVAILABLE UPON REQUEST

Table 4.5

Functional or Achievements-Style Résumé

CHRIS DUMONT
2345 Education Road
Paralegal City, North Dakota 02000
(701) 555-9340

Education
- North Dakota Paralegal College (ABA-approved; Paralegal Certificate to be completed in December, 1998)
- North Dakota University (B.A., History, 1997)
- Voorhees County Community College (A.A., Political Science, 1995)

Honors
- Dean's List, Fall and Spring Semesters, 1996-1997
- "Who's Who in American Colleges and Universities," 1997

Qualifications
- Proficient in Westlaw, Lexis, WordPerfect, Windows, DOS, and Excel
- Award-winning legal researcher and writer
- Familiar with all phases of litigation procedure
- Well-rounded classroom drafting experience (pleadings, motions, corporate formation, partnerships, wills, trusts, closing documents)
- Excellent communication and organization skills
- Extensive experience dealing with the public
- Can work effectively under pressure

Professional Accomplishments

Research and Writing
- Winner of Legal Research Award, North Dakota Paralegal College, 1997
- Authored three pamphlets for Paralegal Speakers' Bureau publications

Organizational Skills
- Implemented computerization of law library records (Voorhees County Community College Library Assistant, 1994-1995)
- Designed a more efficient customer delivery system, increasing revenues by 30 percent (Assistant Manager, Johann's Deli, 1994-1995)

Problem-Solving Skills
- Resolved staff dispute and averted staff walkout (Staff Coordinator, Mount Kuaola Summer Camp, Summer, 1997)
- Responded effectively to emergency calls during understaffed periods, averting possible liability to employer (Night Clerk, Grand Hotel, 1995-1996)

Communications
- Counseled elderly clients on available community services (Voorhees County Elderly Services Bureau, 1998)
- Recruited a dozen new paralegal speakers for educational program (Student Coordinator, Paralegal Speakers' Bureau, 1997)
- Designed and implemented a promotional voters' survey for reelection of State Senator Bob Gordon, 1997
- Created a learning program for making American history more understandable and memorable to sixth-grade students (History Department Faculty Committee, City Township Middle School, 1997)

Personal
- Self-supporting throughout college
- Has own transportation; can travel throughout the region

Available Upon Request
- Writing samples
- List of relevant courses
- Excellent references

things at least *similar* to what the office wants an intern to do? If the answer is highly doubtful, omit the item. But if the answer is yes, then keep the item, perhaps shortening the description to a few key words to save space.

Additional relevant information can sometimes be discretely added in an addendum. For example, a list of relevant courses might be separately prepared, including a short description of each course and of key assignments you performed. To avoid having this taken as a second page of your résumé, let it carry a separate title such as "Paralegal Courses Completed."

Because each internship office is different, your cover letters were tailor-made for each office. You can do the same for your résumés. For example, you may have learned that one office needs research assistance whereas another expects a great deal of client contact. Your prior experience may cover both of these skills. To save résumé space, elaborate on your research experience only in one résumé and include lengthier details about previous client/customer relations in the other. This technique adds details only where they are needed, keeping each customized résumé to a single page.

Using a good word processor makes it easy to customize your résumé. If a master résumé is put on disk, then each printed résumé can be a slightly modified version of the original. Remember though, you are not making things up out of thin air. You are emphasizing different aspects of your training and experience for different internship settings.

Appearance is Critical

Your résumé and cover letter represent you. They convey all that you are as a newcomer to the profession. Consequently, the way these documents *look* is at least as important as what they say. In some ways, their appearance may be even more important. Every legal administrator has a story about otherwise good résumés that were discarded without further thought simply because of a sloppy or amateurish appearance.

Here are some of the résumé-killers that every applicant must avoid:

* Erasures or crossed-out items (this is the equivalent to a sign saying "Don't hire me!")
* Misspellings (use a dictionary, a spell-checker, or both)
* Poor grammar or sentence structure (use a grammar book, a grammar-checker, or both)
* Dot matrix printing (get access to a laser printer)
* Dirt or smudges (this is the "Don't hire me!" equivalent to erasures)
* Improper business format in letters
* Résumés that are poorly organized or hard to follow
* Anything that does not convey real information
* Anything that rambles
* Inaccuracies, such as in dates or names

The three most important things you can do for your résumé and letter are: proofread, proofread, and proofread. Then have someone else proofread these documents for you because most of us miss our own mistakes no matter how carefully we check. Send nothing until you are certain it is letter-perfect.

Use white or ivory-colored paper and matching, standard business-size envelopes. Use good quality bond—never the erasable kind. If you will have several enclosures, such as sample course work or lengthy internship guidelines, use a manila envelope large enough to send these items without folding. Be sure to include a return address and sufficient postage. Do use a word processor rather than a typewriter; it is faster and always results in a better appearance. As noted earlier, do get access to a laser printer for a crisp, professional look. Some copy shops will let you use theirs.

Let your letter and résumé convey the message you are a professional, like everyone else in that office. Prove that you are ready to become a member of the professional environment. Produce a piece of writing that the recipients would be proud to have their clients see.

THE INTERVIEW

Initial inquiries are over. Your résumé and other materials have been sent and reviewed by prospective supervisors. If you are now invited to an interview, you can arrive knowing you are being seriously considered. For the internship to become a reality, you must now make a favorable impression in the most potent medium of all—in person.

Dress and Appearance

As with many occupations, lawyers have a sort of uniform. For men and women alike, it is the suit. It conveys many messages, including authority and confidence. The suit says: "I accept the conventions of the profession. I am a team player. I belong here. I am successful enough to wear this suit, and discreet enough not to wear anything gaudy."[3]

In your initial interview, make your appearance shout "professional!" Your appearance need not be identical to that of a lawyer but, in a law office, it does need to be compatible with the atmosphere lawyers tend to create. If you are interviewing at a private firm where coats and ties—or jackets and skirts—are normally the rule, do not wear anything less formal. If you are interviewing in a more casual, non-law-office environment where coworkers wear somewhat more relaxed attire, such as in a nonprofit service organization, you should still treat the interview as a special, relatively formal event and wear business attire for this occasion. You can always adopt the more relaxed styles of those around you after your internship begins and you are more certain of the office's expectations.

The cost of looking professional is a frightening thought for many students, particularly those who are working for little or no compensation. Do not overlook discount stores and thrift shops where a very professional-looking outfit can be had for a small fraction of the cost others may be paying. The label is not important. What counts is the overall impression you make, and you can achieve that with surprisingly little money.

The following list of "dos" will help you succeed in your interview, perhaps laying the groundwork toward a permanent job.

DO:

- Wear a blazer, sports coat, or suit jacket over a coordinated skirt or dress (women) or dress pants (men) for the best effect. A jacket or blazer conveys authority—similar to a suit—like nothing else you can wear. It can be removed when informality is preferred and put back on again when needed, such as to meet a distinguished managing partner, judge, or official. Most students should always have one, just in case.
- In most offices, men should always wear a tie.
- Wear only minimal jewelry.
- Wear a watch; you will need it.
- Keep hair neat and conservatively styled.

- Wear clean, polished shoes and dress hose.
- Carry a briefcase or portfolio. An inexpensive vinyl or canvas one is fine.

Lawyers of both sexes are very conservative in their appearance. "They're not trendy at all," says a lawyer and former editor of the *ABA Journal*.[4] And they expect the same conservatism from others in their office. Be sure it is your abilities that stand out and get noticed—not your clothes and makeup.

Most students are already aware of the "don'ts" in the following list, but some may need a gentle (and perhaps humorous) reminder.

DON'T:

- Wear "rock star," "rapper," or too-casual styles (spiked hair, baseball caps, etc.)
- Show up in jeans, cut-offs, or sweats
- Carry a large backpack
- Wear sneakers
- Wear white sport socks
- Forget socks or hosiery completely, wearing shoes on bare feet
- Wear pants where most of the women do not
- Wear low-cut or "peekaboo" dresses or blouses
- Wear skirts that are too short (or too tight) to sit opposite a boss or a client without causing distraction or embarrassment
- Dress as you would for a dinner party or wedding (ruffles, bows, satins, sequins, etc.)
- Wear lipstick or eye shadow so bright that it dominates your appearance
- Wear spindly, spike heels that inhibit walking
- Wear several earrings on one ear
- Wear visible body-piercing or face ornaments
- Display tattoos
- Keep fingernails too long for easy keyboarding
- Overwhelm everyone with perfume or cologne
- Forget to shower

Dressing more casually than others suggests you may also be more casual about your work, and that is not the impression you want to make. But do not worry that your clothes may be slightly more formal than the other paralegals or support staff in your office—at least during an interview. You will simply be seen as a serious student concerned about making a good first impression.

Right or wrong, your appearance has a huge impact on how the world perceives everything else you do. Follow the preceding dress guidelines and you will be taking the first step toward establishing yourself as a polished professional.

Preparing for the Interview

Never go into an interview "cold." Several fairly predictable issues are likely to be raised during the interview. Prepare to respond to them smoothly and knowledgeably.

Review each of the following items before interviewing:

- Your immediate learning objectives (established in Chapter 1)
- Your longer-term career goals (established in Chapters 1 and 2)
- Your reasons for wanting to work in this particular office
- Your résumé, particularly the experience and achievements that you can describe in some detail

- Your research findings about this office and the individuals with whom you may be working
- Your program's internship requirements
- Unavoidable limitations that your supervisor needs to know about, such as scheduling restrictions or the lack of a car

As you answer the interviewer's questions—or perhaps when your interviewer is finished asking them—be sure to outline your own internship objectives. *To be fair to yourself and to each office, you need to convey your learning objectives and career goals to the interviewer.* For example, if you are uncertain about the area of law in which you would like to concentrate and you therefore want as varied an experience as possible, this preference should be stated. If you want to fine-tune your research strategies, drafting ability, or client relations skills, say so. The response you receive to these requests helps you gauge the office's value as an internship option.

Prepare your own checklist of questions. Some questions should be geared toward discovering your office's objectives. Why are they seeking a student intern? What do they hope the internship will accomplish for them? This information gives you insight into their motivation and helps determine how compatible their objectives are with yours. In addition, you will probably need answers to the following:

- What work schedule is expected?
- Who will be responsible for your supervision and final evaluation? How often will you be able to meet with this person?
- What kinds of assignments can you expect?
- From what other people might you receive assignments?
- Are there other paralegals there to mentor you—to answer routine questions, provide work samples, and give occasional guidance?
- Is a separate work space available? Where will it be?
- What equipment is available for you to do your work?
- Is any secretarial support available, at least for high-pressure projects? (Do not be too surprised if the answer is no.)
- Will you be responsible for all your own word processing?
- Will your responsibilities require driving to other locations and are travel expenses reimbursed, at least for longer trips?
- Might this office be hiring a paralegal in the near future? (Do not leave without asking this last question!)

Add to this list specific questions for your interviewer pertaining to your learning objectives and career goals. Keep questions simple and polite, focusing only on issues relevant to the internship and to your career.

Unless it is clear at the outset that payment for your internship is available, do not raise the issue of compensation until the internship is offered to you. Even then, do it gently and cautiously. Do not appear presumptuous or pushy.

Do not go to your interview empty-handed. Have several things ready to take with you:

- The name, address, and telephone number of the office and of your interviewer
- Clear directions to the office and a plan (plus pocket change) for parking
- A clear understanding of how your interviewer's name is pronounced
- A few extra copies of your résumé
- Extra copies of relevant work samples from your paralegal courses (even if these were provided earlier)

- A copy of your program's internship guidelines, policies, or internship brochure (even if these were provided earlier)
- Samples of the forms or documents that your program uses for internships, such as a learning contract, internship agreement, or evaluation form.
- The name, address, and telephone number for your program director or your director's business card
- A note pad for taking notes during the interview
- A professional-looking pen (not a chewed-up pencil)
- An inexpensive but professional-looking portfolio for carrying these things—maybe one with your school's name on it

Before interviewing, conduct a trial run. Practice how you will get through the question-and-answer process. You can take turns role-playing with another student or practice interviewing with a relative, an instructor, your program director, or a counselor from your school's placement office. Have someone ask you about the items interviewers often focus on (see Fielding Interviewers' Questions below).

Also, rehearse the questions you have for your interviewer. Try different approaches to your questions and answers and decide what wording is most effective. Videotape a practice interview, if you can, and play it back for yourself. What you see may astonish you. Some schools occasionally make videotaping available for this purpose.

Conducting Yourself Effectively

Appearance and attitude convey an instantaneous impression that can make or break the success of the entire meeting. *Interviewers often make unconscious decisions about a candidate during the first minute of the interview. Make that minute count.*

Plan your trip to arrive at least ten minutes ahead of schedule. The extra minutes give you time to find the right office, stop by the rest room to check your appearance in the mirror, and walk through the office door calmly, composed, and better than on time. Never make interviewers wait for you. With each passing moment, they will become more convinced that you are a poor candidate.

Because the first impression counts so much, rehearse your entrance and greeting. Practice striding into the room confidently, smiling, with arm outstretched for a handshake. Look right at your interviewer and say, "Hello, I'm . . . ." Shake hands firmly, and repeat the interviewer's name when introduced. "I'm really glad to meet you, Ms. (or Mr.) Interviewer." Then pause for a moment to be asked to have a seat.

Allow the interviewer to lead the way with his or her own questions but be prepared to start the conversation if the interviewer does not. You can break the ice with a cheerful remark about your drive to the interview or something you have seen in the office that you like. Remarks and questions from the interviewer will probably follow but be prepared to begin the interview with a relevant opening question of your own, just in case. Something related to your career objectives is the best place to start. Above all, convey the image of someone who is polite, composed, and confident.

Look the interviewer right in the eye frequently while talking. If you are interviewed by more than one person at a time (a multiple interviewer situation), be sure to look at each of them from time to time as you talk.

Answer questions in a clear, firm voice. Do not just say yes and no as answers; elaborate further. With positive responses, add an anecdotal example from your classes, former job, or course assignments. Explain negative answers in as positive a way as possible, mentioning what you are

Table 4.6

Sample Interview Discussion

Receptionist:	Good morning. Can I help you?
Student:	Good morning—yes. I'm Chris Dumont. I have a 10:30 appointment with Attorney Rodriguez.
Receptionist:	Oh, yes, of course. He's expecting you. Go right on in to the office on your left.
Student:	Attorney Rodriguez, hello. I'm Chris Dumont.
Attorney:	Well hello, Chris. It's nice to finally meet you. Have a seat. You had no problems finding our office, I see.
Student:	It's great to meet you, too, sir. No, no problem at all. Your secretary gave me directions the other day—really helpful.
Attorney:	So, tell me, Chris, why did you become a paralegal student? Why not computer science, English, sociology—something like that?
Student:	Actually, those are all interesting subjects. But law has always been my first love, ever since taking a business law course in high school. The entire legal system is fascinating to me, as is lawmaking in general. My dream is to learn as much as possible about how the law works on an everyday basis and really experience that in depth, and then run for legislative office some day.
Attorney:	Yes, you mentioned that in your letter. 'Looks like we have a thing or two in common, don't we.
Student:	(smiling) That's why I'm here!
Attorney:	That's great. There seem to be a lot of things you're good at, Chris. What are the problem areas? Everybody has some. What do you find most difficult in your studies, for example?
Student:	I'll admit that staring at columns of numbers for too long tends to bring on a kind of number blindness after a while. I ran into this problem in an accounting course I had to take. I found that it went a lot better if I just took occasional breaks from the numbers and worked on something else for a few minutes. But even with this problem, I still managed to get a B in my accounting course. So, although numbers are not my greatest strength, I've learned that I can handle them.
Attorney:	Good. Chris, I've looked over the résumé you sent, and I do have a few questions. This is your last quarter at South Dakota Paralegal College, right?
Student:	Yes, which means that I've completed all my required paralegal courses. All I have left is one paralegal elective. I was planning to ask what you would recommend for that—what might be most helpful to this office, for example.
Attorney:	Let's see, have you had environmental law yet? I have a big appeal coming up in that area.
Student:	No, but I believe I can still register for that.
Attorney:	I also need a paralegal with excellent research skills, Chris. Tell me about the research you've done so far.
Student:	Sure, Mr. Rodriguez. I have an extra copy here of a research memorandum I prepared last semester for my Advanced Legal Research course.
Attorney:	Oh, right. I remember seeing that with the résumé you sent. Looks pretty good. Is that all your own work?
Student:	Yes, it is. No two assignments were alike, so we each had to work on our own. This particular assignment required a great deal of research because it involved a novel question of law. There were no cases on point in this jurisdiction—and, believe me, I checked everything. It was quite a challenging project.
Attorney:	Not unlike the appeal I've got coming up. This arrangement is starting to sound like it might work, Chris.

doing to fix the problem or to compensate for it. An example appears in Table 4.6.

When the interviewer seems to have completed the inquiry, ask questions of the interviewer. Have a list of questions ready. Present your questions courteously. Keep them brief and to the point. Try to couch each question in terms of the reason for it, such as: "I will still be attending classes on Tuesday and Thursday afternoons, so, would a Monday and Wednesday work schedule be acceptable?"

Now that you understand what to *do* during an interview, here are some important "don'ts":

DON'T:

- Say negative things about others—instructors, students, previous employers, politicians, famous personalities, or *anyone*—no matter how true your comments might be
- Tell jokes—especially any that are off-color, racist, sexist, or ethnically offensive
- Smoke or chew gum
- Resort to childlike gestures such as rolling your eyes, waving your arms, shouting, or giggling
- Let your eyes wander around the room
- Digress from the subject at hand except to point out something that is important to your candidacy or to this internship
- Ramble; keep the discussion on track

Fielding Interviewers' Questions

Bringing a newcomer into the office always involves risks. Many of the questions put to you reflect unspoken concerns about those risks. The interviewer will be wondering: Are you someone who can get along with the other workers? Will you make an effort to fit into this environment? Can the office rely on you to do what you are asked to do, and on schedule? Can you be trusted to use good judgment? Or will your presence require inordinate amounts of time from supervisors and coworkers? The guiding principle behind every answer you give should be this: that you want to *contribute* to the work of this particular office. You want to be a working member of their team.

Interviewers' questions tend to focus on the following:

- Your relevant achievements and education ("So, tell me a little about yourself" is an invitation to talk about what you know, what you can do, and what you want to learn—not to describe to your childhood or life history)
- Your future career goals ("Where do you hope to be after graduation?" or "five years from now?")
- Your reasons for wanting to intern in this office ("So, what brings you to Garabaldi, Gingham and Girard?")
- Your ability to deal with problems or pressures ("What if . . . ?")
- The professional assets you bring to this position ("Do you have any experience in . . . ?")
- Your limitations or shortcomings ("I see you've never worked in a law-related position before.")

Look for an opportunity to talk about what motivates you toward this office. Are you here because this firm has a reputation as a leader in a certain area of the law? Were you attracted by their commitment to modern technology, to public service, or to leadership in the legal community? Did the experience or reputation of the prospective supervisor make this internship stand out? Know what your motivation is and be prepared to talk about it in specific terms. Candidates who just want "an internship—any internship" are not taken as seriously as those who have researched and selected particular internship offices. Let it be apparent that you have done that.

Take advantage of every chance to elaborate on your own experience and training when that becomes relevant. Remembering the main points in your achievement résumé, offer some detailed examples of past experience that will be helpful in this new setting. Have work samples on hand, even though

THE STUDENT'S PERSPECTIVE 4.2: DEY

"No, I've Never Worked in a Law Office, But . . . ."

Dey took a deep breath and silently counted to three. Until this moment, the interview had been going beautifully. The interviewer had said "Wow, these look really professional" when he saw the documents she had drafted for some of her courses. They even shared the same passion for the rights of children and protecting their interests in abuse cases. Then came the question she dreaded most: "I see you've never worked in a law office before; that's a major handicap, don't you think?"

Rather than talking about experience she lacked, Dey decided to focus on the experience she had. "That's true, but a lot of the training paralegals used to spend years slowly acquiring on the job has been provided to me in my courses. In fact, I think a well-structured educational program gives us a broader and sounder background than coming up the ladder from legal secretary.

"Unlike most paralegals whose training was acquired solely on the job, I have had detailed exposure to *several* major areas of law practice and I have the adaptability that comes with that. What's more, the extensive hands-on experience my instructors have given me is equal to perhaps a full year of work in a general practice firm.

"There will be procedural fine points I'll have to learn, along with nitty-gritty things like how your filing system works and how to find certain courthouses. I look forward to learning those things. But to tell you the truth, I don't feel handicapped at all. Quite the opposite—I believe I have a huge advantage over unschooled paralegals having years of experience but only in one or two narrow areas of law."

She was offered an internship on the spot.

---

some may have been sent in advance. Explain the skills that your work samples demonstrate.

One of the things being tested in the interview is your ability to communicate effectively. Be someone who volunteers useful, relevant, and positive information. Speak in full sentences. Talk in a natural, conversational voice—but clearly, so that each word is understandable.

Another thing that is sometimes tested in interviews is your problem-solving ability. You may be asked what you would do in certain difficult situations or how you would handle certain conflicts. Often such questions come in the form of a "what if" scenario, such as "What if an angry tenant calls demanding immediate advice about his landlord's actions. How would you handle that?" It is appropriate to pause and think for a moment in order to respond with an honest, but helpful answer.

Another variation is the question that asks you to cite your shortcomings. Though not as commonly asked in internship interviews as in real job interviews, an interviewer might use this approach out of habit. If there is a shortcoming that might cause a problem on the job—a difficulty talking on the phone, for example—then it probably should be mentioned honestly.

Then, restore your credibility by describing the efforts you have made to overcome the problem just mentioned. For example, a good response to the telephone difficulty would be: "I'm working to improve my telephone skills by helping with the college's fund-raising campaign. It involves telephoning alumni and reading from a script, but I find it's getting easier to go beyond the script and ad lib sometimes. The other day, I forgot about the script and persuaded a woman to contribute a hundred dollars!" Showing that you work constructively with your shortcomings helps turn them into a plus, rather than a minus, with your interviewer.

 ## FINAL DECISION AND FOLLOW-UP

Even if your first interview went extremely well, the outcome may depend on how effectively you proceed afterward. Each interviewer should be formally thanked in writing. Afterward, evaluate each internship office based on what you learned during interviews.

You might also encounter sudden complications due to one interviewer's need for a speedy response. The rescheduling of subsequent interviews, the acceptance of one internship, and the decision to decline others may have to be timed differently from what you originally planned.

Coordinating Your Response Time

You have your own timetable, and employers have theirs. Although some offices will happily give you all the time you need to conclude your search, others may not. Students not experienced in job hunting need to be aware of the complexities that sometimes arise. You can reduce the risk of problems with clear communications along the way.

At the end of each interview, you should know whether the internship is being offered to you or whether that decision is being made at a later time. If this is not made clear, you must ask about it before leaving—especially if you are interviewing at more than one office. For example, you might say, "I'm really excited about the possibility of interning here, but I do have another interview coming up soon. When do you expect to make a decision about my candidacy for this position?" Offer to follow up with a telephone call to the interviewer at an agreed date and time. And make that call exactly as agreed.

If the internship is offered to you at the end of the interview (or by telephone sometime after that), convey enthusiasm and sincere thanks—even if this office is not your first choice. To all such offers, you might say, "Thank you so much, Mr. (or Ms.) Interviewer. I'm flattered that you want me to work for you, and I'm excited to have an opportunity like this."

If you need more time for additional interviews or to think through your options, you may politely say so and ask for a reasonable deadline. For example: "I'd like to say yes right now, but, unfortunately, I can't do that yet. When do you need a definite response?"

Employers are accustomed to such responses from job candidates. You will almost never be asked to explain the need for more time. If you are, continue to be honest but polite. For example: "It happens that another firm also offered me an internship yesterday. I consider myself fortunate to have two good offers but it creates a difficult decision. I need to think it over carefully." If the interviewer continues to press for an earlier response than you would like, try to reschedule remaining interviews to accommodate the new time frame.

Students fortunate enough to find themselves in heavy demand must be careful not to let it go to their heads. Remain unassuming with prospective supervisors. Do apologize for any inconvenience you are forcing on them.

Table 4.7

Sample Thank-You Letter

2345 Education Road
Paralegal City, North Dakota 02000

August 19, 1998

Gerald Rodriguez, Esquire
Rodriguez & Steinman, P.A.
54321 Career Way
Opportunity City, North Dakota 02222

RE: Paralegal Internship

Dear Attorney Rodriguez:

I want you to know how much I enjoyed meeting you yesterday. Thank you for your time in discussing my internship and for your kind encouragement. The appeal you are working on sounds like a fascinating challenge, and your other litigation work promises to provide invaluable experience. I am excited about your offer to have me intern at your office, and I am grateful to you and Ms. Steinman for this opportunity.

Thank you, too, for understanding my prior commitment to two additional internship interviews and your patience in that regard. I will telephone your office no later than August 26 with a definite response.

Sincerely,

Chris Dumont

Continue to demonstrate your ability to deal with problems effectively and to get along well with other professionals. Those qualities are still being evaluated.

Immediate Follow-Up

Within about twenty-four hours after each interview, send a thank-you letter to the interviewer. Open with a sentence or two thanking the interviewer for the time spent with you and for the information provided. Add a few sentences summarizing, with some enthusiasm, your reasons for wanting to intern in this office. An additional segment can clarify, once again, what you hope to bring to this position. Close with a confirmation of the date and time at which you agreed to telephone (either to learn of the office's decision about taking you or to accept the internship offer that was made). If, on the other hand, an internship was offered during the interview and you accepted it, you can confirm that here, adding details about what further steps are needed. A sample thank-you letter can be found in Table 4.7.

Like your initial letter and résumé, this one should also follow standard business format, typed or word processed on standard business paper. Proofread the letter carefully for correct grammar and spelling. Be sure it is properly addressed and that it gets sent promptly.

This letter accomplishes several things for you. It demonstrates to potential employers that you know how to respond courteously and professionally. It shows initiative and good follow-up, both desirable traits in an intern. And it helps forge cordial bonds with your new contacts in the legal community regardless of ultimate internship placement.

Making Your Decision

Multiple internship offers are a sign that the student identified objectives early and well, researched offices thoroughly, and put real work into the search process. The luxury of deciding between two or more offices is the reward for that effort. If you find yourself in this situation, you can take great pride in your success.

Usually, no single office meets all of your objectives perfectly. Each offers a different combination of advantages and disadvantages that must now be weighed. Begin by comparing the following qualities for each internship option that has been offered to you:

- Which office best meets your immediate learning objectives?
- Which office best meets your longer-term career goals?
- Which office may offer an opportunity for eventual employment?

Next, balance the advantages against whatever drawbacks exist for each office. One may require an unusually long commute; another may involve working for someone with whom you are uncomfortable. Where compensation is an issue, figure this into your evaluation as well, though preferably not as the controlling factor.

Get advice from your program director if the decision is a difficult one. It is not unusual for students to consult others as well, such as paralegal instructors, family members, friends, and graduates of your program.

As you consider your ultimate choice, bear in mind your program's decision deadline and also the deadlines of the offices you have interviewed. You want to begin your internship under favorable circumstances, so do not keep anyone waiting beyond the expected time.

Confirming Your Decision

No matter how you originally communicated your decision to accept an internship—during an interview, by phone, or in a short thank-you letter—internship placement should be formally confirmed in whatever form your program prescribes. Some schools provide a learning contract for you and the office supervisor to complete. Others require something different, such as a placement agreement. Still others have no formal requirements for confirming internship placement. Find out what form of confirmation your school prefers (if any) and follow through exactly as instructed.

If your school has no formal confirmation requirements, you would be wise to obtain confirmation in writing—signed by someone in authority at your internship office such as your immediate internship supervisor or a managing partner of the firm. The writing should confirm the following details:

- The name of the office (if not shown on the letterhead)
- Your name
- The name of your principal supervisor
- The nature of the internship and anticipated assignments
- Your starting date
- The length or duration of the internship

Table 4.8

Sample Supervisor's Letter of Confirmation

Rodriguez & Steinman, P.A.
Attorneys at Law

54321 Career Way
P.O. Box 370A
Opportunity City, N.D. 02222
Telephone: 701/555-3242
Fax: 701/555-7232

August 27, 1998

Professor Damian Dogood
Director, Paralegal Internship Program
North Dakota Paralegal College
Paralegal City, North Dakota 02000

RE: Chris Dumont, Paralegal Intern

Dear Professor Dogood:

This letter confirms that Chris Dumont will be interning at this office beginning on September 15, 1995. Our understanding is that Chris will work at least 200 hours between September 15 and December 15. He has also volunteered to work additional hours, if needed. Working mainly on Tuesdays, Wednesdays, and Thursdays, his schedule will average 20 hours per week.

As his principal supervisor, I am assigning to Chris a major research project in connection with an upcoming appeal. In addition, he will assist with various litigation matters, corporate matters, and occasional real estate closings for both myself and my partner, Attorney Louise Steinman. I think you will find these assignments consistent with the learning objectives that Chris has communicated to us.

We find Chris to be highly qualified. We look forward to having him in our office.

Sincerely yours,

Gerald Rodriguez, Esquire

cc: Chris Dumont

- The total number of internship hours required (if such a requirement exists)
- Your anticipated daily or weekly work schedule

A letter from your office supervisor usually meets everyone's needs sufficiently if it contains the details just stated. To make this chore easier for your supervisor, submit a draft for the office's review and modification. The time this saves will be appreciated.

Ideally, the final version is written on the internship office's letterhead and addressed to the program director at your school. You will want a copy for your own reference as well. See Table 4.8 for an example.

This letter verifies your verbal agreement, clarifying both the student's and the office's basic scheduling and supervision commitments. If things somehow go wrong, it provides some proof of the understanding that was reached. Most importantly, written confirmation helps prevent things from going "wrong" in the first place.

POINT OF ETHICS

The Ethical Applicant

Students are usually alert to the ethical dilemmas that can arise while working in a legal setting. Forgotten, sometimes, are the ethical issues that can develop even during the application process. The first, which sometimes occurs among applicants, is inflated credentials or qualifications. The second—occasionally committed by interviewers and supervisors—is unlawful discrimination. Here are some tips for avoiding both of these offenses.

Avoiding Inflated Credentials

When faced with some shortcoming in their backgrounds, students are sometimes tempted to go beyond the truth in résumés and interview discussions. For example, a course that the student dropped midsemester might be included in a list of completed courses. Or the dates of prior employment might be extended from six months to a year to make experience appear more substantial. Facts should not be stretched in this way.

Students need to know that their claims are often checked. Honesty is a key requirement in law-related positions. When dishonest background reports are discovered, the effect is usually devastating. Applicants can lose much more than the position they applied for. They may also forfeit their reputation in the legal community.

Ironically, misleading statements are often made regarding relatively trivial matters. For example, most internship offices readily understand that courses sometimes get dropped for legitimate reasons, such as financial setbacks or family obligations. Short-term employment is also common among people who are in career transition or attending school; it does not need to be portrayed as something lengthier. Owning up to your own history, whatever it may be, is preferable to allowing a misleading statement to put everything at risk.

There are two ways to handle embarrassing background factors. First, you can report the matter in your résumé accurately, adding a short explanation. Regarding the dropped course, for example, the words "half completed due to financial constraints" (if that was the reason) could be added in parentheses. The short-term employment could be explained by noting in parentheses the reason for its termination, such as family illness, family relocation, or the resumption of schooling.

A second way to handle shortcomings is simply to leave out any written reference to them, instead explaining the situation personally at the time of the interview. Regarding the half-completed course, for example, the student might explain, "I also took Advanced Legal Research last spring along with several other advanced courses. My program director warned me it was a very ambitious schedule and eventually it became obvious that I had taken on more than I could handle at one time. So I dropped Advanced Legal Research halfway through the semester. That's why it's not listed with the other courses. The good news is that I learned a major lesson about realistically managing my time and my workload. I know that lesson will help me in the future." Any qualms an interviewer might have about the unfinished course become trivial compared to the scrupulous honesty—and upbeat ending—of this explanation. Handled this way, a shortcoming can become the basis of genuine admiration.

A Judge's Perspective 4.3: Judge Tina I. Nadeau
Discrimination and Sexual Harassment

Now an Associate Justice of the New Hampshire Superior Court, this remarkable woman began her career in the Homicide Division of the Criminal Bureau of her state Attorney General's Office. One day, a disturbing incident occurred on the job. This is her description of the incident and how she handled it:

"Once, I was at a crime scene with another female lawyer from the Attorney General's Office, preparing warrants and getting ready to make an arrest. I was working with a male officer who was not much older than I was, putting together a search warrant. He made some sort of derogatory remark, describing the way I was putting the search warrant together, in sort of a sexual fashion that was extremely offensive to me.

"I handled it by ignoring him. I talked with my colleague at the time about what to do, and we decided to write a letter to the Chief of Police and explain what had happened.

"I found two things remarkable. One was that it was a rare event, and the other was that our Bureau Chief at the time (who was a man) was extremely supportive of us. He contacted the Police Chief as well, and we got a lot of support at the office. Everybody there thought that it was an inappropriate comment to make to anybody, whether they were male or female. I was pleased with the support from the office, and I also was happy that we decided to take steps.

"I think that women shouldn't hesitate to do that when they think that they have been treated unfairly or inappropriately. I think over the years, we have begun to recognize discrimination when it occurs and we have also been able to react because we are starting to learn that other people don't tolerate it, that it is okay to take steps to do something about it, and that you are not going to receive any negative consequences for doing that. If we perceive discrimination, and if we want to get rid of discrimination, the only way to do it is to take steps."*

Countering Discrimination

Professional interviewers, such as personnel directors and human resource managers, are usually well-informed about state and federal antidiscrimination laws and savvy enough to avoid even the appearance of racial, religious, ethnic, age, or sex discrimination. The more common offenders are those who have little or no interviewing experience. Improbable as it may seem, many of them are lawyers.

The following are examples of questions and remarks which—when made during the application process—reflect unlawful discrimination:

- Questions about whether you have children, how many you have, or their ages
- Questions about your child-care arrangements
- Questions about your marital status or whether your spouse approves of some aspect of your work

---

*Quote reprinted with permission of both the New Hampshire Bar Association and the *New Hampshire Bar Journal*.

- Questions about religious practices
- Questions about your experience as a member of a racial, ethnic, or religious group
- Gender-based questions about your experience as a man or as a woman in this profession
- Questions implying that you are too old to be doing something
- Derogatory comments based on your race, religion, ethnic group, gender, marital status, or (over-40) age group (In many jurisdictions, remarks or questions about sexual preference are also unlawful.)
- Any comment, question, gesture, or physical contact suggesting a sexual relationship

With rare exceptions, discriminatory questions or remarks are generally the product of unthinking mental stereotypes, not an actual attempt to exclude or demean a particular group. In other words, the problem usually is thoughtlessness—a failure to think about the implications—not an intention to offend. The best interviewee responses assume inadvertence, bringing the unpleasant implications calmly but fully to light.

Most unwanted discrimination can be dealt with effectively by following these rules, usually in the sequence they are presented here:

1. Assume ignorance on the part of the interviewer. Do not immediately assume malice.
2. Respond factually. Educate your interviewer, courteously but firmly.
3. Tell the interviewer that the remark could be interpreted as discrimination. You will almost always receive an apology.
4. If no apology is offered for what you believe is an offensive remark, or if such remarks continue, terminate the interview.
5. Report such incidents to your program director, who may want to educate the offender, report the offender to higher management in that office, and perhaps remove that office from the school's internship list.
6. Serious incidents should be reported to the antidiscrimination agency in your state and to the federal Equal Employment Opportunity Commission for further action.

You are not likely to encounter any serious forms of discrimination in your internship search. If you do, your guiding principle should be professionalism. A professional educates and informs in language appropriate for an office setting. A professional checks out actual intentions, waits for an appropriate apology, and takes more serious steps—such as walking out and reporting the incident—when none are forthcoming. You are in the process of building a reputation. Try always to conduct yourself as a professional, even with an interviewer who does not.

EXERCISES

1. With another student, role-play a telephone inquiry to an office with which you and your school have no prior association. Plan several basic questions and comments for the office you would like to call. When you have finished, reverse roles and let the other student role-play a telephone inquiry to you.
2. Draft a mock follow-up letter to the office you have just practiced calling in the preceding role-playing exercise. Ask your student-partner or your program director to critique your letter.

3. Prepare a draft résumé and cover letter. Ask to have it critiqued by your program director or by a career counselor from your school's placement office.
4. With another student, role-play an internship interview with the same office you "telephoned" in the first exercise. Prepare for your interview as instructed in this chapter. Consider dressing for the occasion. Have the other student pose several of the questions mentioned in this chapter as an interviewer would do. When you have finished, reverse roles and interview your partner in the same manner. If possible, have your program director (or other students) observe and critique the mock interview by evaluating your appearance, your responses to the interviewer's questions, and the questions you posed to the interviewer.
5. Draft a thank-you letter for your interviewer. Ask your program director, your student-partner, or a counselor from your school's placement office to critique the letter.
6. Draft a mock letter confirming internship arrangements with the office you "interviewed" in Exercise 4, as if you were submitting it to a prospective internship supervisor for his or her modification and use. Have the letter critiqued by your program director, a student-partner, or a counselor from your school's placement office.

ENDNOTES

1. It was reported on October 13, 1994, in "Academic Internship Programs," a seminar of the 1994 Annual Conference of the American Association for Paralegal Education in San Francisco, California, that the University of Central Florida requires paralegal candidates to provide an acceptable research paper to prospective internship supervisors on whatever topic each supervisor assigns.
2. Mailing out unsolicited résumés fails to lead to a job for ninety-two out of every one hundred job hunters who try it, reports Richard Nelson Bolles in what is often referred to as "the Bible for job hunters," *The 1994 What Color Is Your Parachute?* (Berkeley: Ten Speed Press, 1994), 25.
3. Paul Reidinger, "Dressing Like A Lawyer," *ABA Journal* (March 1996): 78.
4. Ibid.

ACTION FORMS

Possible offices

1. _____ 2. _____ 3. _____

Office type

_____ _____ _____

Background research

Martindale-Hubbell	_____	_____	_____
Yellow pages	_____	_____	_____
Dun & Bradstreet	_____	_____	_____
Other	_____	_____	_____
Telephoned on	_____	_____	_____
Spoke to			

_____ _____ _____

Résumé sent on	_____	_____	_____
Enclosures			
Work samples	_____	_____	_____
Policies/brochure	_____	_____	_____
Course list	_____	_____	_____
Other	_____	_____	_____
Follow-up call	_____	_____	_____
Interview on	_____	_____	_____
Interviewer			

_____ _____ _____

Thank-you letter	_____	_____	_____
Follow-up call	_____	_____	_____
Decision deadline	_____	_____	_____
Notified of decision			
Date	_____	_____	_____
Letter or phone	_____	_____	_____
Internship confirmed in writing?			

_____ _____ _____

Form 4.1

Plan of Action

Form 4.2

Office Contacts Worksheet

Office number _____ (1, 2, 3, etc.)

Name of firm or company _____

Address _____

_____

_____

Phone ( ) _____

Contact person(s) _____

Name _____ Title _____

Office type _____

Area of specialization _____

Probable supervisor _____

Other attorneys I have met there or would work with

_____

_____

Other paralegals I have met there or would work with

_____

_____

Other professional contacts at this office

Name _____ Title _____

_____

_____

Notable features/characteristics of this office

_____

_____

Fulfills the following learning objectives

_____

_____

Probably fulfills the following career objectives

_____

_____

Drawbacks

_____

_____

Preference rating (first choice, second choice, etc.)

_____

Form 4.3

Job-Finder's Skills Diary

Telephone inquiry techniques that worked

1. _____
2. _____
3. _____
4. _____
5. _____

Telephone inquiry techniques I will avoid in the future

1. _____
2. _____
3. _____

Interviewer's questions to be ready for

1. _____
2. _____
3. _____
4. _____
5. _____

Interviewing techniques I'm glad I tried

1. _____
2. _____
3. _____
4. _____
5. _____

What I will avoid doing in an interview in the future

1. _____
2. _____
3. _____

Other strategies that helped

1. _____
2. _____
3. _____
4. _____

Form 4.4

**Checklist for Preparing
Your Own Internship
Information Sheet for
Prospective Supervisors**

Name of school _____

Address _____

_____

_____

Paralegal internship director _____

Telephone _____ Fax _____

Number of academic credits to be earned _____

Number of internship hours required _____

Date internship begins _____

Date internship ends _____

List of paralegal courses completed

1. _____   6. _____

2. _____   7. _____

3. _____   8. _____

4. _____   9. _____

5. _____   10. _____

Student's internship learning objectives

1. _____   5. _____

2. _____   6. _____

3. _____   7. _____

4. _____   8. _____

Evaluation by supervisor (sample form attached, if available)

When _____

How _____

Site visit(s) by school representative

When _____ Conducted by _____

Approximate length _____

Student's reporting obligations (log, journal, reports, work samples, etc.)

1. _____

2. _____

3. _____

4. _____

General description of anticipated supervision/training

_____

_____

_____

General description of anticipated assignments

_____

_____

_____

Paralegal program's work restrictions/limitations

_____

_____

_____

Program's policy on compensating interns

_____

_____

_____

Student's concurrent classroom obligations

_____

_____

_____

Ethical considerations

The intern will cooperate fully with supervisors and coworkers in (1) protecting clients' confidentiality, (2) safeguarding privileged information, (3) avoiding conflicts of interest, and (4) avoiding the unauthorized practice of law.

Other matters _____

_____

_____

The following may be added for students in special situations:

This internship is combined with a regular, on-site work schedule in the following manner:

Regular employment schedule   Internship work schedule

_____   _____

Supervisor _____   Supervisor _____

Letter of permission _____   Letter of permission _____

Part II

Beginning the Job

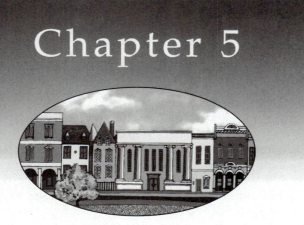

Chapter 5

Ensuring a Smooth Start

You have researched, planned, telephoned, written, and interviewed with care. As a direct result, you have landed what may be the ideal internship for launching your career. You probably want to celebrate—not pause to identify obstacles that may still exist. Nevertheless, that is what the smart career planner now does.

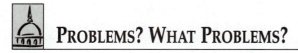 ## PROBLEMS? WHAT PROBLEMS?

Potential obstacles can often be averted early on, and that is the focus of this chapter. By checking certain things in advance, you can eliminate the more common difficulties interns sometimes encounter during their first days on the job. An unfamiliar computer system, awkward work-space adjustments, or the unexpected apprehension of a coworker can cloud an otherwise sunny start. Discovered ahead of time, however, such circumstances need not become problems at all.

Other normally preventable complications include

- The unavailability of instruction and feedback
- Redundant assignments that fail to provide good learning experience
- Competing demands of multiple bosses
- The "Monday Morning Syndrome" or a lack of assignments at the beginning of the internship or—worse—at the beginning of each week

The key to averting these problems is twofold. First, try to arrange a preinternship meeting with your supervisor to work out a fairly specific internship plan, preferably on paper. (A subsequent section shows you how to confirm those details in a learning contract.) Second, request a tour of the facilities and a brief introduction to coworkers and office staff, perhaps right after your meeting with the supervisor.

The preinternship meeting, tour, and introductions might take place during your first-day orientation, where interns and employees alike normally find out where their desk is, briefly meet some of their coworkers, and receive their first assignment. However, your purpose is to accomplish more than that. By sitting down with your supervisor for about a half hour and finalizing the items outlined below, you can avoid many of the false starts and lost time that are sadly common in internship situations. You can create a situation that allows you to learn and perform productive paralegal work from the first day right up to the last.

By meeting coworkers and touring the facilities ahead of time, you will learn about your new environment well before the first day on the job, while you still have time for whatever adjustments are needed. Adjustments can include seeking better work-space arrangements, arranging a regular conference schedule with your supervisor, or gauging the need for instruction on the computer network system. Adjustments can also include intangible things, such as the chance to visualize yourself in your new surroundings and to experience in advance the personalities and idiosyncrasies of those with whom you will work. A good preview allows you to begin your internship with much greater insight and self-confidence—already knowing what to expect.

To begin with these advantages, you should not leave these meetings for the first day on the job when important details might be presented hastily or not explained at all. Instead, try to schedule your orientation meetings *before* the internship starts. If you have any concerns about the internship office you have chosen, plan these meetings for three or four weeks before your starting date to allow time for returning to your second or third choice, if that can be arranged. But do not begin your internship "cold." You want to "hit the ground running," as employers like to say.

A word of warning: in a small or solo law practice, you may have difficulty getting a harried lawyer to agree to a formal preinternship meeting and tour. Anticipate that possibility. Explain that finding time for this process early on ensures a productive start and good use of work time when the internship begins. And be prepared to compromise. With an overburdened lawyer-supervisor, focus mainly on your half-hour, face-to-face meeting. In a solo office, the facilities and staff will be limited and your tour a rather short one in any event.

If your internship is for academic credit, you need to make every day and every hour count as a productive learning experience, no matter what the setting. That means having at least a tentative plan agreed upon by you and your supervisor. And it means getting oriented (and getting the office somewhat oriented to you as well) before you start working.

ORIENTATION MEETING WITH YOUR SUPERVISOR

The letter of confirmation you requested from your supervisor (see Chapter 4) verified for your school's internship director the minimum information needed for administrative record keeping and follow-up: the name of the professional for whom you will work, the office, the starting date, the expected number of hours, and generally the kind of work you will perform. However, to begin the internship with confidence, you need to be sure of even more than that.

When you call to schedule an orientation meeting with your supervisor, ask for a half hour of his or her time, privately. If you need to justify the time you have requested, emphasize that the purpose of this meeting is to make the internship as productive as possible—not just for you, but for the entire office. Mention a few of the italicized phrases in the following list as examples of things you need to discuss together. And be sure to thank your supervisor for accommodating this request.

When you finally sit down with your supervisor for preinternship orientation, here are some of the issues that should be confirmed *before* the internship begins:

1. What will be *your work area* and how does the arrangement affect coworkers? Is an employee moving elsewhere to accommodate you? If so, perhaps extra courtesy should be shown to that person.

2. What hourly schedule works best? Agree in writing on a definite *work schedule.* Calendar in several "flex" days to cover possible storm cancellations, car breakdowns, or a bout of the flu. Double-check the office's work calendar, too, for holidays and vacations.

3. What *equipment* is available for your use on the job? Do you have ready access to a telephone, computer, printer, copier, fax machine, and the right paper for these things? What is the procedure when others need the same equipment at the same time?

4. Are you among the fortunate few paralegal interns who will have occasional *secretarial support?* If so, what secretary will be accepting your work?

5. Are there rules regarding use of the *law library, conference room,* and other shared spaces? Get such rules in writing so you can consult them later.

6. What is the plan for overall supervision and review of your work? Ask for a regular schedule of *meetings with the supervisor* who will evaluate your performance. Try for at least a half hour per week—more if possible. If your supervisor will often be out of the office, be flexible about accommodating his or her schedule.

7. If your *day-to-day supervision* and training are being partly delegated to others, get their names and verify when they are usually available.

8. In the event of *a client's emergency,* whom should you consult if your attorney-supervisor is out? The name and number of another responsible attorney should be available from the beginning.

9. What *assignments* can be given to help you meet your learning objectives and career goals? With your supervisor, rough out a plan for mutually beneficial assignments and experiences.

10. Will you be receiving assignments from more than one person? To avoid being overwhelmed by competing demands, ask *how your work will be prioritized* among two or more supervisors.

11. With multiple assignors, agree on a *system for tracking assignments* from various sources in the office and periodically informing all assignors about them. Consider using the Multiple Assignors Report Form at the end of this chapter.

12. In this office, who are the best people to go to for various kinds of *advice or guidance?* Different coworkers have different areas of expertise. For example, whom should you see about computer advice, or for sample documents and forms, or just for routine help?

13. Does the office have *a procedures manual* for support staff? If so, it serves as a valuable reference on the office's systems, policies, and protocols.

14. *Who evaluates your performance?* If your school provides an evaluation form for supervisors to use, allow all evaluators to become familiar with it in advance.

When you meet with your internship supervisor, take along a note pad or use the Orientation Form (Form 5.2) at the end of this chapter. As you ask the fourteen questions listed above, write down the answers. Try to get the correct spellings for coworkers' names. Ask whether printed sheets or officewide memoranda are available on any of these subjects, such as employees' work schedules or the use of facilities or equipment. Keep these materials together with your notes for future reference.

Find out whether any coworkers are from paralegal programs like yours. Make it clear that you are looking for whatever affinities exist—not implying that other kinds of training are less acceptable.

If responsibility for your routine, day-to-day supervision and training is being delegated to someone else, explore this situation with some care. Is the person assigned to oversee your work completely comfortable with that arrangement? Probably so—but if not, you now have the chance to resolve any misgivings before difficulties arise.

If a happy resolution of the matter is not clearly conveyed, ask whether you might assume some of this person's workload in return for the training

---

THE STUDENT'S PERSPECTIVE 5.1: CORI
The Unwitting Supervisor

Cori was one week into the internship when a certain tension became apparent between her and Susan, her day-to-day paralegal supervisor. "I'm not sure what the problem is," she confided to her program director, "but I'm feeling a bit of resentment from this woman, and I don't know what to do about it.

"When I go to Susan with a question about my assignment from Attorney Vigeant—like I was told to do—she seems rather annoyed. She keeps telling me how busy she is and that I'll just have to wait. Yesterday, she stalled me for almost an hour. I'm now wasting time because of this problem."

A few questions from Cori's program director revealed the difficulty. Cori had been accepted into the office by Attorney Vigeant, who thought a paralegal intern would be a useful addition to the office. A week before Cori was to begin, he put his paralegal, Susan, in charge of Cori's routine training and supervision.

"It may have been Attorney Vigeant's idea to take you in," the program director speculated, "but not Susan's. Meanwhile, Susan has been given the daily responsibility of your supervision and training. Susan may wish she'd had the chance to participate in that decision, and she may see you mostly as an extra burden on an already heavy workload. It's too bad Attorney Vigeant didn't get Susan's input and cooperation *before* you began the internship.

"But, for now, let's focus on finding a solution," the program director continued. "I think you need to talk to Susan. Without being accusatory or complaining, let her know you realize this arrangement puts extra demands on her time. See if she'd like to give you some of her work in return and review it when you're done."

A week later, Cori was smiling again. "I did what you suggested," she reported to her director. "It went well. I'm doing some of Susan's work now, as well as Attorney Vigeant's research. I'm no longer kept waiting and I'm learning a lot more than I was before. Even Vigeant likes the arrangement. He says he wishes he had thought of it sooner. So do I!"

he or she provides. Such an exchange often works well. Just be sure that your broader learning and career objectives are not being overly compromised as a result.

ORIENTATION TO OFFICE AND COWORKERS

At least a half hour should also be requested for an orientation to the office. This session normally consists of a tour of the facilities and an introduction to coworkers as you make the rounds. Ideally, an introduction to important office equipment is included. If requested ahead of time, this introduction might include a few demonstrations. A demonstration (of the computer system, for example) is less likely to be disruptive to coworkers if it was arranged in advance.

Your orientation tour can be conducted by anyone who is knowledgeable about how the office functions and about the people who work there. Particularly in smaller offices, orientation tends to be a loosely structured affair. It need not include a formal, sit-down conference with anyone. It could be led by the attorney-supervisor who brought you into this office, your day-to-day paralegal-supervisor, an office manager, a legal administrator, a paralegal coworker, an associate, or an experienced secretary. Or, one coworker may turn you over to another for certain portions of your tour.

You might be introduced to a coworker who wants to take you aside and talk for a while. You may even want to suggest a personal chat yourself if introductory comments lead to a subject of common interest. One-on-one conversations can provide helpful insights about the office you are joining and the expectations of the people who work there. Allow extra time to take advantage of such opportunities, if they arise.

You must be an active participant in this introduction process. Have your list of new names (learned from orientation with your supervisor) handy as you now make the rounds. Begin mentally putting a face to each name. Ask questions and share information as you go. Use these conversations to create a bridge to future working relationships. Here are a few rules to follow with everyone you meet:

- Repeat your name clearly to each person you meet as you smile and extend your hand for a firm handshake—just like you did in your interviews.
- Tell everyone that you look forward to working with them. They will be more likely to look forward to working with you, as well.
- When meeting someone you may come to for advice at some point, let them know that and ask if that is all right with them. (They will undoubtedly say "sure!")

As you gain your first, insider's view of the facilities and the people who work there, be prepared to raise certain questions. For example, share your learning objectives and career goals with some of the individuals you meet. See whether they may be able to give you assignments to develop the skills you need. When introduced to someone with computer expertise, ask whether you might spend some time observing some of this person's skills and techniques. Ask the secretary or receptionist about the office's preferences on handling incoming and outgoing calls. And finally, note how other professionals of your gender and status are dressed. Is your appearance already compatible with theirs? If not, what changes do you need to consider?

THE STUDENT'S PERSPECTIVE 5.2: LAMBERT
Straightening Out a Strained Relationship

It was Lambert's turn to report to the class in the Senior's Internship Seminar. "I have to tell you about one of the associates at my office," he began. "This guy is barely one year out of law school and, in the beginning, he was bossing me around more than the partners who have been practicing for twenty years! Truth is, he was kind of cold to me since we were first introduced. Eventually, I asked him if something was wrong. Had I offended him without realizing it, or something?

"Well, he said 'no, of course not,' and walked away. Later, he came back—and that's when it all came out. It turns out that he's afraid that someone like me might replace him at the office! He thinks paralegals are gradually replacing new associates at a lot of law offices." The class laughed and a few students cheered.

"So I said, 'Not if they want somebody to go to court, because I can't do that. And I see you doing that pretty regularly!' I also told him that, in some ways, I envied him (his paycheck, mostly) but that I never want to be a lawyer. I like dealing with clients a lot, doing behind-the-scenes fact gathering, and the like. Also, I have no great love for judges.

"Anyway, we've been getting along fine ever since. Now he's got a new 'judge joke' for me every time I see him. I think it helped to get the problem out in the open in a friendly way. Having a sense of humor about it really helped, too."

At the end of your office orientation, write down any new names you have learned. Add these names to the list you created during your earlier meeting with your supervisor. You can use the Office Personnel Form (Form 5.3) at the end of this chapter to develop a complete, permanent record. Review all the names, clarifying the position held by each person listed: secretary, law partner, associate, paralegal, administrator, and so on.

Also, jot down anything about each individual that could be helpful to you later. A law office associate, for example, may have offered to let you sit in on a trial or an initial client interview. Someone else may have offered to give you a lesson on the office's new word processor. Be sure these offers are noted so you will not forget to act on them.

Your list of names has double value to you. First, knowing who these people are will make your early days on the job far more productive and fun than they would otherwise be. You will want this list to refer to every day, at least in the beginning. The value of these names goes beyond your internship, though.

These new acquaintances are also the beginning of a professional network that will multiply many times over in the months to come. Your new coworkers are a source of job references and letters of recommendation. More importantly, some of these individuals may be potential future employers or the colleagues of potential future employers. They could become your links to eventual employment opportunities—not just after graduation, but three, five, and ten years from now.

Learn to enjoy and respect your new acquaintances as people. Cultivate these working relationships with genuine care. And do not lose that piece of paper on which their names are written!

DEVELOPING YOUR OWN LEARNING CONTRACT

A learning contract is a written agreement between the intern and the on-the-job supervisor which describes the learning objectives of the internship experience, listing specific ways in which those objectives will be achieved. Some paralegal programs require a learning contract for all their interns, as do many training programs in other fields—psychology and social work, for example. *In programs in which a learning contract is required, you must use the form that your school prescribes and follow your director's instructions carefully.* Other paralegal programs do not require such a document but may encourage students to develop a learning contract on their own.

The advantages of having an agreement are incalculable. It outlines not only what you will do, but also what your supervisor and coworkers agree to do. It gives your supervisor the occasion to fully understand and make a commitment to many of the internship goals that you developed in Chapters 1 and 2. It helps you discover which learning objectives, if any, cannot realistically be pursued in this setting, and it gives you the chance to negotiate other learning options with your supervisor. In short, solid opportunities for achieving important goals are agreed upon *before* the internship begins—not left to chance.

In addition, a written agreement on learning objectives clarifies an understanding of the internship's purposes, which can then be conveyed to others in the office as well. Once written, the learning contract also becomes everyone's reference point for evaluating your progress throughout the internship.

A personal learning contract can be drafted in any format that seems convenient as long as it contains the following elements:

1. Dates on which the internship begins and ends
2. A list of learning objectives and/or career goals that are acceptable to both you and your supervisor
3. Planned assignments (or other learning experiences) that correspond to each goal or objective
4. The name of the person who will direct each of these assignments if it is someone other than your principal supervisor
5. The work schedule you and your supervisor agreed upon
6. A description of how and when you will be evaluated, and by whom (especially if you are reporting to more than one person)
7. An agreed schedule of meetings with your supervisor for answers to your questions and feedback on your work
8. Other items that you or your supervisor want to add
9. A signature line for you and your supervisor, with the date of signing

If your school does not prescribe a form, follow the nine elements listed above to create your own agreement. These elements can be modified in whatever way you and your internship supervisor are comfortable. If your school has a prescribed form for such agreements, know that it reflects careful thought and planning, consistent with your school's particular academic requirements. Do not modify your school's form without clear, prior permission from your program director.

Usually, lawyer-supervisors are very receptive to the idea of a learning contract.[1] The ideal of a contract draws heavily on their own background and their notions of thoroughness and care. And because this agreement relates to learning experiences—not professional services or remuneration—issues about legal enforceability or liability for breach of contract do not merit serious concern. A reasonable disclaimer can be added in any event. An example appears in the sample learning contract in Table 5.1.

A rough draft of your learning contract can be developed during your orientation meeting with your supervisor. Later, during your orientation meeting with staff and coworkers, you may discover several additions or changes that you want to propose. If your supervisor agrees to those changes, you can then prepare a final draft and put it in the mail for your supervisor's review and approval.

Do not be surprised if your supervisor also proposes a modification or two before agreeing to a final version. Such negotiations make agreements workable for the long haul.

With your learning contract in place, you have the closest thing possible to a "guarantee" that this internship will do for you all that you want it to do. Now you have *real* reason to celebrate!

 ### POINT OF ETHICS
Sufficient Supervision

Many of the ethical issues that paralegals can encounter—such as conflict of interest, breach of confidentiality, professional negligence, and the unauthorized practice of law—could be avoided if supervising attorneys lived up to their responsibility of proper delegation and supervision. The ABA Model Code and Rules of Ethical Conduct recognizes lawyers' responsibility in this regard in Ethical Consideration 3-6, which states:

> A lawyer often delegates tasks to clerks, secretaries, and other laypersons. *Such delegation is proper if the lawyer maintains a direct relationship with his client, supervises the delegated work, and has complete professional responsibility for the work product.* This delegation enables a lawyer to render legal service more economically and efficiently. (Emphasis added.)

In addition, the Codes of Ethics and Professional Responsibility of the National Association of Legal Assistants and the National Federation of Paralegal Associations both indicate that the obligation to ensure adequate supervision is shared by the law office paralegal (see Appendix 3). Although you may only be an intern at this stage, you nevertheless need to be aware of this responsibility and learn to implement it.

When paralegals risk unethical conduct, it is often because of a supervising attorney's chronic unavailability, which leaves the paralegal to make decisions and handle matters that actually should be handled by a lawyer. Failure to review a paralegal's work before sending it out and unavailability for a paralegal's questions about how to proceed can be harmful to clients. It can also be harmful to a paralegal's career.

Fortunately, paralegal interns can prevent such problems. The key is to ensure adequate supervision and guidance from the beginning. In your first meeting with your supervisor, particularly emphasize items 6, 7, and 8 of the fourteen-item list found earlier in this chapter. Those three items involved creating a regular meeting schedule with your supervisor, knowing how to reach others who assign you work, and the availability of an outside attorney in emergency situations. The last point is especially important for students interning with sole practitioners. It can also be crucial for anyone whose boss is planning a vacation.

Table 5.1

Sample Learning Contract

_____ (student) of _____

(school) has established the following as learning objectives for an internship with the office of _____

Learning Objectives

1. _____   5. _____
2. _____   6. _____
3. _____   7. _____
4. _____   8. _____

To the extent permitted by the exigencies of day-to-day office operations and assuming the student's full cooperation, this office agrees to give the student as many opportunities as reasonably possible to achieve the learning objectives just stated. Specifically, this office anticipates giving this student the following kinds of work.

Anticipated Work Assignments

1. _____   5. _____
2. _____   6. _____
3. _____   7. _____
4. _____   8. _____

The person responsible for supervising the student during the internship is:

Name _____

Address _____

Phone _____

Fax _____

E-mail _____

The student's work schedule will be as follows:

_____

_____

_____

_____

The student will report to _____

(school's internship director) on internship work in the following ways:

1. _____
2. _____
3. _____
4. _____

Upon completion of the internship, this office will evaluate the student's work on the form prescribed by the school. The completed, signed form will be returned to

_____ by _____ (date).

(Continued)

This office is also invited to convey additional comments on the student's performance—in writing, by telephone, or in person—at any time. Comments on the student's work, as well as questions about internship arrangements or requests for assistance, should be conveyed to:

Name _____

Address _____

Phone _____

Fax _____

E-mail _____

Additional stipulations

_____

_____

_____

_____

_____   _____

Student's signature   Supervisor's signature

_____   _____

Date   Date

Get clear answers to all three of the issues just mentioned. Write the answers on your Orientation Form at the end of this chapter. You can include some of those answers in your learning contract as well.

Taking these steps will prevent major headaches later on. Even your supervisor will appreciate the professionalism and good ethical sense shown by raising these issues. Your concern for adequate supervision demonstrates that you are a serious worker—someone who understands and respects the supervisor's responsibility for your work.

EXERCISES

1. Find the Lawyer's Code of Professional Conduct for your jurisdiction. What provisions does it contain regarding lawyers' supervision of paralegals and staff? What implications does this have for you?
2. Survey recent graduates or the paralegals in your local paralegal association with these questions:
   a. When they began their present positions, who in the office was most helpful to them in learning their job?
   b. Who is the first person they would recommend that you get to know in any law office? Why?
   c. What was the one thing they most wish they had known about their office before starting their present job?
   d. Is there someone in their office who seems to have a good deal of power over how work gets done even though that person does not carry an

THE STUDENT'S PERSPECTIVE 5.3: JOYCE
Negotiating for Better Experience

Jerry knew that Joyce had landed an internship with a top litigation firm, and he was curious about how she found a slot that would give her such great litigation experience.

"Be careful," she warned. "Being in a well-known litigation firm in no way guarantees the experience you want. I found that out the hard way."

Then she explained. "During my orientation, I discovered that what they really wanted was help with a major class-action suit that was getting bogged down. Not knowing much about class-action suits, it sounded fine until I asked what I would be doing. What they then described was repetitive, almost identical paperwork for hundreds of plaintiffs. There was so much I wanted to learn besides that!

"So I tried to strike a bargain with them. I would work on the class-action suit—and it turns out there was quite a bit to learn about how that works, too. But I also asked for substantial assignments related to other cases in different subject areas. Because I was there for an education, and not for money, they felt they had to agree. It has worked out really well for everyone. I received challenging and varied experience, but I also helped the office a lot, too.

"The key is to have these things understood before you start, if possible. I'm sure glad I did. I wouldn't have lasted very long if all I did was the same thing over and over again!"

important title? What position does that person have? What seems to be the reason for that person's power or influence over others?

e. What would be their main advice regarding surviving office politics to someone beginning an internship like yours?

ENDNOTES

1. Reported October 13, 1994, by Pat Medina, Field Studies Placement Director for the Paralegal Studies Program at San Francisco State University, in "Academic Internship Programs," a panel presentation at the 1994 Annual Conference of the American Association for Paralegal Education (AAfPE).

ACTION FORMS

Form 5.1

**Multiple Assignors
Report Form**

To _____

_____

_____

From _____, Paralegal Intern

Date _____

Re   Current Status of My Assignments

Date Assigned	Assignor	Project	Completion Deadline	Current Status
1. _____	_____	_____	_____	_____
2. _____	_____	_____	_____	_____
3. _____	_____	_____	_____	_____
4. _____	_____	_____	_____	_____
5. _____	_____	_____	_____	_____
6. _____	_____	_____	_____	_____
7. _____	_____	_____	_____	_____
8. _____	_____	_____	_____	_____

Work Schedule

A. Internship begins on _____ and ends on _____

B. Agreed hourly schedule

Mondays _____   Tuesdays _____   Wednesdays _____

Thursdays _____   Fridays _____

Weekend hours _____

C. Office holidays/vacations

_____

Work Area Will Be _____

Equipment Availability

	Know How to Use	Will Receive Instruction	Instructor & Date
Computer network	_____	_____	_____
Word processor	_____	_____	_____
Printer	_____	_____	_____
Typewriter	_____	_____	_____
Fax	_____	_____	_____
Copier	_____	_____	_____
Other	_____	_____	_____

Secretarial Support?

___ Available   Name _____   ___ Not available

Limitations _____

Restrictions on Use Of

Conference room _____

Law library _____

Other area _____

Weekly (Or Other) Meetings with Principal Supervisor _____

_____

Name(s) of Day-to-Day Supervisor(s) _____

_____

Other Assignors _____

_____

(Continued)

Form 5.2

(Continued)

Who Determines Priority Among Competing Assignments?

_____

Additional Sources of Advice and Assistance

Sample forms/documents _____

Computer _____

Other equipment _____

General guidance _____

Other matters _____

_____

Who Is Responsible for My Evaluation? _____

Others Who Will Participate in My Evaluation _____

_____

Backup Attorneys for Emergency Situations

Name _____   Phone _____

Name _____   Phone _____

Name	Position	Possible Assistance
1. _____	_____	_____
2. _____	_____	_____
3. _____	_____	_____
4. _____	_____	_____
5. _____	_____	_____
6. _____	_____	_____
7. _____	_____	_____
8. _____	_____	_____
9. _____	_____	_____
10. _____	_____	_____
11. _____	_____	_____
12. _____	_____	_____
13. _____	_____	_____
14. _____	_____	_____
15. _____	_____	_____
16. _____	_____	_____
17. _____	_____	_____
18. _____	_____	_____
19. _____	_____	_____
20. _____	_____	_____

Form 5.3

Office Personnel Form

Chapter 6

The Meaning
of "Professional"

L ike a butterfly emerging from its cocoon, you are about to shed your identity of "student" and assume, instead, the identity of "professional." With a little effort, you will develop the same air of professionalism and authority that distinguishes everyone in the office as trained professionals. Achieving this new persona is critical to your success as an intern. This chapter shows you how to achieve the professionalism you need to win the respect of clients and colleagues alike.

ADAPTING TO LAW OFFICE CULTURE

An old adage advises, "When in Rome, do as the Romans do." Students who have visited other countries understand what it takes to become accepted in a new culture. It begins with learning the language, customs, and mannerisms of those around you. Gaining acceptance in a law office begins much the same way. *Speaking and behaving similarly to the other professionals in your office makes you less of a stranger and more like a member of the working community.*

The transition from school to office may be easy for students who have worked in other professional environments. But for young interns lacking a professional work history, entering a law office or other fast-paced, structured setting can be somewhat like entering a new culture, perhaps worlds apart from the student culture they have always known. Inexperienced interns may need to prepare themselves for some degree of what sociologists call *culture shock.* The strangeness of it all can be highly energizing—or downright discouraging. It all depends on the intern's flexibility and willingness to adapt.

In the sections that follow, you will learn about dressing appropriately, developing courtesy and credibility, knowing how to be flexible, and earning respect from your professional peers.

DRESSING FOR YOUR PARTICULAR JOB

When you interviewed for your internship, you dressed professionally for the occasion. For a majority of students, the advice offered in Chapter 4 on dressing for interviews continues to apply throughout their internships. Students who did not have to interview for their internship should review that section for guidance on the job.

In a private law firm, the business suit (or its "blazer" facsimile) described in Chapter 4 usually prevails. However, in offices serving middle- and low-income populations, such a formal appearance can alienate clients. In those settings, attorneys and paralegals sometimes dress more informally for meeting with clients. For the legal aid assistant interviewing an elderly couple at their home or the public defender intern interviewing a defendant in prison, the often-recommended blazer might occasionally be worn over a pair of jeans. Attire in other offices, such as government agencies, falls somewhere between these extremes.

The key is to observe how the professionals in your office tend to dress and take your cues from them. Imitate your most respected coworkers. If you ever accompany an attorney to court or have to meet an important official, be prepared to make a crisp, professional appearance regardless of what else the day may hold.

COURTESY AND CREDIBILITY

In law offices and other professional settings, a high level of courtesy is expected from every staff member, including interns. Courtesy is shown in how you relate to others, by the words you choose in communicating with those around you, and in the manner in which you resolve conflicts that arise. Courtesy and consideration to others help create a reputation of credibility among your coworkers. So does your ability to meet deadlines successfully. These elements of courtesy and credibility are explained in the sections that follow.

The Power of Words

The words you use and the way in which you use them may have a greater impact than you realize. For effective communications at the office, be conscious of the words you use and chose them wisely.

You must be genuinely pleasant to everyone you meet at the office. A friendly "hi" or "good morning" to the people you know and occasional social chitchat make it that much easier to ask procedural questions or get help from them later.

In work-related conversations, never forget those mundane but crucial words *please, thank you,* and, when needed, an honest *I'm sorry* said with a smile. Use those words with everyone in the office, from cleaning staff to managing partner. Become known as someone who treats coworkers with courtesy and respect regardless of their position, and you will be treated the same.

When misunderstandings occur (and they inevitably do), there are three responses to avoid: (1) saying nothing; (2) saying too much; and above all, (3) assuming the worst without verification. For example, Susan worked late into the night to complete a deposition summary for her supervising attorney, Charles. She proudly left it on his desk for him to find on Monday morning.

She later stopped by his office for comment, but he was in court. She tried again the next day but he was still out. Days went by without acknowledgement or response from Charles—only new assignments left on her desk for completion, as he often did. None of the new assignments were depositions for her to summarize, and she mused about the possible significance of that. Increasingly, she worried that something must have been wrong with the summary on which she had worked so hard. By Friday, she was fuming with anger that he had delayed his comments and left her in doubt all week. The following Monday morning, she confronted him angrily about his "unwillingness to provide feedback and convey criticism appropriately."

It turned out that Charles actually had no criticism at all to relate. He had seen her deposition summary and was pleased with it. Unexpected trial developments had simply kept him from the office longer than expected. They both quickly apologized and appeared to smooth things over. But he was not pleased with the assumptions she had made about him. Her sharp words had cut deep and he would not easily forget them.

How could Susan have handled this better? She could have begun her encounter with Charles not with assumptions and accusations but by (1)

Table 6.1

Penetrating the Fog

Sometimes the reactions of supervisors and coworkers are hard to understand. Rather than assume the worst, do two things: (1) briefly mention the words or actions you noticed and (2) ask a *neutral* question about them—implying nothing negative about you or the other person.

For example, you might begin: "You seemed worried when we discussed my new assignment." Then comes the neutral question: "Is there something unusual about this case or maybe something I should do differently?"

This will elicit the accurate feedback you need. Often, you will be surprised to learn that the problem had nothing to do with you at all.

---

explaining and (2) asking neutral questions (see Table 6.1). In other words, she could have explained how important his evaluation and comments were to her, and then asked when might be a good time to discuss the deposition summary. He would have undoubtedly apologized for the delay and complimented her efforts right then and there. All hard feelings would have been avoided.

Honoring Work Schedules and Deadlines

Imagine that your supervisor gives you your first assignment with instructions to have it completed by Thursday of this week. Do you nod in agreement, thinking, "I suppose I can do that if nothing else comes up in the meantime . . . "? If your internship schedule calls for your arrival at the office by 1:00 P.M., do you saunter in around 1:20? An intern who fits either of these descriptions has not yet become part of the professional culture and can anticipate serious problems.

In the classroom, schedules have to be honored and, if they are not, your grade usually suffers for it. In the office, the consequences involve far more than grades. Not honoring work schedules and due dates can have catastrophic results. For example, your delayed arrival delays others who are waiting for you. Missed due dates create embarrassment to your office. Even worse, a major transaction may be lost, a statute of limitations deadline might be missed, and the office may be liable to the client for the harm this caused.

Meeting deadlines is a key feature of all law-related services. From the very beginning, one of the main things your supervisor will want from you is an appreciation for the potential seriousness of work schedules and of every deadline. An intern who fails to take these things seriously will never be considered for permanent employment and will have difficulty winning positive recommendations for employment elsewhere.

If you are unable to begin your workday on time or if it becomes apparent that you cannot complete an assignment on time, do not keep the problem to yourself. Let your supervisor know of the difficulty right away so that adjustments can be made. By making the problem known early enough for something to be done about it, you can prevent a host of problems for yourself and others. You will also be seen as more responsible and professional than if you had silently allowed the deadline to pass.

The intern who completes assignments fully and on time is valued by supervisors and coworkers alike. When this intern says an assignment will be done by a certain date, everyone feels secure in knowing that it will be done as promised. This is the intern who wins glowing letters of recommendation, a sound reputation in the legal community, and eventual job offers.

> **QUICK TIP 6.1**
>
> The key to professional credibility is making every promise count. Carry to completion whatever assignments you have agreed to perform—and avoid accepting assignments you know you cannot carry out.

THE STUDENT'S PERSPECTIVE 6.2: DAWN
Paralegals and Single Parenthood

The young mother of two girls ages 7 and 4, Dawn was determined to enter a career that would support her and her daughters comfortably. Approaching the end of her schooling, this internship seemed the last obstacle to fulfilling Dawn's long-held goal. At her internship office, she quickly befriended Jennifer, another single mom who had been working at the same office for three years. They often shared experiences over coffee during their brief breaks from work.

"Ordinary students have no idea how hard it is to be available for your kids, make sure they're cared for, and also show up at work regularly when you're supposed to. I always feel like I am being pulled in several directions at once," Dawn confided to Jennifer.

"It's so different from school," Dawn continued. "At school, I can miss a class when one of my girls is sick without a lot of fuss being made. The professors understand and are sympathetic. But that's not always the case here. Did you see how upset Attorney Tremont was when I went home early on Wednesday and took Thursday off? Doesn't this guy have kids?"

"Yes, he does. It wasn't your kids or the fact that they were sick that made him angry. It was the fact that his client's motion for custody was in danger of being dismissed, and he was counting on your help to finish the paperwork by Friday. The day you were out, I heard him say 'Great—she's home with her kids and, because of that, my client could lose hers!'"

The irony of that situation had visible impact on Dawn, who knew what it was to treasure one's children above all else. "Well, what am I supposed to do?" she moaned.

"I can only tell you what I do," Jennifer sympathized. "I've worked at creating an elaborate support system for me and my kids. I've made arrangements with neighbors for backup child care when school closes or when one of my boys has a cold. When a neighbor helps me out, I return the favor by babysitting to give them a free Saturday night out. At those rare times when no neighbor can help, I call a group at my church to see whether one of the retired ladies can give me a hand.

"So I have Plan A, Plan B, and Plan C," Jennifer concluded. "It's a lot to deal with, but that's what it takes for this single mom to be able to be here every day.

"It's hard to play so many competing roles, but that's a big part of who I am. I'm proud of doing it as well as I do."

Conflict Resolution in a Nutshell

Resolvable conflicts arise from time to time in every work setting. Normally, such conflicts occur when a coworker's professional interests appear to be at odds with yours. For example, a secretary may resent the additional workload your temporary presence represents. A law associate may see you as competition for the office's limited hiring options. A paralegal with less education may feel threatened or intimidated.

With ordinary conflicts such as these, *you almost always have the power to resolve conflicts and turn them into something positive.*

Effective conflict resolution involves four steps: (1) listening to the concerns of the other person, allowing him or her to express those concerns freely; (2) acknowledging the validity of the other person's feelings and getting an accurate understanding of them; (3) evaluating competing interests for a way to resolve them; and (4) negotiating a solution.

Imagine, for example, that tension has developed between you and Rebecca, a more experienced paralegal on the staff. Rebecca began as a legal secretary seven years ago and, through on-the-job training and lots of hard work, gradually assumed all the responsibilities of a bankruptcy paralegal. One of your internship goals is to acquire some experience in bankruptcy work. But Rebecca has been strangely cold, distant, and unresponsive to your interest in her work. What can you do?

Listen

Many newcomers might take Rebecca's aloofness personally, believing that Rebecca dislikes something about them. That is probably not the case. More likely, the problem stems from something Rebecca perceives about *herself*.

Knowing that, you strike up a friendly conversation with Rebecca when you notice her headed for the coffee machine. You let her know that you admire her obvious capabilities in a field you have always wanted to know more about—bankruptcy. You tell her you would enjoy the chance to talk to her about it sometime, maybe at lunch or during a break. Flattered and not wanting to appear rude, she says, "All right, but I can't take too long. I've got a lot of work to do." You have now succeeded in opening the door to a possible solution to this conflict.

Over coffee, you thank her for meeting you and begin the conversation with an open-ended question: "What is it like being a bankruptcy paralegal?" The open nature of your question allows her to discuss whatever she chooses. Not surprisingly, she sighs and zeros in on the source of tension between you. "I enjoy my work most of the time, but after seven years of the same thing day in and day out, I sometimes feel trapped," she admits. It eventually becomes apparent that she has been rather jealous of you. You have broad paralegal training and, consequently, a wide variety of career options. She believes she has neither of these things.

By giving her a chance to talk and by listening patiently to all she has to say, you have uncovered the problem. You may also have begun a new friendship.

Verify and Acknowledge

You may assume that you now understand the situation completely, but you probably do not—not yet. Acknowledge her feelings and invite her to explain further. "I can see how it might get tiring doing the same things over and over," you agree. Then pose another question or two: "Have you thought about any other options or asked your supervisor to give you different work sometimes?" It turns out that she has done that, but with no success. Her boss values her mainly for the work she is presently doing. Freeing Rebecca for other work means training someone else to do at least part of her bankruptcy work and he cannot afford to do that. Hiring another paralegal is financially impossible for the office. And she has no other paralegal experience on which to base a broader job search. Her frustration spills over: "I would love to get into litigation support. But how can I break into a different area of work if I have no experience in it? You're so lucky! You have training in lots of practice areas. You can go almost anywhere."

Evaluate and Propose

Pause for a moment and evaluate what has been accomplished so far. Which of your initial goals have you achieved and, most importantly, which still remain to be accomplished? On the positive side, the resentment she once showed seems to have melted away. That is an accomplishment in itself. On the debit side, you still have not achieved your larger goal, which is to gain experience in bankruptcy work. So there is still more to do.

Next, ask yourself the following question: Is there anything that could be worked out to give both of you what you need? Brainstorm the situation, either in your own mind or together with the other person. A possible solution may suddenly occur to you. You could begin explaining: "Remember when I said I wanted experience in bankruptcy work? Maybe we could trade on our different backgrounds to the benefit of both of us." Then propose your idea.

"Tell me how this sounds," you begin. "I'll share some of my litigation assignments with you and you share some of your bankruptcy work with me. We'll each start with very simple tasks and gradually move to more complicated ones. It will take some extra time at first, but we could have our discussions in the staff lounge over a bag lunch. Also, I can loan you my litigation textbook, and maybe you have some bankruptcy manuals that I could borrow. That way, we both get what we want!"

"I don't know," she responds. "I'd love to do that but it's not that simple. For example, we can't take files out of the office without permission. Our supervisors might not like us using our time this way. And I have to account for my billable hours."

Negotiate and Resolve

Obviously significant fine points need to be resolved and, as often happens, resolving them requires the cooperation of others. A tentative plan is needed, perhaps with a backup plan ready to go in case the first one fails. Both plans should also serve the broader needs of the office.

The next day, you each speak to your supervisor about your idea and ask whether a short meeting could be held to explore it. You emphasize to your supervisor how important this is to your internship. Rebecca emphasizes how important more varied experience is to her long-term career. You both describe how it could benefit the office.

At the meeting, two alternate plans are proposed. The first is exactly as you initially proposed it to Rebecca, with the added assurance that work exchanges will only take place in the office and only during nonworking hours. This ensures that files will not be compromised and Rebecca's billable time will not be reduced. The second plan is Rebecca's idea—that she enroll in a litigation course at your school and that you tutor her in the course material in exchange for weekly instruction in bankruptcy work. Stress the benefits of these arrangements to your internship. Also note the advantage it has for the office: better staff preparedness for a wider variety of clients' needs.

The supervisor is impressed with how thoroughly you have analyzed the matter and pleased with your awareness of the office's needs. Thanks to your skillful use of conflict resolution techniques, the supervisor allows both options!

Conflicts You Cannot Resolve Alone

When difficulties with a supervisor, coworker, or client are more serious, the intern may need the advice and support of the school's program director. If an intern faces what appears to be sexual harassment, discrimination, unethical or criminal conduct of a coworker, or a pattern of verbal abuse, expert advice is required. Moreover, the school's program director needs to know about such conduct—to assist the intern effectively and also to protect the integrity of the school's internship program.

 ## THE IMPORTANCE OF BEING FLEXIBLE

QUICK TIP 6.2

If others are busy and you are not, do not wait for someone to stop and tell you what to do. Look to see where help is needed, and volunteer.

Experienced paralegals understand the need to be flexible about work assignments. In a small or solo law practice, everyone has to be prepared to assume different roles at different times. In any office, the paralegal has to anticipate emergency developments and changing circumstances.

The paralegal intern has additional reasons for being adaptable. Unyielding expectations about what you will do blinds you to new learning opportunities. Rigid expectations can also label you "uncooperative" and unwilling to pitch in when needed. These results seriously undercut your on-site learning as well as your long-term career objectives.

The Dangers of the "I Don't" Syndrome

Most of the "I Don'ts" held by paralegal interns are easily understood on a symbolic level. Usually aimed at making coffee, typing other people's work, running simple errands, and long stints at the copier, "I don't" targets chores a lesser-trained person can perform.

If such tasks are virtually all that you are ever asked to do, then you have ample reason to complain; and if your supervisor does not remedy the problem, you should bring it to the attention of your internship director at school. But do not complain until you have the full picture. Under some circumstances, complaining will only earn you the reputation of a whiner.

Cooperation may be called for when any of the following situations exists.

- A seemingly demeaning chore (such as making coffee) is performed by virtually everyone in the office at different times.
- "Typing" means drafting your own work at a computer (a valid paralegal task)—not transcribing someone else's dictation (a secretarial task).
- At your office, all paralegals "type" their own work.
- The internship position is actually that of paralegal/legal secretary—a valid job description at many small and solo firms.
- A seemingly simple errand takes you to a courthouse or other outside location that you want to know more about.
- An occasional clerical task brings clearer insights to important office procedures.
- You are filling in for a file clerk, messenger, or secretary who is out sick or overloaded—and only for a short time.

When you are assigned a task that seems beneath you, a good rule of thumb is: do not overreact. It may be worth cooperating one time until you can determine whether any of the above-listed circumstances exist. If you are put in the same position again without justification, then you may need to use your conflict resolution skills to resolve the matter. If that fails, report the problem to your internship director at school.

Be a Team Player

Students who have played soccer, basketball, or similar sports understand the team concept. No one operates alone. Goals are achieved through the collaborative efforts of the entire team. Each player has a constant eye on whoever has the ball, ready to enter the action and lend support to another player the moment it is needed. Working in an office requires the same spirit.

Particularly in a small office where there are fewer resources and not much support staff, there is no time for worrying about what is or is not in your job description. If there is a gap to be filled, simply fill it as quickly as possible. With eyes open to all that is happening around them, paralegal interns can spot *many* gaps to fill.

When one experienced paralegal switched to a small firm, she found that this environment "... put an end to any illusions she had about 'who did what' in the office. You either rolled up your sleeves and pitched in, or there was no job."[1] Because so many paralegal interns have their first experience in a small or solo law practice, this advice is worth remembering.

Members of a law office team do not wait for an invitation to help out. They volunteer of their own initiative to do whatever appears needed. For example, in the file you are organizing, what document or discovery procedure appears to be coming up next? Offer to do the necessary drafting. In the witness statement you have just summarized, what legal issues seem to emerge? Offer to research them. If your boss is not immediately available, you might even go ahead without prior permission. Just do not let it interfere with current assignments.

This is flexibility at its finest. It is the kind of self-starting, collaborative teamwork that lawyers and supervisors love. It can earn you the status of "most valuable player" in your office and make you someone others want to recruit for their legal team as well.

 ### POINT OF ETHICS
Clients Count on You

Canon 1 of the ABA Model Code of Professional Responsibility (Model Code) and Rule 1.1 of the ABA Model Rules of Professional Conduct (Model Rules) both require competence in legal representation. Specifically, Canon 7 of the Model Code requires zealous representation within the bounds of the law, and Rule 3.2 of the Model Rules requires lawyers to expedite litigation consistent with the interests of the client. Both the National Association of Legal Assistants (NALA) Model Standards and Guidelines for Legal Assistants and the Model Code of Ethics and Professional Responsibility of the National Federation of Paralegal Associations (NFPA) echo these objectives for paralegals as well (see Appendix 3). Working competently, meeting deadlines, and cooperating to give clients the best legal services possible are not abstract goals. They are *required* of everyone in the law office.

The unanimity of all organizations on these points is not surprising. A client's personal and financial welfare depends on how effectively everyone in the office collaborates to get the job done. All members of the law office team must give their best effort. They must also be willing to take on whatever tasks are needed and within the scope of their training and experience. Always remember: A client is depending on you.

EXERCISES

1. Outline how you would handle the following situations, including what you would say, how you would say it, and to whom.

a. The secretary who types much of your work seems to give your work lower priority than anyone else's. Recently, her delay in typing your work made you late in turning in an assignment. You want to prevent this from happening again.

b. You arrive at the office before 8:00 A.M. to get a head start on your work, hoping to leave ahead of schedule that afternoon for a dentist's appointment. As you sit down to work, the cleaning staff begins vacuuming the area, making it impossible to concentrate.

c. You have finished your last remaining project and have become bored. There seems to be nothing for you to do. You want to make good use of the rest of your day at the office.

d. After a brown bag lunch in the staff lounge, a secretary turns to you and says, "Well, it's your turn to clean up the kitchen!" You do not know whether she is serious or joking.

e. You are working at top speed to finish different projects for two attorneys in the office. Both projects are due first thing tomorrow. One of the two attorneys suddenly calls you from court. "Drop everything," he says. "I need you to pull the old Browning file and bring it over here right away." The courthouse is more than an hour's drive from the office. This errand will make it impossible to complete both of your two projects on time.

f. You have worked for three days on a complex project that is due at the beginning of next week. You figured it would probably take all this week to complete it. Then a snowstorm closes down the office (and the entire city) for a day and a half. Now you may not have enough time to finish the project by the due date.

g. You have been asked to pick up your supervising attorney's dry cleaning on your way into the office—for the second time.

h. You have just finished a project and given it to a paralegal on whom you frequently rely for guidance. She seems very annoyed as she glances through it. You have no idea why she is annoyed. You are concerned that there might be something wrong with the way in which you completed the project.

2. Practice finding the best words for handling these client situations:

a. Days ago, Mrs. A said she would personally bring her financial records to you right away. She never did. You need them to draft her claim, which may soon be barred by the statute of limitations.

b. Mr. B is on the phone. He wants to know why your supervising attorney (who is presently at a real estate closing) failed to return his telephone calls yesterday. Mr. B has been extremely concerned about a dispute with his landlord and now he is angry that he got no response from this office.

c. In a follow-up interview with Mr. C, you ask if he brought copies of his correspondence from the defendant. He says he has and hands you a bundle of letters from someone completely unrelated to the case.

d. You suspect Ms. D may have omitted certain details about her auto accident for fear that they might damage her case. You and your supervising attorney need to know the full truth about what occurred in order to prepare her case effectively.

e. You have been asked to explain upcoming discovery procedures to Mr. E. He has no prior experience with law offices or litigation procedures.

ENDNOTE

1. Chere B. Estrin, "Life in a Small Firm: Who Will Make the Coffee," *Legal Assistant Today* (September/October 1995): 70.

Chapter 7

Building Alliances

Your internship will bring you into contact with many different professionals from both in and out of the office. Most of these professionals are described in this chapter. Dealing effectively with their diverse expectations is more than a necessary part of doing your job. These professionals can also influence your career beyond this internship.

Each person you meet is a potential ally—someone who may be able to help you in the future. You may have to rely on one of them again some day to carry out your responsibilities in a future paralegal position. One of these people may even become instrumental in helping you find that position. Such prospects makes each professional contact doubly important and exciting.

Take every opportunity to get personally acquainted with coworkers. If you are invited to lunch, a reception for clients, an office party, an interoffice softball game, or other recreational event, make every attempt to attend. Socialize and broaden your range of acquaintances. Outside of their work setting, coworkers may turn out to be a lot more down-to-earth than you imagined. Real friendships are often formed this way.

AUTHORITY, STATUS, AND ROLE EXPECTATIONS

Every office has its own hierarchy. In a solo law practice, the "pecking order" may be very simple: lawyer is in charge, paralegal supports lawyer, secretary supports both. But the larger the office, the more complex the hierarchy becomes. Medium-sized and large offices can be highly stratified, with different roles played by many employees at each level.

Outside of the office and on the phone, you will come into contact with personnel who are also conscious of a certain hierarchy among legal professionals. Their perceptions may or may not be compatible with yours.

Nevertheless, you must anticipate the probable expectations of coworkers and outsiders alike, so that you can respond to them effectively. Many of the possibilities are covered in the following subsections.

Attorneys

In most law offices, no paralegal is hired or even retained from year to year without the approval of the attorneys with whom that paralegal works. For the majority of career paralegals, lawyers are the professionals on whom future employment depends. So you may need to understand them well.

All lawyers have at least one thing in common: the law school experience. This means that lawyers have had to be highly competitive and surmount some daunting hurdles in life. They have had to perform exceptionally well in college, endure a grueling law school admissions process, work extremely hard through three additional years of law school (or longer if they attended part-time while remaining employed), and spend months preparing for one of the most difficult exams in existence: the state bar exam. Younger lawyers are also likely to have incurred seven years' worth of educational loans and will be paying them off for perhaps a full decade of their careers. As a result, they anticipate respect from those around them, regardless of the work setting. They believe they have earned that respect and they are right.

As law students, they also learned early to make good use of every available moment. So, as a rule, they may also be a bit impatient. They want their time treated as if it were a precious commodity, like money. For many attorneys, that is precisely the equation that exists. Their livelihood depends on it—and so may yours.

The following rules of thumb will help you navigate your way through any lawyer relationship:

- Be respectful of a lawyer's time. You may be clearly entitled to some of that time but convey the need graciously.
- Because of their greater education and responsibilities, lawyers traditionally expect some degree of deference from nonlawyer staff. You will be appreciated for showing them special courtesy.
- Most lawyers also value coworkers who (like them) are confident about freely speaking up, telling the lawyer all that she or he needs to know. Do this often.
- Take the initiative in thinking of ways to be helpful to any lawyer you work with. They will value that above all else.
- Do not assume all lawyers are extremely well off or envy them for things they may not have. Today's lawyers are not as smugly secure, financially or socially, as lawyers may have been in the past.[1]
- Do not judge all lawyers by television portrayals or by the news headlines a few of them make. The overwhelming majority of lawyers are hardworking people, quietly doing a difficult job for people who need their help.

Beyond the considerations just outlined, lawyers' expectations may vary considerably, sometimes depending on the work setting. For example, in corporate legal departments where hourly billing is not a factor, a lawyer-supervisor may be able to show greater patience. In public service settings, lawyer-paralegal relationships may have a somewhat more egalitarian spirit.

A lawyer's expectations also depend on personality factors. Understanding personal variations requires getting to know each attorney individually.

Some differences in a lawyer's expectations can often be foreseen based on the lawyer's role in the office. In private law firms, the expectations held

THE STUDENT'S PERSPECTIVE 7.1: PAT

Connecting with Coworkers

After her first week at the office, Pat's supervising attorney asked how things were going. "I have to admit that, when I first started working here, I was a little afraid of you all," she answered candidly. "Everybody seemed so formal and businesslike. I wasn't used to that and I was afraid I'd never fit in. But the end-of-the-week socializing in the office lounge really showed me a different side to everyone here! Mr. Beel, for example, with his incredible jokes—I couldn't believe this was the managing partner I was so worried about meeting. And Ms. Elliot, the legal administrator, asked me about school and the courses I've had. She was genuinely nice. And you know Joanna, the paralegal I worked with on my first day? During that gathering in the office lounge, she asked me to join her and another paralegal from Barney, Small, and Goldmintz for a sandwich at the neighborhood deli next Tuesday. I said I would check with you and let her know. Would it be okay if I left a little before noon that day?"

"I think it's a great idea," was the response. "I'm glad you're making an effort to get to know people. It helps make things go more smoothly for everyone in the office. Meeting as many people as you can in the legal community is also a very good idea for someone hoping to launch a career. So by all means, go! Enjoy yourself. And tell your friend from Barney, Small, and Goldmintz to say hello for me to my old law school buddy, Jonathan Barney."

QUICK TIP 7.1

Forget most television portrayals of lawyers. In reality, lawyers work very long hours. They face a tight job market and may be paying off huge educational loans for years to come. Their lifestyles tend to be quite middle class. Increasingly, lawyers are also women—and mothers.

by managing partners, associates, and law clerks will differ in somewhat predictable ways. Many of these distinctions also apply in corporate and public service settings where lawyers and paralegals work together.

Managing Partners

Also known as "equity partners," managing partners own a significant partnership share (or a large portion of outstanding corporate shares) of a private law firm and have a voice in the overall management of the business. This is the highest level a lawyer can attain in any firm. In larger offices, only a relatively small number of lawyers will have achieved this status. In a very small or solo practice, every lawyer may be, in effect, a managing partner.

In their firms, managing partners function similarly to the board of directors of a corporation. They are the ultimate bosses and decision makers for the office. They are often mature, experienced attorneys who are known and respected in the legal and business communities. Colleagues tend to treat them with considerable deference. Being older than many of the other lawyers in the office, they may also be more conservative than others in dress, behavior, and attitude toward change.

Because the managing partner's status is higher than that of other lawyers in the firm, paralegals who work for managing partners may also enjoy greater prestige than other paralegals in the office. A letter of recommendation from a managing partner of a widely known firm can be an impressive door opener to many offices in your region.

Associates

Associates are salaried attorneys. Their status is that of employee—not partner. In a large firm, they may serve on committees to whom a narrow range of decision making has been delegated—such as a committee on office technology. Experienced and trusted associates may influence other aspects of the firm's decision making as well. But generally, associates have no control over how the office is run, who gets hired or fired, or what policy decisions are made.

Many associates aspire to becoming partners themselves some day. They achieve that not just by winning cases and serving clients, but also by bringing significant client business into the firm. Called "rainmaking," increasing the firm's client base is an important part of what most attorneys are expected to do. The pressure to produce billable hours while also producing new clients can be great.

Although he or she may be more highly paid than a paralegal, a new, young associate sometimes does work that an experienced paralegal can do just as well. Consequently, a new associate may see paralegals as competition for the firm's limited hiring dollars. If aloofness or resentment is occasionally encountered in a young associate, this may be at the root of it. Guidelines for addressing this problem are offered in the section below on law clerks, who may also see themselves in competition with paralegals.

Nevertheless, most associates can be wonderful teachers. They can also be highly instrumental to your career development. As associates grow in their own careers, moving up to partner or opening their own offices, they can also become valuable to your future job prospects.

Law Clerks

Law clerks are usually "lawyers-to-be," often in their last year of law school, working part-time or temporarily during summer vacation. Some are recently graduated and waiting for the results of their bar exam. They may be found in any office. Struggling learners like yourself and usually not much older than college students themselves, law clerks have a natural affinity for paralegal interns.

Normally, paralegal interns and law clerks get along extremely well. Paralegals often find that they are better acquainted with procedural basics than a new law clerk who is steeped in legal theory but may never have even seen a will, a contract, or state court pleadings. So, your relationship with this fellow newcomer stands to be mutually helpful.

Despite their more extensive education, an occasional law clerk perceives the paralegal intern (or any paralegal in the office) as competition for his or her job prospects. This is because opportunities for law school graduates are not as plentiful as they once were. In fact, it is no longer unusual to see recent law school graduates applying for paralegal positions as a last resort.[2] Future paralegals are wise to be aware of this.

If you believe a law clerk or new associate sees you as a competitor for future job openings, try the following—in the order they are given:

- Do not be the one to make this a personal issue. See the problem on the abstract level where it truly begins. Neither you nor the law clerk are the cause of this problem. The overabundance of law school graduates is the cause, and the clerk or new associate probably stands to lose the most because of it. Remember this whenever you feel yourself becoming defensive.
- If a law clerk or new associate makes it a personal issue and becomes antagonistic (which is unlikely), simply minimize your interaction with this individual without comment.
- If your responsibilities require frequent interaction with this person, try the four conflict resolution steps outlined in Chapter 6. This may put the two of you back on a more cooperative track.

- Report the problem to your supervisor *only* under the following circumstances: (a) your own honest efforts at conflict resolution have not succeeded, and (b) the law clerk's actions have begun to interfere with your work or with your agreed-upon learning opportunities in the office.

Be assured that most paralegal hiring decisions still favor paralegals over law school graduates who are often seen as high turnover risks, taking a paralegal job only until something better comes along.[3] In reality, real competition between a law clerk and a paralegal intern for the same job slot is fairly rare.

When a trusting work relationship is established, a law clerk is someone from whom you can learn and share exciting new experiences. As future lawyers, law clerks may also be in a position to help you greatly in your career some day. Most of the time, they become valued friends as well.

Legal Administrators

Also known as law office managers, law office administrators, or legal assistant managers, legal administrators oversee many of the day-to-day operations of the law office. *A "second boss" to the paralegals in your office, this person may be every bit as important to the success of your internship as your supervising attorney.*

Firms hire legal administrators to bring in strong business and organizational skills that lawyers often lack and do not have time to develop. Legal administrators take direction from the managing partners, so they wield considerable power and influence in the law office hierarchy. They are not usually law-school-trained and may never have practiced law. Often they have a prior background in an unrelated business setting such as a corporate personnel department. Sometimes they are former paralegals who have moved up to this position, perhaps after acquiring an advanced degree.

Typically, legal administrators screen new hires, carry out employment procedures and policies, and—most important to the paralegal intern—assign work to support staff. Newcomers are sometimes surprised to learn that, in many law offices, it is the legal administrator, rather than an attorney, who decides which paralegal (or intern) gets assigned to which projects. If this is the practice in your office, you must get the legal administrator's approval if you want certain assignments. It also means that the legal administrator must be treated with the same respect normally reserved for one's boss, because that is exactly what he or she is.

If a legal administrator helped select you for this internship, then the legal administrator will probably play a role in your evaluation as well, perhaps equal to that of your supervising attorney or paralegal. Therefore, you must keep this person informed of your achievements and successes along the way. Also, let your legal administrator know of any logistical difficulties you are unable to resolve on your own.

As with your supervising attorney or paralegal, try to communicate with your legal administrator at least weekly—either in person or in a short memo—about your progress, your accomplishments, and your changing needs. As with any supervisor, keep these communications courteous, serious, and businesslike. This person may have considerable influence on your job search in the future.

The difficulty interns most often encounter with legal administrators has to do with the complexities of having two "bosses": the legal administrator on the one hand, and the supervising attorney or paralegal on the other. With two supervisors overseeing your work, who is in charge of what? If this becomes an issue, follow these guidelines:

- As a general rule, only a lawyer can make decisions about the *content* of legal work being prepared for a client. For questions on how to proceed with law-related tasks that are assigned to you, check with your supervising attorney or supervising paralegal.
- A legal administrator may be authorized to decide *what assignments* are given to you. To request new or different assignments, try checking informally with the attorney in charge of the project to see whether he or she is even willing to supervise such an assignment. With that attorney's agreement, approach the legal administrator with your request.
- Do not appear to sidestep the administrator's authority. Make it clear you understand the need for the administrator's approval and that there may be larger scheduling issues to be considered.
- Take time to help your administrator understand the reasons for any request. Make your reasons objective rather than personal. For example, cite your agreed-upon internship goals rather than personal preferences.
- When in doubt, ask who is in charge of a particular issue. Begin with the person who seems closest to it.
- A legal administrator can also be very helpful in devising a solution to conflicts with law clerks or others when you have been unable to resolve such problems on your own.
- Report an administrator's actions to the internship director at your school only if a major, agreed-upon internship goal is being seriously thwarted.

Legal administrators from different offices in your region usually know each other personally. They check with each other about the work histories of job candidates. They may attend local and national meetings of the Association of Legal Administrators (ALA), the Legal Assistant Managers Association (LAMA), or similar groups in which they share experiences and information. Consequently, your reputation with one administrator may become your reputation among many. Do everything you can to make this relationship a strong alliance for the future.

Other Paralegals: Coworkers and Supervisors

No one is a more natural ally in the office than a paralegal coworker. *Experienced paralegals are your most valuable role models and the people from whom you will probably learn the most.* Do seek out their guidance as often as you can without infringing too greatly on their time. These are also the professionals to whom you may be able to relate on a social level, as long as you keep it fairly businesslike. Consider inviting them to join you during your lunch hour or coffee break. They, too, may welcome the chance to socialize.

In most areas, paralegals tend to know each other either from prior work experience or from paralegal association meetings. Consequently, they are often the first to know of upcoming paralegal job openings. Making a favorable impression on your paralegal coworkers often has the same advantages as favorably impressing lawyers and others.

Do not limit your contacts to paralegals in your own office. Get to know paralegals at neighboring offices as well. Attend local paralegal association meetings. Volunteer to work with other paralegals on one of the association's projects. Take a copy of your résumé with you to meetings in case some interest is expressed in your background. Find out other paralegals' viewpoints on their work and on future career prospects. Widen your network for additional role models and more numerous sources of future job news.

In larger offices, paralegals may have a hierarchy of their own. Beginning paralegals may be called "document clerks." More experienced paralegals may have another title along with more challenging responsibilities. Interns should try to observe workers at each level and learn as much as possible about what these distinctions entail. Higher-ranking paralegals may also expect a degree of deference from those at less experienced levels. The intern should be sensitive to this possibility.

Sometimes, an intern's immediate supervisor is a paralegal. If this is your situation, you should count yourself as very fortunate. You are being taught by someone who knows—probably better than anyone else in the office—what being a paralegal really is all about. You have an experienced role model virtually all to yourself. Take full advantage of this special relationship and do not hesitate to show your gratitude often.

Legal Secretaries

The best advice that can be given about legal secretaries is this: *never assume a secretary knows less than you about any subject. Do* assume that, in many situations, the secretary may actually know quite a bit more.

New paralegals need to understand that many legal secretaries have already been doing paralegal-level work for years, but without the benefit of the proper job title (and perhaps also without appropriate pay). Even if they are not doing paralegal work, they may know more about nitty-gritty procedural details than almost anyone else. They may also know more about what is happening in the office than some managing partners!

Perhaps because they work for so many in the office, the legal secretary is an informational gold mine to be treasured. For example, this is the person to see for assistance when no paralegal or attorney is available, such as to help you locate samples when you are drafting a document for the first time. It is the secretary who probably knows where your supervising attorney is and when he or she will be back. When you get to know this person well enough, the secretary may also be the one to fill you in on the idiosyncrasies of coworkers you have had trouble understanding.

The legal secretary is the person on whom many interns depend to process their documents quickly, file them properly, or mail them out on time. This is someone who can save interns from embarrassment by catching drafting errors and other mistakes while they are still correctable. Many times, this is also someone who can relieve the day's tensions by making you laugh.

If you are lucky enough to have the services of a secretary, you will probably be sharing those services with others in the office. Know that yours is not the only work waiting to be processed and that the secretary's workload may be quite heavy. To help ensure the cooperation you want, routinely ask how much lead time the secretary needs to fit your work in with other projects that are waiting. Alert the secretary several days in advance of an unusually large project. Accommodate the secretary's workload as best you can.

Occasionally, one hears stories about a secretary refusing to process an intern's work on time. When this happens, it is usually because the paralegal has treated the secretary disdainfully or has been insensitive to the other demands on the secretary's time. You know to avoid doing that. If resistance still occurs in spite of your best efforts, here are a few ideas for getting better cooperation:

- Try the four steps toward conflict resolution outlined in Chapter 6. This effectively solves most problems.
- If faced with a rare instance in which conflict resolution fails, discreetly share the problem with your attorney or paralegal supervisor in a neutral, factual manner. Ask for his or her advice in dealing with it.

- If there is an office administrator, you can share the problem with this person in the same neutral, factual manner and ask for suggestions.
- If all else fails, submit your work to your supervisor in the form it would normally be presented to the secretary—untyped or unprocessed—and let the supervisor assign it to a secretary for processing. But save this as a last resort; it could cause further conflict and hard feelings in the future.

Never condescend or "talk down" to secretaries. Treat them as professional equals. Cultivate the secretary's friendship as perhaps the most essential person in the office, without whom no other worker would survive professionally.

At the Courthouse

Several activities may take you to the court house: filing and researching court documents, observing court proceedings, and assisting at a trial or hearing. For the paralegal intern, these can be exciting, eye-opening experiences.

The Clerk's Office

Unless electronic filing and retrieval are available (at a limited number of courts), the filing, retrieving, or researching of court documents requires a trip to the court clerk's office. These visits allow students to learn the intricacies of court processes and also get an insider's view of another potential employment setting.

Portions of the clerk's office are often open to the public. Lawyers, paralegals, *pro se* (unrepresented) plaintiffs and defendants, newspaper reporters, and other researchers are among those who may be waiting in line with you.

As in other offices, a hierarchy exists in this setting. The clerk's office is normally overseen by the clerk of the court. This professional is elected or appointed to the office and, in higher courts, may be a trained lawyer. Most routine matters will not bring you into contact with this person— only with assistant clerks and other clerical personnel. But the clerk of court is someone you might politely ask for in the event of serious problems or confusion.

The clerk has ultimate control over how paperwork is handled in that office. In all probability, he or she also makes the hiring decisions for the office; you may want this person to consider your résumé one day. Clearly, this is someone to treat with respect. If the opportunity arises, you would be fortunate to count the court clerk among your professional acquaintances.

Rules for preparing, filing, copying, and researching court documents can be enormously complex. The clerk's office is a priceless source of assistance in getting it right. Interns should never hesitate to telephone the clerk's office for instruction on these sometimes confusing details. Your call will be no surprise to them; most court office personnel are accustomed to taking procedural questions on the phone. Calling will also save you wasted trips for a document that cannot be processed due to, say, a newly increased filing fee or failure to have the correct number of copies.

In the same way that you are building a reputation among coworkers, you are also building a reputation at the court clerk's office. In time, you may be recognized there. Make sure you are remembered favorably. Never risk alienating court clerk personnel. Your office depends heavily on their cooperation and also on clerks' willingness to help the law office overcome procedural errors sometimes. So, no matter how brusque or unpleasant an assistant court clerk may be, always remain courteous and professional.

THE STUDENT'S PERSPECTIVE 7.2: DANIEL
Coping with "Red Tape"

Speaking to next semester's interns, Daniel was asked to describe one of the most difficult experiences of his internship. "We were suing a landlord for injuries caused by unsafe conditions, and we heard that the same landlord had been sued by someone else a year earlier for a similar problem. My supervising attorney thought this was useful information and wanted to know more.

"Normally, we would have called the lawyer involved in the earlier case but that wasn't possible here. The earlier case was brought by a *pro se* plaintiff—she had no lawyer. We didn't even know who the plaintiff was. The lawyer who defended the landlord in that case was the same one who opposed us now. He certainly wouldn't help us. So, somehow, I had to track down the pleadings and motions filed in that case.

"I went to the district court clerk's office with only the name of the land-lord and a rough idea of when the earlier case was filed. The clerk I spoke to was curt and uncooperative. She kept asking why I wanted this and why didn't I have a specific date, the plaintiff's name, or a docket number. I explained the situation but it didn't help. She was very busy and didn't have time to 'plow through a year's worth of files,' as she put it. The situation really looked hopeless.

"Now, most clerks know that, with few exceptions, court documents are public records. Anyone should have access to them. I'm sure this clerk knew that, too. But I decided not to lecture her about my legal rights. Instead, I told her about the horrendous injuries our client suffered and asked what she needed to be able to help me out. I said I would do whatever the office's procedures required. I guess my polite persistence and my appeal to her sympathy worked because she said, 'Okay, here's what you can do.'

"She put me at an out-of-the-way desk and handed me the index for the preceding year's cases with instructions not to disturb the order of anything it contained. In a few minutes, I found what appeared to be the name of the case, with the docket number. She pulled the case file and there it was—everything I needed!

"When I returned to the office, my supervisor was thrilled to see the docu-ments. He said I had saved the case. And when I told him about my experi-ence at the clerk's office, he laughed. 'Oh, you met my friend Dot!' he said. 'She does that to everyone the first time they come in. When she gets to know you, though, she's the most helpful person around. I'm glad you kept things on a professional level. She'll remember that and, next time, you'll find her to be far more pleasant. Nice work, Daniel!'"

The Courtroom

Whether you are assisting a lawyer at trial or simply there to observe the pro-ceedings, going to court can be one of the most exciting things you do as an intern. Whatever your purpose in being there, you must understand that this is the most formal, and also the most hierarchical, of all law-related work settings.

Personal behavior and attire must be impeccable. Wear your best business outfit. Follow all instructions from your supervising attorney and certainly any from the judge. Once the proceedings have begun, remain absolutely quiet.

In some courtrooms, even whispering might be considered disruptive and can bring a harsh reprimand from the judge. With relatively little provocation, a judge can order an uncooperative person to be physically ejected from the courtroom or even taken into police custody. If you must communicate with your supervising attorney while court is in session, do so in writing and preferably without leaving your seat. (Have paper and pencil handy for this purpose.)

During court proceedings, the judge has control over everyone in the courtroom. To show respect for the judge's position, everyone stands when the judge enters and leaves the courtroom. Lawyers and others also rise to their feet when speaking to the judge. No one but lawyers or *pro se* parties may speak directly to the judge in court, unless the judge directs otherwise. Even then, one does not speak until after the judge acknowledges her or him and indicates permission to speak. Even in noncourt settings, always remember to address a judge as "Your Honor."

If you are fortunate enough to accompany your supervising attorney to a conference with the judge *in chambers* (in the judge's private office near the courtroom), greet His or Her Honor with a smile, a handshake, and a cordial "good morning" or "good afternoon." Then allow the judge and attorneys to confer without interruption.

The courtroom hierarchy is strikingly apparent in the surroundings. Typically, the judge's *bench* is placed higher than all other seating in the room. A railing or *bar* often separates the general public from the area where the lawyers and their clients sit. This is where the term member of the bar originates. *Jury seating* is normally on the working side of the bar as well, but always off to one side, perhaps implying detached objectivity.

Table 7.1

Diagram of a Courtroom

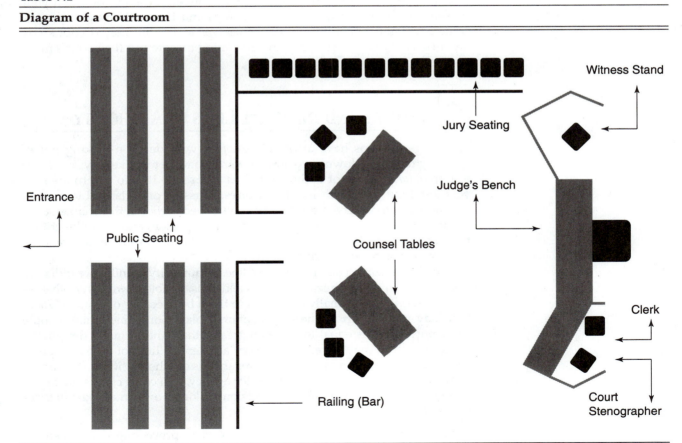

Illustrated by Cassie McInnis

Two large *counsel tables*—one for the plaintiff and one for the defendant—face the bench. These tables are occupied by the lawyers and clients presenting a case. In some courtrooms, there may also be a *lectern* for the attorneys to use in presenting arguments to the court. Adjacent to the judge's bench is the *witness stand*, a partially enclosed area where each witness sits while delivering testimony. In most courtrooms, the witness stand is also somewhat elevated. The *court stenographer*, who makes a verbatim record of everything said in the proceedings, is usually positioned to one side, at the front of the courtroom.

Most judges are accustomed to seeing a paralegal seated next to an attorney at counsel table, assisting the attorney with documents, evidence, visual aids, or note taking. However, not all judges are equally accepting of this practice.[4] Therefore, sit with your supervising attorney at counsel table only if it is certain that the judge approves of the arrangement. If you are assisting in court for the first time, ask your supervising attorney in advance about the judge's expectations in this regard.

Paralegals who are not assisting counsel and only observing the proceedings usually sit in the public seating area. This is where witnesses, family members, and other interested persons sit until called upon to participate. You may be providing a service by keeping them calm as they wait.

Other professionals in the courtroom may include (1) a uniformed (and often armed) *bailiff or court officer* who maintains order and handles security matters, and (2) a *court clerk* or assistant clerk who assists the judge in following the docket and processing paperwork.

The bailiff, in particular, should never be given reason to question your presence in court. Prior to the proceedings and before the judge appears, some paralegals like to introduce themselves to a bailiff they do not know and briefly explain their role in the upcoming case, to put the bailiff's mind at ease.

FORMAL AND INFORMAL LINES OF AUTHORITY

Most organizations have a formal structure with decision-making power typically radiating downward and outward from the top, like a pyramid. For example, *formal* lines of authority tell us whose job it is to determine next year's staffing budget, to select new hires, to assign projects, and to oversee the completion of a given project. As you learned earlier in this chapter, each of these responsibilities may fall to a different person, and it can be critical to your future to know who each one is. However, these are not the only lines of authority worthy of concern.

Every organization also has *informal* lines of authority or influence radiating from people in the organization who wield considerable power over others—not because it was formally delegated to them but because of circumstances that may not be part of the organizational plan. Sometimes these people carry power that is equal to, or even greater than, the formally designated authority others may have. Informal or "accidental" lines of authority probably exist in your own organization, regardless of whether it is a law firm, a bank, a real estate office, a social service agency, or a court clerk's office.

Significant sources of informal decision-making power may exist in these kinds of situations:

- When bottleneck sites exist, such as a word processing department or copying center, through which all work must pass

- When financial approval must be separately obtained for all decisions involving expenditures
- When one person's expertise on a subject is greater than everyone else's and that expertise is needed
- When someone with formal power and authority, such as a senior managing partner, is actually relying on the advice of a trusted colleague
- When someone with formal power and authority has informally delegated responsibilities to someone else
- When many procedural requirements ("red tape") exist and someone is in charge of either accepting or rejecting submissions based on whether the procedural requirements are met
- When a particularly well-liked or charismatic person —who may have little or no formal authority—is listened to and taken seriously by others in the office

Interns should watch for informal power sources and seek out their assistance when it is needed. For example, knowing who controls the paper flow in the copying center may make the difference between getting your copies done on time or getting them back late. Knowing who in the court clerk's office is most experienced may mean getting timely instructions on difficult procedural requirements. And knowing who has the ear of the firm's financial decision makers may mean that a new paralegal position could be created a bit sooner than you (and others) first believed.

 **OFFICE POLITICS**

To cope effectively with this phenomenon, interns must recognize what office politics is, and what it is not.

First, office politics is *not* what we euphemistically call a "personality conflict"—a personal dislike of certain individuals who think or behave somewhat differently from you. There will always be a few people to whom you do not relate very well. Occasionally, such incompatibility is the result of cultural distinctions and minor differences in upbringing, both of which can only be resolved through tolerance and flexibility. More often, incompatibility may be the result of a clash in work styles. The following subsection explains how to deal with certain recognized differences in work styles.

Second, office politics is not simply gossiping. Rightly or wrongly, gossip takes place to some extent in every work environment. The universal attraction that gossip holds and the many dangers it creates are discussed in the next subsection.

Real "office politics" is power brokering within the organization. This subject is explored in the last subsection.

Recognizing Different Work Styles

Not everyone approaches work the same way or works well under exactly the same circumstances. When your work or an office relationship is not going well, the problem may be due to differing work styles. The solution lies not in making excuses, of course. It lies in changing your timing or adjusting your approach to accommodate your or your colleague's particular work style as much as your job allows.

The Myers-Briggs Type Indicator (MBTI) is a widely recognized system for identifying personality-linked approaches to work.[5] It divides people into sixteen types based on their opposite preferences in four categories. The categories are Extraversion versus Introversion, Sensing versus Intuition, Thinking versus Feeling, and Judging versus Perceiving. None is "good" or "bad." Each simply has a different mode of operating and brings different strengths to the task at hand.

As you review these various styles of fact gathering, decision making, and relating to others on the job, you may recognize yourself and some people you know. The questions found in Appendix 1 will help you tentatively to determine what is most likely to be your MBTI type. For conclusive identification of your MBTI type, you need to be properly tested by an authorized MBTI test administrator.

Extraversion versus Introversion

Extraverts (psychologists retained the nineteenth-century spelling of this word to distinguish it from the everyday term *extrovert*) need to be among people, tend to think out loud, often seek others' reactions before acting, and usually need excitement in their work. Introverts, on the other hand, work best in one-on-one situations and prefer to think things through on their own before acting. They also require periods of privacy in their daily lives to reflect quietly and "refuel" themselves.

In American society, Extraverts outnumber Introverts by about three to one.[6] So it surprises many to learn that *most lawyers—about 57 percent—fall into the less common Introvert category* (see Table 7.2).[7] If your next boss strikes you as a pensive "loner," now you know the reason.

Successful employees eventually develop some degree of versatility, using their Extravert tendencies when assertive communication is needed, for example, but also learning to work in a more introverted style when the situation calls for it. You can learn to do this, too. You may also have to learn to accommodate the coworker or boss whose approach to work is different from yours.

Sensing versus Intuition

Sensing workers seek hard data, physical facts, practical solutions, and tangible results. They work well with details and with numbers. In legal work,

Table 7.2

Type Preferences of Lawyers

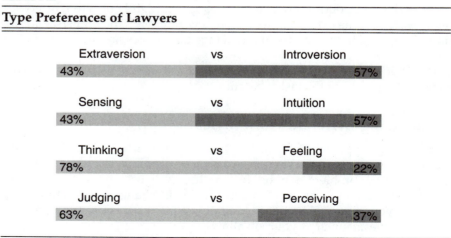

From "The Lawyer Types" by Larry Richard, *ABA Journal* July, 1993. Copyright © 1993. American Bar Association. Reprinted by permission of the *ABA Journal.*

Sensers are usually comfortable with tax matters and real estate transactions, for example. Intuitives, on the other hand, are more comfortable with interpretation, analysis, and abstract ideas. They can be quite original and creative.

Lawyers are almost evenly split between these two categories, with a slight majority preferring Intuition over Sensing. The differences become apparent in the kind of legal work they prefer. For example, litigators are often Intuitives (and also Extraverts).[8]

Being aware of these differences will help you choose assignments in which you are most likely to succeed. It may also help you to communicate with clients and coworkers in a way they are more likely to understand. When asked to "find the answer," for example, it will help tremendously to know whether your boss wants to hear about ideas and ambiguities or "just the (tangible) facts!"

Thinking versus Feeling

In Myers-Briggs terms, these words do not have their usual meanings. By Thinking, we mean being able to approach a problem in a detached, objective manner and not being prone to personal judgment about the issue at hand. Thinkers usually base their reactions on logic, rather than personal values. Feelers, on the other hand, tend to make decisions based on personal values and judgments. The Feeler is directed strongly by personal likes and dislikes, whereas the Thinker normally is not.[9]

Being Thinkers makes it possible for lawyers to participate in heated adversarial conflicts, for example, and find it stimulating rather than stressful. A Feeler, on the other hand, tends to take such conflicts personally. Also, being a Feeler often leads workers toward humanitarian pursuits and into service-related fields.

Students who fall heavily into the Feeling category probably should avoid litigation or else develop very thick skins to survive in an intense, adversarial environment. Such students may also need to learn greater objectivity and tolerance in office relationships to avoid unnecessary personality conflicts. Students who are Judgers (see subsection below) may need to show sensitivity to the Feelers around them, be more liberal with praise, and limit criticism to that which is genuinely helpful.[10]

Judging versus Perceiving

Again, the MBTI terms mean something different from what one might expect. In this case, the category can often be identified just by peeking into a worker's office. Judgers are methodical, orderly, on time, and like having everything under control. Their work spaces are usually neat and well-organized. Perceivers, on the other hand, like to keep all their options open, so decisions come slowly. They tend to be informal, impromptu, and procrastinators.[11] The cluttered office often belongs to the Perceiver.

Most (but not all) lawyers fall under the Judging category—and expect their employees to do the same. A student who falls into the Perceiving category must learn to maintain at least an appearance of orderliness—and above all, respect deadlines! Conversely, if your boss is a Perceiver, you will probably be appreciated for bringing order to his or her work.

Rumors and Gossip

Privately discussing the behavior of others, sharing opinions about coworkers' actions, and exchanging information on developments in the office are

> ## THE STUDENT'S PERSPECTIVE 7.3: TARA
> ## When Work Styles Clash
>
> During her internship, Tara learned a valuable lesson about herself. Working in a general practice law firm, she was asked to develop asset lists for estate planning clients. "I couldn't believe how detailed that was," she confided. "Some of these clients owned a lot of stocks and other investments that I, unfortunately, didn't understand and had absolutely no interest in. One day, I felt like I would scream if I had to calculate the value of shares in one more mutual fund."
>
> Tara had the good sense to calmly discuss her frustration with her supervisor, who understood the problem. Performing methodical, detailed work just was not Tara's strength. "I like work that draws on my imagination or has me out and about, talking to people, looking at problems, and trying to come up with solutions," she told him. Seeing intelligence of a different kind, the supervisor put Tara on a criminal defense matter.
>
> "It was a fascinating case. I had the chance to do some creative research on arrest and search procedures. I also interviewed a witness and participated in strategy-planning discussions. I absolutely love my internship now, and they seem to like my work a lot, too.
>
> "I now have a clearer picture of what kind of work best fits my own work style. That, in itself, made this experience worthwhile."

all commonplace. On its most innocent level, gossip is a way to keep informed of what is going on around you. It helps relieve the tensions of everyday work. It promotes social bonding between like-minded coworkers. Unfortunately, it also presents many dangers.

Gossips pay a high price when critical remarks—made privately—fail to remain private. Interns should always assume their words could reach the ears of the very person they are talking about, no matter what assurances are made to the contrary. When privately discussing a coworker or an office development, say only what you could bear to have repeated throughout the office.

Repeating office rumors begun by others is also dangerous. Although many rumors contain some thread of truth, they tend to be embellished or modified each time they are told. As a result, most rumors are fraught with inaccuracy. Confusion and misunderstanding are compounded as a rumor gets passed from person to person. When you hear a rumor, end what may only be a chain of confusion. Simply do not pass it on.

Power Brokering

Genuine office politics is quite different from personality conflicts or gossip. Office politics is really power brokering. It is the deliberate manipulation of the organization's power structure to promote certain organizational decisions or to further personal career goals. For example, an associate who hopes for promotion to the status of partner may engage in some degree of office politics. So may support staff who want management to purchase and install a new computer network system. You may engage in office politics yourself, at some point, in pursuing better assignments or in seeking permanent employment at your internship office.

This practice in and of itself is not evil. Power brokering is a reality—perhaps even a necessity—that exists in every organization. At times, it can be positive and productive. Other times, it can be ugly and destructive. It depends entirely on what tactics are used.

According to Eileen Rosenberg, legitimate political tactics in the office include

- Using outside experts or factual research
- Cultivating a favorable impression
- Developing support among others in the organization
- Getting your matter on the agenda at meetings
- Selecting (or helping to select) the criteria on which a decision will be based
- Aligning yourself with those who have power

Illegitimate tactics include

- Showering decision makers with undeserved flattery ("bootlicking")
- Withholding full information about a matter
- Scapegoating—blaming the wrong person or blaming one person for problems that are caused by many
- Overwhelming decision makers with irrelevant information[12]

Legitimate tactics are honest, straightforward, and essentially fair to others. Illegitimate tactics involve some level of deception and are deliberately misleading to others. Misleading people undermines the operations of the office and ultimately weakens the integrity of the work being done there. Misleading people can also backfire when the truth later becomes known. Interns should never engage in illegitimate tactics; and if they see coworkers engaging in them, they should distance themselves from that behavior.

Is it ever permissible for interns to "play politics" in the office? When fair, aboveboard tactics are used to achieve positive, professional goals, then of course it is. After all, building and maintaining influence in your surroundings are important to your success as a newcomer in your work environment. Any of the strategies listed under "legitimate political tactics" may be tried as long as they are used responsibly and as long as the goals involved are compatible with your office's objectives.

EXERCISES

Test your understanding of status, authority, and alliance building by answering the following multiple choice questions. There may be more than one acceptable answer to each problem, but one answer will be *better* than the others. Compare your answers with the suggested responses in Appendix 2.

1. There is an office Christmas party at a nice restaurant next Friday evening and you are invited. The party costs nothing to attend, but you had other plans for that evening and you dislike formal social events. You also find the prospect of attending a party with a room full of lawyers a bit intimidating. You
   a. Decline the invitation, saying that you are sorry but you have already made other plans.
   b. Attend the party and take full advantage of a great opportunity to get to know coworkers outside of the office environment.
   c. Make an appearance at the party, stay for less than an hour and leave early, apologizing for having other obligations that evening.

> **QUICK TIP 7.3**
>
> The level of "politicking" in the office may indicate the level of stability (or instability) in the organization. Political struggles tend to be minimal when resources are sufficient, jobs are secure, and employees have meaningful influence over their work—important factors if you are thinking about permanent employment.

2. You are drafting a complex will. You expect the draft to be done in about three days. Your supervising attorney has told you that when your draft is finished, you should give it to the secretary to have it typed and that the secretary should deliver the final copy to your supervising attorney. You have never had anything typed by the secretary before. The best way to handle this situation is

   a. Finish the draft and leave it on the secretary's desk when you are done.

   b. When the draft is completed, take it to the secretary and explain your supervising attorney's instructions in case the secretary is unaware of the arrangement.

   c. Call or see the secretary soon after your meeting with your supervising attorney. Alert the secretary to the instructions you were just given and let the secretary know that, in about three days, a complex will must be typed for your supervisor.

3. You are accompanying your supervising attorney to court for the first time. You are seated with your supervisor at counsel table. The court proceedings have just begun. Suddenly, the judge points at you and says to your supervisor, "Counselor, is this cocounsel you have with you and, if so, why wasn't I informed?" You

   a. Immediately jump up and explain to the judge who you are and what you are doing there.

   b. Stare at the table in terrified silence.

   c. Turn to your supervising attorney, look him or her in the eye, and wait for the attorney to explain.

4. You are being introduced to Robert Wickham, a senior managing partner of the firm. He is a distinguished man in his sixties whom you have never seen before. You

   a. Reach out for a handshake, smile, and say, "Hi, how are ya?"

   b. Stand respectfully still and say, "Hello, Sir."

   c. Reach out for a handshake, smile, and say, "How do you do, Mr. Wickham. It's a pleasure to meet you."

5. You have just been introduced to a paralegal from another office, who is also vice president of the local paralegal association. After the introductions, there is an awkward moment of silence when no one seems to know what to say. You

   a. Break the ice by talking about yourself, your school, your internship, and the kind of employment you hope to find in the future.

   b. Say, "I'm always so glad to meet an experienced paralegal. What area of law are you working in, Jeannette?"

   c. Wait for someone else to begin talking, because you do not know this person and you do not want to seem pushy.

6. Your supervising attorney has asked you to work with Scott, a new associate just out of law school, to research a case for possible appeal. The supervisor instructed you as follows: "Let Scott determine what the issues are and where you can be helpful. You may have suggestions, too, but generally I want you to follow his lead on this, okay?" As you begin working with Scott, it becomes evident that he does not know as much as you do about certain procedural questions involved in the case. You

   a. Do not contradict Scott's direction; he is the one in charge of the project.

   b. Take control of the situation; list the procedural issues you see and tell Scott what needs to be done. The project is more important than Scott's ego.

   c. Tell Scott that together you make a good team because of his in-depth knowledge of legal theory and your practical training in procedural matters. Then suggest that you be given the task of researching the procedural issues you have noticed.

7. You have been asked to find out what forms to file when a legal heir cannot be found. You work in a solo law practice and no one is in the office this morning except the secretary. You hardly know where to begin. You
   a. Research your state's statutes and probate court rules on your own.
   b. Ask the secretary if this has ever come up before and, if so, what forms were filed.
   c. Call the clerk's office at the local probate court and ask what forms are required for this purpose.
   d. Contact an attorney you met recently from another firm in the same building; you happen to know she does a lot of work in decedents' estates.
   e. Call a probate judge that you met last week at a local bar association picnic.

8. You have heard rumors that several associates are dissatisfied with their salaries and that they may be leaving at the end of the year to start their own law firm. Paralegals and support staff seem to be taking one side or the other, either voicing agreement with the unhappy associates or dismissing the complaints as the product of ambition and large egos. One of the reportedly dissatisfied associates is Linda Hartmann, a lawyer whom you respect very much. The views of other lawyers in the office are not known to you. You
   a. Verify the rumor with Linda Hartmann, letting her know that if it is true, you support the move she is making.
   b. Let it be known to anyone who asks that the dissatisfied associates are people you admire, and they must have good reasons for being dissatisfied.
   c. Voice no opinion on the matter and stay out of the controversy for the duration of your internship.

9. Working under very rushed circumstances, your supervising attorney overlooked what might be an important aspect of a developing case. You want to bring it to his attention, but he is tired and anxious to complete another matter before ending the day's work. You
   a. Let it go until another day, realizing that he is tired and that his time must be treated with respect.
   b. Explain the overlooked factor in full detail, right then and there.
   c. Stop him long enough to say you noticed an important development that he will want to know about; then ask if he has a minute to talk about it.

ENDNOTES

1. According to Hindi Greenberg, career consultant and head of "Lawyers in Transition," the median income of lawyers in the United States is under $60,000 a year. See H. Greenberg, "Career Satisfaction in the Law," *The Compleat Lawyer—The Magazine of the ABA General Practice Section* (Spring 1996): 36.
2. For a more detailed discussion of this problem, see Cheryl Rogovin, "J.D.'s Accepted, Paralegals Preferred," *Legal Assistant Today* (July/August 1996): 27.
3. Ibid.
4. See, for example, Gina Farrell Gladwell, "Philadelphia Paralegal Barred from Counsel Table Raises Controversy," *Legal Assistant Today* (July/August 1995): 12.

5. The Myers-Briggs Type Indicator (MBTI), was developed in the 1940s, building on Carl Jung's theories about normal personality differences among people. According to Otto Kroeger and Janet M. Thuesen, *Type Talk at Work* (New York: Dell Publishing, 1992), p. 7, it is one of the most widely used psychological testing instruments. The MBTI is copyrighted by Consulting Psychologists Press, Inc., of Palo Alto, California.

6. Kroeger and Thuesen, *Type Talk at Work,* 28.

7. In a 1992 study, the MBTI was administered to 3,014 lawyers. The results were compiled and reported by Larry Richard in "The Lawyer Types," *ABA Journal* 79 (July 1993): 74–78.

8. Richard, "The Lawyer Types," 75.

9. Ibid., 76.

10. Ibid., 77.

11. Ibid.

12. Eileen Rosenberg, *Principles of Law Office Management* (St. Paul: West, 1993), 132–133. Rosenberg does not specifically characterize any of these tactics as either good or bad. She does state that we should distinguish beneficial behaviors from those that are organizationally dysfunctional and unethical. That distinction is attempted here by labeling some of these behaviors as "legitimate" and others as "illegitimate."

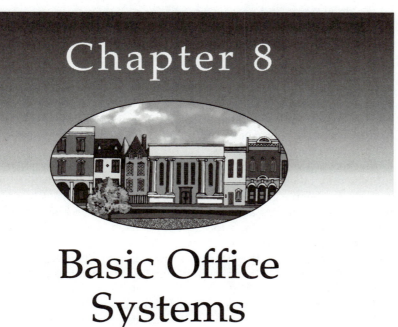

Chapter 8

Basic Office Systems

In any office providing law-related services, the intern's first challenge is mastering the procedures used for handling paperwork, preserving clients' files, and tracking deadlines. In a private law firm, interns may also have to keep time records and understand the office's client-billing system. All offices do not use identical systems for these procedures, but all systems do have certain things in common. What follows is an introduction to the principles involved in each of these systems, explaining the *whys* as well as the *hows*.

 ## FILING SYSTEMS

No matter what kind of office you work in, it will have a filing system. To work effectively, interns must know how to navigate that system. This section explains how most filing systems work. In any office providing law-related services, interns must also be aware of the confidentiality issues surrounding client files. Those issues are also explained in this section.

How Filing Systems Work

Lawyers sometimes joke about how their salaries could be calculated by the number of documents they create. Indeed, legal services produce prodigious amounts of paper. Every document provides a record of something that could assume great importance at any time, not only to a client but also to the office itself in the event of malpractice claims, financial audits, or future litigation. Virtually everything must be kept for anywhere from three to seven years, sometimes indefinitely. Simply retaining them is not enough. Documents must also be organized for easy identification and retrieval. It takes a fairly elaborate setup to accomplish that—hence, the filing system.

QUICK TIP 8.1

A textbook overview of office's systems will make your office's systems easier to understand and will help you adapt to different employment settings in the future. Nevertheless, every intern needs on-site instruction on the particular systems he or she will use during the internship.

The files that interns work with most often are client files, containing all the documents and notes prepared for a client's court case, transaction, or business operations. (Other office files might include employees' personnel files, vendor files and office purchases, financial records such as payroll and billing, forms files, and timekeeping records for attorneys and paralegals.)

One client's file may consist of dozens or even hundreds of *subfiles*. Subfiles contain specific categories of work prepared for the same client. Subfiles may contain only pleadings, discovery, correspondence, or research. Inside the front cover of each subfile, a *file index* lists the contents so that documents can be located quickly.

Marked *tabs* on the end of the folder identify each subfile. Alternatively, subfiles may be color-coded for easy identification. For instance, pleadings may always be in a green folder and correspondence always in a yellow one. Sometimes documents are copied onto colored paper, instead, for the same purpose. (In some offices, colored paper is used not for subfiles but to identify documents as office copies rather than originals. Other offices use colored paper to identify the attorney responsible for the case.)

Each new client file begins with a *client information form,* which may have another name such as "intake form," "new matter memo," or "new file memorandum" (see Table 8.1). This form contains key information on the client and the case such as the client's address, phone number, the nature of the matter, and the name of the attorney responsible for it. The client information form provides a starting point for familiarizing yourself with a new file. The file contents that follow are usually kept in reverse chronological order with the most recent document on top.

Many offices accompany the client information form with a *tickler list:* a checklist of upcoming deadlines to ensure timely progress on the client's case, business, or transaction. The tickler list in the client's file will be coordinated with the office's general tickler system (see the Calendaring and Tickler Systems section below).

Each client file is also marked with a *file number* to identify its place in the filing system. To avoid disclosing a client's identity to outsiders, most offices do not mark file folders with clients' names. Instead, the office may use a number, a series of letters, or a combination of the two.

The file number is based on a system chosen by each office for identifying new files—such as a combination of the date the case was taken and the initials of the responsible attorney. For example, a file opened on January 3, 1997 and assigned to Attorney Maria Bellinni might look like this: 1-3-97MB. File numbering systems vary from one office to the next, and your office may have a somewhat different method.

In large offices, files may be *bar coded,* using the same kind of small black and white lines we frequently see on supermarket merchandise. Bar coding allows office files to be scanned with a handheld scanner for rapid inventorying and easy identification. Each client's bar code may also be transferable to envelopes for mailing correspondence and documents to clients, taking advantage of discounts available from the U.S. Postal Service to offices using this system.

Offices also maintain a *master list* showing the file number of each client and the name of the attorney to whom the client's matter has been assigned. To find out a certain client's file number, an intern can check the master list or ask the file manager to check it.

The master list also becomes the basis of conducting a *conflicts-of-interest check* for every new client. When expanded to show the names of opposing

Table 8.1

Sample Client Information Form

NEW CASE MEMO

Client Information

Client _____   File no. _____

Address _____   Date opened _____

_____   ☐ New client   ☐ Present Client

Phone(s): Home _____   Business _____

Case Information

File title _____

Matter _____

_____

_____

Type of case _____

Referred by _____   Obtained by _____

Responsible attorney _____   Assigned to _____

Adverse party _____

Address _____

Phone(s) _____

Opposing attorney _____

Address _____

Phone(s) _____

Fee Arrangements

☐ Fixed fee of $ _____   ☐ Hourly rate at $ _____ Per hour

☐ Hourly rate at $ _____   Per hour plus _____% of amount ☐ Recovered ☐ Saved

☐ Estimated fee in the range of $ _____ to $ _____

☐ Contingent fee of _____ % of amount ☐ Recovered ☐ Saved ☐ Other _____

☐ Fee to be determined on basis of all relevant factors ☐ Retainer of $ _____ Per ☐ Month ☐ Year

    Number of hours of service covered by retainer: up to _____ Hours per ☐ Month ☐ Year

    Excess hours to be billed at $ _____ Per hour

☐ Other _____

Billing Arrangements

Bill ☐ Monthly ☐ Quarterly ☐ On completion ☐ Other _____

                                         ☐ Toward fee & costs

☐ Retainer of $ _____ Received on_____   ☐ $ _____ toward fee

                                           ☐ $ _____ toward costs

☐ Client's deposit account of $ _____ Received on

    Toward fees and costs as incurred. Account to be maintained at $ _____ until completion.

Notes

_____

_____

_____

_____

_____

parties and related data, the master list allows each new client matter to be compared with cases that the office's lawyers and paralegals have handled in the past (even in previous employment settings), so that potential conflicts of interest can be spotted.

If the master list shows that a new client may be suing the former client of any attorney in the office, then the case may have to be referred elsewhere. In many offices, these comparisons are now being done by computer with software designed specifically for checking conflicts of interest.[1]

Files that are currently being used by lawyers or others in the office often have to be located quickly. To ensure that a needed file can be easily found, large offices may have attorneys and staff sign an *out card* for each file they have in their possession and an *in card* each time a file is returned to the files.

"Where is the Jensen file?" is a typical question in many law offices. Few things cause as much panic as a missing file. Although it may be annoying to sign a card each time a file is taken or returned, this practice protects more than just the file. It also protects you by providing proof that you returned it properly.

Where no sign-in system exists, protecting yourself from responsibility for files that someone else may have misplaced can be difficult. In small and solo offices where in cards and out cards are not used, *consider keeping an accurate list of all files in your possession,* along with the date when each file was received and the date when each was returned for refiling. This is especially important if you are not recording time and tasks for client billing and lack the advantage of having such records show who last worked on a given file. In your own record, indicate the location of files that are currently in use, such as "my office," "supervisor's office," or "at home." (An example of daily notes on the location of current files is shown in Table 8.6.)

THE STUDENT'S PERSPECTIVE 8.1: HEATHER

Risky Exposure

Before leaving her weekly meeting with her supervisor, Attorney Schumann, Heather decided to share an experience she had earlier that week. "Remember when I went to the law library at the courthouse the other day to do some research on the Lawrence case? Well, you wouldn't believe who I saw there—our illustrious opposing counsel, Gerald Ferraro! Since I'm new around here, he didn't know who I was. But I knew who he was as soon as I passed the table where he was working. His files were open and papers were scattered all over the place, with his name and law office letterhead on them, of course."

"So was he working on the Lawrence case, too? Did you scope out his trial strategy?" Attorney Schumann joked.

"Right," she responded, "and then the Supreme Court Ethics Committee would swoop down on us and we'd lose a lot more than this case. No—fortunately for Ferraro, I know my ethical limits. But he could be a lot more careful about exposing his clients' files to everyone around him. If he plans his trial strategy as carelessly as he handles his files, I wouldn't worry too much about our winning the Lawrence case."

"I hope you're right. By the way, I'm glad you didn't take unfair advantage of his sloppiness, and even more glad you don't put the contents of our files on public display."

POINT OF ETHICS
Confidential Client Files

A misplaced file or a file left open to the view of outsiders easily leads to a breach of client confidentiality. When working with a client's file, interns should be conscious of where the file is at all times. They should also be thinking about who may get a glimpse of what it contains. To protect clients' privacy and to ensure the integrity of the records you are using, you should develop the following good habits.

- When working outside of the law office (at the courthouse or registry of deeds, for example), do not leave a client's file unattended. Protect client confidentiality and safekeeping of the file by taking it with you on lunch breaks and the like.
- Avoid leaving unattended files in your car. If your car is struck, towed away, or broken into, much needed files may suddenly be inaccessible.
- When finished working at an outside location, check carefully before leaving to be sure you have all client files, documents, and notes with you.
- Never take client files home unless you have the express permission of your supervising attorney.
- Close the file folder, turn client documents over to their blank side, or cover them with a legal pad when talking to anyone from outside the office—even another client.
- Do not remove documents from a folder unless doing so is necessary to your work.
- When removing a document from a thick folder, tab the document's original position with a self-stick note for easy replacement in the correct sequence.
- Avoid removing documents from more than one folder at a time; this helps prevent accidental misfiling when you are finished with them.
- Never place loose papers on top of an opened file folder; the papers may be lost forever when the folder is closed!

TIMEKEEPING AND BILLING

In an internship for credit, students are usually required to keep a record for their schools of time spent in the office to verify how the program's internship requirements have been met. This record may be a daily log, a journal, a weekly summary, or other reporting system. Each school has its own procedures, and interns should follow whatever format their school requires. For many interns, no other timekeeping records are needed.

Among students working in law firms, however, additional timekeeping may be required for the office itself. If clients are billed by the hour for work done on their behalf, detailed time records are needed to calculate the client's bill. Lawyers and paralegals may have to keep careful track of at least three things: (1) the amount of time spent, (2) the kind of work done for each client, and (3) the date on which the work was performed. These details are then reported on clients' bills (see Table 8.2).

Even when hourly billing is not a factor, offices may have other reasons for requiring paralegals to keep time records, such as the following:

- Corporate legal departments may need to prove that in-house legal work is economically preferable to hiring outside counsel; internal time records make that comparison possible.

Table 8.2

Sample Client Bill

Able, Baker & Charley, P.C.
987 Value Place, Suite 5
Enterprise City, NE 00023

To: Penny Pincher
    12-A Duquesne Street
    Enterprise City, NE 00022
    Date: 8/30/97

Re: Rental Property at 12-B Duquesne Street, Enterprise City

For Professional Services Rendered—August, 1997

Attorney Ann Able   1.6 hours @ $125/hr $200.00
8/2/97:   Conference with client; review correspondence with
          prospective tenant; prepare list of issues to be covered
          by revised lease agreement.
8/12/97: Review preliminary draft of revised lease agreement.
8/27/97: Follow-up telephone conference with client.

Paul Paralegal   2.7 hours @ $65/hr $175.50
8/4/97:   Prepare preliminary draft of revised lease agreement.
8/17/97: Prepare final draft of revised lease agreement; send final
          draft to client with letter of explanation.

Total for Professional Services: **$375.50**

- Law offices that bill clients on a contingency fee basis (such as in personal injury work) may nevertheless want to document hourly costs to ensure payment if the law firm withdraws or is dismissed from a case.
- Time records may be needed to justify even flat fees when clients' fees are subject to a court's review—in bankruptcy and probate matters, for example.
- Some offices keep time records for management purposes, to determine the efficiency of their methods or gauge the profitability of certain work.
- Offices that depend on legislative funding or on private grant money may also monitor efficiency and work output to justify future funding.
- Time and output records may be kept in anticipation of audits by an outside agency or parent organization.

Keeping Time Sheets

Each office has its own method of tracking lawyers' and paralegals' time. Increasingly, time records are logged in on a computer,[2] but many offices still use written time sheets in various formats. Traditionally, time records have consisted of commercially preprinted sheets, each containing a series of smaller perforated forms, or time slips, to be completed for each task being reported. When computer software is used instead, the format presented on the computer screen contains essentially the same information as the printed sheets and may even resemble them visually. An example appears in Table 8.3. Ask for instruction on the method used in your office early on—preferably during the first or second day on the job.

Table 8.3

Sample Computerized Time Sheet Entry

```
Timekeeper   [1  ]   MJB              125.00 = 62.50       ◄bill by
Client       [1  ]   Refrig.          125.00 = 62.50
Activity     [1  ]   Telephone Conf.

│ Telephone conference with Stefenson re: June, 1996 minutes¶              │
│ │..........................................................              │
│
│
│
│ Reference   [                  ]       Time estimated        [
│ 0:30:00]

 Slip 1 of 1           BILLABLE   TIMER: OFF


 ►MAIN MENU◄          Go to slip [          ]

 F1  Help             F2  Edit              ↓↑          Scan slips
 F3  Create slip      F4  Define names      Exc         Quit
 F5  Timer on/off     F6  Get active slips  Alt-F5
 Delete/Undelete
 F7  Find a slip      F8  Last active slip

                                  6:32:27  ► Timeslips S4.00C ◄
```

Source: Courtesy Timeslips Corporation, Essex, MA USA

Whether computerized or handwritten and regardless of format, time sheets generally have spaces marked for filling in the following information:

- Your name
- File number or other identification code for the client
- A description of the client's matter (one client may have several matters, such as a divorce and a real estate transaction)
- The date on which the work was performed
- The total time spent on this client matter on that date
- A brief description of the work performed, such as a telephone conference or legal research

The description of each task justifies the time being reported and the amount being billed. Today, clients are more likely to question their fees than in the past, so the basis of every fee has to be clear. The description need not be lengthy, but it should be detailed enough that the client reading a bill or a court reviewing the office's fees will understand what work was done and how that work relates to the case or transaction. For example, the phrase "reviewed documents" would not be sufficient. Instead, the time sheet should state what documents were reviewed—such as, "reviewed 1997 corporate minutes."

With computerized record keeping, prescribed abbreviations or codes are used for describing routine tasks. For instance, "telephone conference with client" may be indicated by selecting (from a menu) the code number for that activity. Recording the work you perform is easier and faster if timekeeping software is used. Its use is increasing for that reason.

Table 8.4

Time Billing Increments

One-tenth-hour increments	One-sixth-hour increments
.10 = 6 minutes	.10 = 10 minutes
.20 = 12 minutes	.20 = 20 minutes
.30 = 18 minutes	.30 = 30 minutes
.40 = 24 minutes	.40 = 40 minutes
.50 = 30 minutes	.50 = 50 minutes
.60 = 36 minutes	1.0 = 1 hour
.70 = 42 minutes	
.80 = 48 minutes	*Quarter-hour increments*
.90 = 54 minutes	.25 = 15 minutes
1.0 = 1 hour	.50 = 30 minutes
	.75 = 45 minutes
	1.0 = 1 hour

Similarly, handwritten abbreviations or symbols are often used to stream-line the use of printed timekeeping sheets. For example, the phrase "with client" might be written as "w/c" or "wc." "Phone conference" might be abbreviated to "pc," and "letter" might be abbreviated to "lt." Your office may have its own shorthand references.

Shorthand references must be uniform throughout the office so the book-keeper will know how to interpret them. Rather than make up their own, interns should inquire about the office's preferred shorthand references for handwritten time records. A list of your office's preferred abbreviations is probably available.

The amount of time spent on a client matter is recorded in increments such as one-tenth, one-sixth, or one-fourth of an hour (see Table 8.4). For example, a half hour is usually reported on time sheets as ".5." Two and a half hours would be "2.5." In offices using one-tenth increments, "1.7" represents one hour and forty-two minutes. In offices using one-sixth increments, the closest equivalent would be "1.4," which represents one hour and forty minutes. Each office uses one of these incremental methods consistently, so interns need to know which method is preferred.

Hourly segments are easier to add and subtract than actual minutes, so bills can be calculated faster and with fewer errors. Using hourly segments simplifies the bookkeeping process and provides uniform billing records that are easy for clients and courts to interpret. Of the three segmented timekeeping methods just mentioned, one-tenth-hour (or six-minute) increments offer the greatest precision and may be the most commonly-used method.

Of course, no one works in six-minute bursts, so it is often difficult for newcomers to adapt to this rather unnatural segmenting of their time. Lawyers and paralegals handle this by rounding up or rounding down their actual time to the next closest increment. For instance, a 10-minute phone conversation with a client might be rounded up to two-sixths of an hour or ".2" (actually 12 minutes). A forty-five-minute conference might be rounded down to seven-sixths of an hour or ".7" (actually forty-two minutes). Some offices have the policy of always rounding up to the next increment.

Billing decisions are the lawyer's responsibility, so interns should *check to see what the office's policy is regarding the rounding up or rounding down of time spent on client tasks.* If continual rounding up makes your reported times seem overly high to you, discuss this concern with your supervisor. He or she may suggest adjustments that are appropriate for someone whose assignments are naturally slowed by on-the-job learning.

For many interns, simply *remembering* to record tasks and the time spent on each is the greatest stumbling block to good timekeeping. Juggling several cases and moving rapidly from one to another, a busy intern easily forgets how much time was spent on each task. Without an ongoing record, the time spent on each activity has to be estimated long after it took place. By the end of the day, remembering what activities were performed for which clients—much less how many minutes were spent on each—may be impossible.

A good practice is to keep a note pad handy for jotting down each new activity as you begin it, noting the time it was begun and the time it was put aside. The day's time sheets can then be completed at the end of the day, all at once. Your notes make it possible to complete them accurately.

Timekeeping notes can be one of several important items you keep in a *personal calendar or planner*, in which many job-related details are recorded. (An example of one day's entry appears in Table 8.6.)

 ## POINT OF ETHICS
Reporting Time Accurately

Paralegal interns need to be aware of at least three ethics issues in tracking and reporting their time for client billing. These issues are double billing, padding your time, and appropriate billing for internship work. Regarding the first two issues, the rules governing lawyers are universally clear and are also reflected in all major codes of ethics and professional responsibility for paralegals (see Appendix 3). The third issue is less clear-cut but nevertheless deserves consideration.

Double Billing

Double billing occurs when the time spent on a single task is attributed (and therefore billed) to two or more clients. For example, suppose an intern spends one hour in the law library researching a new appeals procedure and the research is useful to the cases of two clients. Can the intern report one hour for the first client's case and another hour for the second client as well? This has been the practice in many law offices but, increasingly, the answer is no.

The American Bar Association issued its first formal opinion on the practice of double billing in 1993, stating that *law offices may not charge more than one client for the same hours of work.*[3] In offices where time and billing are computerized, the software system may detect double billing automatically, warning the user that "this is a duplicate entry." When that occurs, you need instructions from your supervisor.

To avoid possible ethical problems, the best approach is usually to apportion the time (and the hourly bill) between the two clients that benefited from it. Ask your supervising attorney to suggest a fair apportionment.

Padding Your Time

Working paralegals are sometimes under great pressure to produce a certain number of billable hours. Interns who are also paid employees may face similar expectations. In offices relying primarily on hourly billing for their income, a paralegal's quota can be high, amounting to a billable sum that is typically three times the paralegal's salary.[4]

In response to these pressures, lawyers and paralegals are sometimes tempted to inflate their time records, reporting significantly more time than what was actually spent working for a client. Although rounding up to the next closest increment is normally permitted, reporting completely fictitious segments of time constitutes deception. Billing a client for work not done is *fraud*. It can be a criminal offense as well as the basis for civil suit by a client. Clearly, no intern should report segments of time that were not spent on a client matter.

Billing for Internship Work

The office's billing policies are not determined by staff, of course, but by the managing partners of the firm. The intern has little choice but to carry out those policies. Unpaid interns are not always comfortable having clients billed for their work, so it may be helpful to understand the issues involved.

Billing clients for work done by a paralegal intern—even though the intern may be working without pay—is not an unusual practice. It does not create for the office the kind of windfall profit that interns sometimes imagine. The income it produces is usually less than what an experienced paralegal could produce. In fact, billing clients for internship work helps pay the overhead expense of having an intern in the office. (Overhead costs include such things as insurance, space, use of equipment and resources, and time spent training the intern.) Billing for the intern's work may be what makes the internship possible. Indeed, the prospect of producing billable hours is a bargaining point students often use to land an internship.[5]

A separate issue, however, is the *rate* at which clients are billed for an intern's work. Normally, interns do not have the expertise and efficiency of an experienced paralegal, so their billing rates tend to be lower than those of more experienced paralegals. Clients who are aware of the status of billing parties listed on their bills often expect a lower rate for someone whose position is clearly that of a learner. Probate courts, bankruptcy courts, and other forums with authority to approve (or disapprove) bills for legal services are even more likely to insist on reduced billing rates for personnel in training. Some have begun creating guidelines requiring it.[6]

In companies to which the U.S. Fair Labor Standards Act (FLSA) applies (businesses directly engaged in interstate commerce with annual sales of $500,000 or more, including public agencies and medical and educational institutions), billing clients for work done by *unpaid* interns may indicate a violation of federal *minimum wage guidelines*.[7] Other factors are also considered under the FLSA, such as the degree of training benefit to the intern (as opposed to benefit to the employer), and the extent to which on-the-job learning is comparable to the learning experience found in a vocational school program. A few large employers have been prosecuted under the FLSA for billing clients for unpaid internship work, so this may be an issue to bring to the attention of some offices.

State minimum wage laws may also restrict client billing for internship work. Because state laws on this subject vary considerably from state to state, the law in your state should be checked.

Students with questions about an intern's role in the office's billing practices should consult the following individuals for clarification:

- The supervising attorney
- The legal administrator or office manager
- A managing partner of the firm
- The internship director at school

Table 8.5

File Card Tickler System

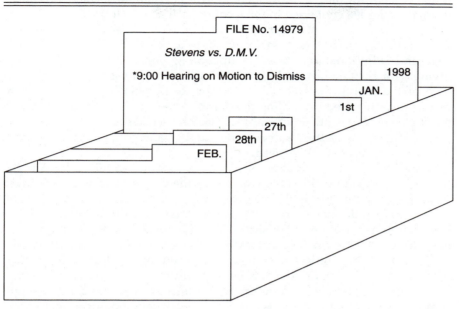

Illustrated by Rebecca Post Corliss

CALENDARING AND TICKLER SYSTEMS

Because deadlines so thoroughly rule legal work, every deadline must be continually and meticulously monitored. Again, different methods are possible and not all law offices use the same systems. But, as with filing and time-keeping, all calendaring or "tickler" systems have certain things in common.

Most offices have at least two such systems in place for monitoring deadlines and upcoming obligations. Having multiple systems operating simultaneously provides an important safety net; it is also a common requirement for lawyers' professional liability insurance. Typically, a centralized docket control system for the entire office is supplemented by individual calendaring or diary systems maintained by each lawyer. The centralized and individual systems are frequently cross-checked. In some offices, a third backup system (usually centralized) exists as an additional safeguard.

Centralized Docket Control Systems

A centralized docket control system may go by any number of names, including *suspense system, tickler system,* and *time control system.* Centralized systems monitor upcoming obligations and provide reminders to the attorneys and paralegals responsible for them. One person usually has the task of maintaining the office's system, adding new deadlines to the system as they become known, and sending out periodic reminders. This person may be the docket clerk (in a large office), a secretary, or (in a small office) a paralegal who also assumes administrative responsibilities. A second person (such as an attorney or secretary) is responsible for cross-checking the centralized system against other systems also in place.

In a small or solo law practice, the centralized system may be as simple as a large, erasable *wall calendar* showing upcoming appointments and deadlines. The entries on the wall calendar will correspond to (and be drawn from) a tickler list contained in the front of each active client file.

More often, a *file card tickler system* is used (see Table 8.5). File cards are kept in a long file box with major dividers for each month of the current year and additional dividers for upcoming years. Between the major dividers for each month, additional dividers are numbered 1 to 31 for each date of the month. Between the appropriate number-dated dividers are cards indicating meetings, filing deadlines, response dates for discovery or other procedures, and other obligations for each date. The name of the responsible attorney, the client and file number, and perhaps other descriptive data also appear on the card.

Some offices use a collection of file folders instead of file cards. The *file folder system* is set up the same way as the file card system but on a larger scale. Full-sized copies of memos or notices are placed in each dated file folder. Other offices use commercially prepared and sold *perpetual calendar systems* with tear-out reminder slips. The reminder slips are prepared in triplicate for sending to the responsible attorney as a due date approaches.

Nowadays, most offices are replacing their manual systems with *computerized calendar systems*. Professional liability insurers often give credits or discounts for their use, so computerized systems are becoming increasingly common. With these systems, lawyers and paralegals enter deadlines onto a master calendar for the office using the networked computer terminals on their desks. Most computer programs automatically add each entry onto individual task lists. Using this system, lawyers and paralegals not only check the master calendar but also print out their individual task lists as often as needed.

Regardless of what system is used, it is only as reliable as the information put into it. Interns who are managing client files must be diligent about entering all upcoming deadlines into the office's tickler system, without delay. When a new client file is created, the following things should be done:

- Check the statute of limitations that applies (if any) to the case. In the client's file, note the date on which the statute tolls. Enter this date into the office's calendaring system as well.
- Make a list of the procedural steps needed in the client's matter and find out the dates by which each step should occur. Enter these deadlines into the file and the office's tickler system.
- Do a periodic review—weekly or monthly, depending on how fast the case is moving—of files you are managing for checking and revising deadlines in the light of new developments.
- Schedule these periodic reviews in the tickler system right along with other deadlines, and also in your personal calendar or planner (explained below).

Pocket Planners or Calendars

Most professionals carry a pocket calendar (also known as a daily planner, yearly planner, or business diary) with them every day. It may be a bound, wallet-sized book or a larger spiral-bound affair. Whatever their size or appearance, *daily planners or pocket calendars* contain pages for every day of the year with spaces for writing in appointments, assignments, meetings, and other obligations. Often, they contain separate sections in the back for important addresses and phone numbers and for recording mileage traveled on office business and out-of-pocket expenses. Personal calendars or planners can be purchased at stationery, business supply, department, and discount stores for anywhere from $5 to $35.

Every paralegal intern needs a planner or pocket calendar. You can create your own using an inexpensive spiral-bound notebook—the kind stenographers use. A planner you create for yourself may actually work better than any you could buy at the store (see Table 8.6). It can be customized to give you as much space as you need to record whatever categories of information you prefer.

Here is how to create your own pocket calendar or planner for your internship using a spiral-bound notebook:

- Put your name, address, and phone number inside the front cover in case the book is ever misplaced.
- Allow about two pages for each workday. Date each page at the top, near the outside corner.
- Use stick-on tabs to mark each week at the side of each Monday's first page.
- Draw a line separating the top one-third of each day's first page. Mark this section "Deadlines and Due Dates." Use this section as a personal tickler system. Write in upcoming work deadlines and other reminders under the appropriate date just as soon as they become known.
- Use the rest of each day's pages as a work diary. In the left-hand margins, list the hours of the workday in half-hour segments.

Use the half-hour time slots in your planner to note upcoming appointments and meetings. You can also use these time slots as a personal record

---

THE STUDENT'S PERSPECTIVE 8.2: TAYLOR
Getting Assignments on Track

A recent graduate visiting with a new group of paralegal interns, Taylor shared the first important thing she learned from her internship. "I started out thinking that assignments would come one at a time, like they do at school," she laughed. "So, on Monday, I got a drafting assignment and went to work on it. That afternoon, I got a new, completely unrelated file to organize—and the drafting still wasn't finished. The next morning, I was told to begin a research project, with the drafting and the unorganized file still undone. Pretty soon, I was juggling more than half a dozen assignments. I started to lose track of which assignment was due on what date and which one I should be working on at any given time. As if that wasn't enough, the phone kept ringing and people kept walking in with questions and comments, and I was beginning to go crazy! By the end of the week, I hardly knew which end was up. Somehow, I had to get control over my work.

"So I bought a pocket calendar with each day divided into half-hour segments. I started dividing up my longer assignments into manageable steps or pieces. I wrote those steps into the time segments of my pocket calendar. For example, I'd schedule in one hour of drafting work, then a half-hour for organizing a file, then several phone calls, and so on. I also noted each due date in my calendar; that helped me pace my work better. That silly calendar saved my internship and my sanity!

"I carry a fancier, leather-bound planning book now, but I'm still doing basically the same things with it. It really works."

Table 8.6

Sample Entry in Personal Calendar or Planner

Monday 9/8/97

Deadlines & Due Dates
- *Balderman* complaint: First draft by Wednesday, 9/10
    About 2 hours to complete
- *Halley* will & trust: First draft by next Wednesday, 9/17
    About 6 hours to complete—more? Allow extra time
- *Gertwood* interrogs: Final draft by Friday, 9/12
    About 3 more hours to complete
- *Office library*—insert pocket parts—finish TODAY

Schedule & Work Done

9:00   Conf w/Atty. Wong re *Balderman* case. Ended 9:20.
       Instructions: Draft complaint. Include P.I. claims against both codefendants.
       See notes in file; incorporate those points in complaint. Finish first draft
       before Wednesday.
       (Coffee w/Laura; discuss holiday scheduling changes.)

9:30   Tel conf w/*Balderman* for additional info. Research in state practice & proce-
       dure manual. Draft Balderman complaint. Finished 10:45.
       (File statutory pocket parts in law library—15 minutes.)

11:00 Resume revisions to *Halley* will and trust. Done at 12:15—delivered to Susan
       for typing final drafts. Says she'll have them done tomorrow before 5.
       (Lunch)

1:00   Resume prep of pltf. interrogs for *Gertwood* case.

1:15   Call from *Balderman*—routine questions. 10 minutes.

1:25   Resume *Gertwood* pltf. interrogs.

1:50   Tel call from *Halley*'s beneficiary—questions. 5 minutes. Told him I'd have
       Atty. Wong call him tomorrow.

1:55   Resume *Gertwood* pltf. interrogs.

2:15   Stop Gertwood. Do memo for Atty. Wong re questions from *Halley*'s
       beneficiary—5 minutes.

2:20   Do today's time sheets. Leave for school at 2:30.

Reminders for Tomorrow
- First thing—remind Atty. Wong to call *Halley*'s benefic.
- Have Atty. Wong review draft of *Balderman* complaint.
- Check with Susan—*Halley* doc's typed before 5?
- Finish *Gertwood* pltf. interrogs.
- If time, start drafting letter re *Halley*'s completed docs.

Files: Balderman, Gertwood, Halley. Still on my desk, except for final draft of
        Halley doc's—Susan has that.

---

of time spent on each client matter. You can transfer that information to time
sheets later, at the end of the day or the workweek.

At the back of this book, reserve a page or two for the following kinds of
information. Mark additional sections with tabs on the side of the first page
of each section for recording the following items.

- Out-of-pocket expenses with the date and reason they were incurred
- Mileage, if this is reimbursed by your office or tax deductible to you, with
  the date and reason for travel
- Frequently needed phone numbers and addresses
- Useful e-mail addresses and work-related Internet sites

Save a sizable section in the middle of the book—about one-third of available pages—for writing down on-the-spot instructions given to you by your supervisor or other coworkers. Tab and label this section "Assignments." This will help you capture the details of hastily given instructions that might otherwise be misunderstood or forgotten.

Keep your pocket planner, calendar, or notebook-facsimile with you at all times. You will need it as a reference throughout your day as you continually record new assignments and due dates. Also, remember that it contains the names of clients and details about work being done for them—confidential information that should not be seen by anyone from outside of the office.

Interns quickly discover that a pocket calendar or planner is indispensable. It is far more reliable than memory alone, and you will depend on it heavily to guide you through each work day. Additionally, it provides a valuable reference for later reporting your activities to the office supervisor and the director at your school. When the internship ends, your planner also provides the specifics you need for an impressive, skills-based résumé and for detailed discussions in future job interviews.

USING OFFICE FACILITIES

Despite the apparent chaos of some offices and the seeming calm of others, there is a rhythm and pattern to workers' use of office facilities. There may also be a certain protocol involved in the use of those facilities. This section helps you find your way through such issues as defining your own work space, using common areas such as the law library and conference rooms, and gaining access to the equipment you need to do your job.

Defining Your Own Space

In large firms, in some corporate settings, and in major governmental offices where internships may always be taking place, a designated work area may be readily available for the new intern. Students in such settings often move right into their own room or cubicle and find a phone, a computer terminal, a desk, and supplies at their immediate disposal. However, this is probably the exception rather than the rule.

In solo practices, municipal offices, charitable and nonprofit organizations, and other offices operating on tight budgets, space is often scarce. In these settings, work space may be shared with another part-time worker. In offices where even this kind of sharing is not possible, interns may find themselves working in temporary, improvised settings.

If you verified your work-space arrangements in your interview as suggested earlier in Chapter 5, then your assigned area is known to you and you have ensured its suitability. If you were not able to clarify these arrangements in advance or if you have been given something less than what you were promised, you may need to negotiate a better arrangement.

At minimum, your work space should provide the following:

- A reasonable degree of peace and quiet, so you can concentrate
- An undisturbed place for keeping client files, books, and papers
- Ready access to a nearby phone if making and receiving calls is part of your job

- Access to a word processor on a predictable (if not constant) basis
- Basic desk supplies such as notepaper, pencils, paper clips, and stapler
- Enough ventilation to avoid unhealthy conditions

As long as you have these essentials, you should be able to perform your internship as well as anyone. But if any of these elements is missing, bring it to the office supervisor's attention right away. Pleasantly but firmly point out that you need these thing to carry out your assignments and to fulfill the educational goals of your internship. Once this is understood, most offices will do everything possible to accommodate your basic needs. If not, and if the situation is indeed hindering the success of your internship, inform the internship director at your school.

In many ways, the space in which you work reflects your personality and your work ethic. Let your space reflect concern for the work you do, care for the clients you serve, and awareness of those around you. As files and papers accumulate, try to keep them organized so that, in your absence, others can find anything that might be needed. If you share a desk with another worker, reach a clear agreement about where each of you keeps working files and papers. And keep your space neat enough that colleagues passing by your area will be favorably impressed—not appalled—by what they see on your desk.

Using Common Areas

The conference room and the reception area or waiting room are used mainly by outsiders, including clients and professionals from other offices. The law library is used by others in your office, usually on an unpredictable basis. At times, the library may even double as a conference room for meetings with clients and outside attorneys. So any of these places may be crowded and busy at times.

Reception Area Discussions

The reception area or waiting room is where you may occasionally meet a client for the first time. This is the office's most public area, so friendliness and cordiality to strangers are the rule here. Most importantly, the reception area also invites serious risks to client confidentiality.

Anxious clients sometimes want to discuss their cases before the "hellos" have hardly been said. Other clients and outside attorneys may also be waiting in this area, and they may overhear details that should not be shared.

For this reason, receptionists and staff greeting a client in the waiting room try to *immediately discourage conversations about a client's case in this setting.* "Attorney Green (or Paul Paralegal) will talk to you about that in his office," or words to that effect, gently bring clients' personal questions temporarily to a halt. Pleasantly changing the subject further ensures that there will be no talk about the client's case until later—and no hard feelings either. For example, "Is it still raining pretty hard out there?" directs the client's thoughts elsewhere for the moment.

The Law Library

A solo practitioner sometimes keeps a collection of law books in his or her own office, but most often, the law library is in a separate room, used by all the attorneys and paralegals in the office. Large firms may have a librarian who keeps the volumes updated, maintains books in their proper order, assists researchers, schedules special use of the room (such as for conferences), and perhaps schedules use of the library's computer-assisted legal research terminals. Smaller firms assign some of these responsibilities to a legal secretary or paralegal.

In office suite arrangements in which certain facilities are shared by numerous (usually solo) law firms, the law library may be used by people from outside your office. Sometimes the law library doubles as a conference room. Consequently, interns whose jobs include legal research sometimes find themselves competing with others for access to certain books, space at the library worktable, or even entrance to the room itself. Meeting your project deadlines while others are also trying to meet theirs can suddenly become complicated. To help your research go smoothly while not interfering with the work of others, a few guidelines should be kept in mind:

- If your office has a librarian, get to know this person early on. He or she can be a great help to you.
- Ask your supervisor to explain any rules regarding use of the office's law library.
- If your library is sometimes used for conferences, check the conference schedule when you first arrive each day so you can plan your research around it.
- Do not remove books from the library unless you know that is permitted; follow any customary sign-out procedures and return the books as soon as possible for others' use.
- When working in the library, have with you only the papers you actually need; leave space at the worktable for others who may come in to do research as well.
- Be gentle with books you are photocopying. Do not break a book's binding or spine.
- Before leaving the library, return books to their proper sequence on the shelves so that others can find them.
- Take all papers and files with you when you leave.

The Conference Room

An intern will not usually have much involvement with conference rooms except perhaps to assist the supervising attorney at a meeting. However, when you have a big project involving many files and papers, the conference table can be a great place to spread things out. Before doing so, make sure that the room has not been booked for a meeting during the time you will be working.

Computers and Office Equipment

Most paralegal interns have already had some experience with computers, copiers, answering machines, and perhaps fax machines. Nevertheless, interns may find that office versions are more complex and sophisticated than what they have used in the past. New operating methods always have to be learned. If you did not receive instruction on using the office's computers and other equipment during your initial orientation, then you need to do so right away. Practice and become comfortable with your office's computer system before using it for serious work.

Regarding computer usage, some issues to clarify include:

- Which computer(s) are you permitted to use?
- If you are sharing a computer with someone else, what schedule can be worked out for predictable access?

> ### QUICK TIP 8.2
> No matter what you are sharing—a desk, a computer, a book, or a room—try to agree on a schedule for its use. A schedule helps ensure that your needs are accommodated with minimal inconvenience to all concerned.

- If your office's computers are networked, what is your password and how do you log on?
- If the office's word processor is new to you, can someone instruct you on using it? Is a manual available?
- From whom can you get instruction on other computer programs you may need to use, such as for timekeeping, calendaring deadlines, and e-mail? Are manuals or written instructions available for these programs?
- If you have access to computer-assisted legal research (CALR), who authorizes its use and what time constraints apply?
- Must the use of CALR facilities be scheduled in advance? What about research by CD-ROM—must this also be scheduled in advance? If so, what is the scheduling procedure?
- Never eat or drink around computer equipment.

During their first days at the office, interns should also get instruction on using the office's copier and fax machine. Some offices require users to record certain information each time these machines are used. When sending a fax transmission, for example, certain information may have to be recorded in a fax log kept by the machine. Such information typically includes the date, the user's name, the client's name or file number, the fax number being called, a description of the document being faxed, and the number of pages faxed. In other offices, data may be punched into the machine itself and a record is printed by the machine. The printout may be added to a client's file or sent to the bookkeeping office, or both. Eventually the fax transmission is included in the client's bill as a reimbursable expense.

In some offices, computer-drafted documents are faxed by modem. If an intern is permitted to do this, instruction will be needed on using the office's particular system.

Copies are also a billable expense in many law offices, so similar records may be made each time someone makes copies. Again, the record may be prepared by the copy machine itself (using data the user punches into the machine) or handwritten into a nearby logbook.

The intern may be assigned a personal code number for using the copier and will probably need a few minutes of instruction on how to operate it. Alternatively, an instruction manual may be kept right near the machine and this can be consulted.

In a busy office, interns may sometimes find themselves waiting in line for access to the copier or fax machine. Saving your faxes or copying chores for when the machine is free helps use your time to best advantage. Otherwise, patience is the only recourse—along with courtesy to those who are waiting behind you. An offer to assist the current user may make things go faster.

 ## POINT OF ETHICS
Other People's Money

Scrupulous honesty and care are required whenever one person is responsible for another person's money or property. Students learn this basic ethics principle as a part of their paralegal education. Putting the principle into practice may be a bit more difficult, however, when faced with the complexities and fast pace of office life. The following sections address this issue in the context of (1) client funds and client trust accounts, and (2) expenses for which clients are billed or for which interns may be reimbursed.

Client Funds and Trust Accounts

Law offices everywhere have a minimum of two separate bank accounts. One is the office's *operating account,* which may also be known as the "office account." Income (or earned fees) are deposited into this account. The office's expenses are paid from this account including, for example, the rent, utilities, salaries, and other operating costs. Some offices may have several operating accounts for different purposes—a separate one for payroll, for example. The fact that it is the office's operating account is usually made apparent on every check and deposit slip, usually by showing the name of the law firm on top.

The second account required in virtually all private law firms is the *clients' trust account.* (Only firms that never accept client funds would be excused from having such an account.) This account is for funds being held by the office for a client pending the conclusion of a transaction or the outcome of litigation. Escrow accounts, in which deposits for real estate purchases are held, are one kind of client trust account. Retainers, or fees paid in advance by a client, are also held in a client trust account until the fee has been earned. For example, if a client pays a retainer of $1,050 to an attorney whose fee is $150 per hour, then $1,050 cannot be transferred in full to the office's operating account until the lawyer has performed seven hours of legal work for that client. The sum may be transferred sooner, of course, if the retainer also covers a paralegal's hourly fees or other expenses. As with the office's operating account, the nature of these accounts is usually identified on each check and deposit slip. In this case, they would show the words *trust account* at the top.

In every state, the rules of professional conduct governing lawyers prohibit the comingling, or combining, of any clients' funds with the office's or attorney's funds. Clients' funds must be kept separate from the attorney's or the office's funds at all times. In addition, meticulous records must be kept on the amount and location of each client's funds at any given time. State supreme courts or committees governing lawyers often conduct random audits—compulsory reviews of all the office's financial records—to ensure that these rules are being followed.

As the keeper of clients' money, the office performs an important fiduciary role, or function of trust. That means special care must be taken to safeguard and preserve a client's money for the client's benefit only—not for the benefit of anyone else. Taking money from a client trust account for personal or office use is theft, pure and simple, and it is punishable as such. *Even temporarily borrowing money from a client trust account is flatly prohibited.*

Only one nonclient use of client funds is legally permitted. In every state but Indiana,[8] trust account programs allow the automatic transfer of short-term interest on client trust accounts to a bar association or state supreme court fund for educational or charitable purposes. Accumulating fairly small amounts of interest from many client trust accounts throughout each state, these are know as IOLTA (Interest On Lawyers' Trust Accounts) funds. They are used to support legal services to the poor, provide grants for special educational and research projects, and facilitate other public services.[9]

Interns should also be aware that the office may have more than one client trust account. There may be dozens of them. One trust account may hold short-term deposits of funds from many clients—retainers, for example. Other trust accounts may each contain a significant sum being held for an individual client pending a particular transaction. Trust accounts created for individual clients must also be kept separate and never comingled, even with each other.

Some interns—particularly those in small offices—may be involved in depositing or writing checks on the job. The following guidelines should help avoid even the accidental breach of the office's fiduciary responsibilities regarding client trust funds:

- When depositing a check written by a client, get clear instructions about which account it goes to.
- When writing a check for filing fees or other litigation expenses, ask what account it should be written against —the client's or the office's? Be sure to follow instructions exactly.
- When writing a check for any office expense, always be sure you are writing it against the office's operating account, unless specifically directed otherwise.
- Never write a check for bar dues, continuing legal education seminars, or professional liability insurance against a client trust account! As obvious a breach as this seems, it has happened in some offices—perhaps inadvertently.[10] It can result in immediate disciplinary action and other serious consequences.

Tracking Expenses

Law office clients are becoming savvy consumers, increasingly sensitive to the high costs of legal representation. They examine their law office bills more closely than ever and often challenge items that seem excessive. Interns should keep expense records as if the client being billed were constantly looking over their shoulder. In a way, the client may be doing exactly that. Accuracy is essential.

Clients are not the only ones to whom accuracy is important. The office's economic success depends on being compensated fairly, too. Balance clients' spending concerns against the office's need to have expenses covered by keeping your expense records as reliable—and verifiable—as possible.

Here are a few tips for ensuring accuracy:

- Have your personal calendar or planner with you whenever you go out on office business.
- Know that travel by auto is customarily reported as the distance from the *office* and back—not from your home or school. If you are unsure which distances to report, ask your supervisor.
- When accounting for travel by auto, use the trip odometer if your car has one. When your trip ends, *immediately* write down the number it shows.
- If you have no trip odometer, simply write down the number shown on the general odometer as you prepare to leave. Write down the number shown when you return. Subtract the first number from the second to get the actual number of miles traveled. Keep all three numbers in case they are needed for verification.
- If distance by auto has to be estimated, check a road map or call your local office of the Automobile Association of America (AAA), which provides information on mileage between cities and towns.
- When combining errands, prorate your mileage to reflect travel for each client involved.
- Always travel with an envelope marked "Receipts."
- Request and keep receipts for everything: meals on the road, tolls, out-of-office copying costs, parking, etc. Mark each receipt with the client's name or file number and the date if that is permitted, or note each expense in your planner under "Expenses" and flag it with the phrase "receipt available."
- When an element of choice exists, try to keep expenses reasonable. For example, avoid the most expensive restaurant or the highest-priced items

---

THE STUDENT'S PERSPECTIVE 8.3: ROBYN
Avoiding Reimbursement Disputes

Upset with her law office manager over expense issues, Robyn went to the internship director at her school for advice. "I was told I would be reimbursed for all travel outside of the office. Now they are refusing to reimburse me and it just doesn't seem fair." Her internship director asked for more details. "Tell me what travel you reported, and what it was for."

"I had to go to the Secretary of State's office for corporate filings from several businesses," Robyn explained. "The office needed them quickly. Although it's not very far from the office, it's 30 miles from my house. I did these errands from home on days when I didn't have to go to the office."

"Would they have had the filings soon enough if you did this on a workday when you were nearer the Secretary of State's office?" the director asked. "Yes, I suppose so," Robyn replied. "But it was easier for me to do this on a nonworkday. I didn't think it made that much difference."

The director probed further. "What did you mean when you said 'errands'? Did you do this more than once?" Robyn sighed. "Well, I forgot one of the filings they wanted and I had to go back a second time. But everybody forgets things now and then. That's no reason to refuse me the reimbursement I'm entitled to, is it?" "I'm afraid it may be," was the reluctant reply.

The director continued. "In the future, Robyn, remember that businesses normally reimburse only for travel from the office, even if the travel was actually begun from home, much further away. This is a customary practice based on tax considerations. Employees everywhere learn to live with it. At 20 to 30 cents per mile, the difference can be significant over time. So try to plan your travel around this rule.

"Also, many employers are facing tight budgets and won't reimburse workers for travel that the employer didn't require. The office did not create the need for your second trip to the Secretary of State's office—you created that yourself.

"There's no crime in what you did, Robyn. We all make mistakes from time to time. But we also have to accept the consequences. If you made a fuss about this, an apology is probably in order.

"The next time you anticipate an unusual reimbursable expense, check office policy before incurring it. Knowing how to be conservative about accumulating such expenses may be valuable to you in the future."

---

when having lunch on the road. If asked to locate potential experts for a trial, include some who will not need a big travel budget.

EXERCISES

1. Practice rounding up and rounding down your time with the examples below, referring to the charts in Table 8.3. State the nearest increment for both a one-tenth-hour timekeeping system and a one-sixth-hour timekeeping system. After doing exercises a through j with the help of Table 8.3, try doing k through p without consulting the table. After you have finished, check your answers with those listed in Appendix 2.

	One-tenths	One-sixths
a. Four minutes	_____	_____
b. One hour and forty minutes	_____	_____
c. Seven minutes	_____	_____
d. Two hours and ten minutes	_____	_____
e. Thirty minutes	_____	_____
f. Forty-one minutes	_____	_____
g. Thirteen minutes	_____	_____
h. Twenty-five minutes	_____	_____
i. One hour and fifteen minutes	_____	_____
j. Two hours and twenty-two minutes	_____	_____
k. Fifty-three minutes	_____	_____
l. Eighteen minutes	_____	_____
m. Thirty-eight minutes	_____	_____
n. Two hours and thirty minutes	_____	_____
o. Fifty-one minutes	_____	_____
p. Thirty-five minutes	_____	_____

2. Ask your supervising attorney, supervising paralegal, or legal administrator to explain the office's docket control system and to show you how it works.

3. Survey several other paralegal interns in your school to find out what kind of docket control system is used in their offices. Ask each to explain how it works and what it requires paralegals and lawyers to do. How do these other systems compare with the one used in your office? Are there significant similarities? Significant differences?

4. If you were asked to set up a docket control system in a new office (for an attorney opening a solo practice, for example), which kind of system would you choose? Explain the reasons for your choice.

5. If there are other paralegals in your office, ask one or two of them to explain the personal calendaring systems they use to track assignments and due dates. Then ask: Are additional kinds of information integrated into the paralegal's pocket calendar or planner, such as out-of-pocket expenses, travel, and time spent on each task? If not, how does the paralegal track these items?

6. Ask your supervising attorney, or another attorney in your office, the same questions stated in question 5.

7. How does the attorney's personal calendar system compare with that of the paralegal? In what ways are they similar or different? Which would you prefer to use for your own work? Why?

8. Ask your supervisor or legal administrator if you may be shown how client trust fund records are kept. Explain that you fully understand the confidential nature of these records and that you would like to understand this aspect of law office record keeping as a part of your education for future employment. Most offices will accommodate this request.

ENDNOTES

1. Tracking your own potential conflicts of interest is discussed in Chapter 14.

2. Close to 40 percent of those responding to a 1995 *Legal Assistant Today* survey reported keeping time records on computers. See Gina Farrell Gladwell, "From Networks to the Net: CD-ROM, Network and PC Usage Grows at Law Firms," *Legal Assistant Today* (November/December 1995): 15.

3. American Bar Association Formal Opinion 93-379, December 6, 1993.

4. A guideline adopted in many private law offices, the "Rule of Three" suggests that associates, law clerks, and paralegals should produce a billable amount that is three times their salary. One-third of the billable amount covers salary and benefits, one-third covers overhead, and one-third is profit. Using this formula, a paralegal billing clients at $60 per hour would have to produce fifteen hundred billable hours a year to justify annual compensation of $30,000. That translates to about thirty billable hours per week. See, for example, Charlotte W. Smith, *Law Office Dynamics* (Dallas: Pearson Publications, 1993), 96, and Dana Graves et al., *How to Survive in a Law Firm* (Somerset, NJ: Wiley, 1992), 81.

5. See Chapter 4, "What Should I Say When I Reach Them?"

6. For example, the U.S. Trustee's Office in Los Angeles recommended that firms not charge for educating junior personnel in basic substantive or procedural rules, law, or principles. See "Billing Guidelines Drawn Up in Central District," *California Law Business* (Daily Journal Corporation, 10, Feb. 1992): 6.

7. Donald T. O'Connor, "The Price of Free Labor," *ABA Journal* (January 1997): 78. See also Provision 106.11 of the U.S. Labor Department's Wage and Hour Field Operations Manual (1990).

8. Jill Schachner, "Not with My Money You Don't," *ABA Journal* (November 1997): 42.

9. Some groups have claimed that IOLTA programs violate clients' property rights under the Fifth Amendment by taking interest earned on clients' money. The 1st and 11th U.S. Circuit Courts of Appeals ruled against these claims of unconstitutionality. *Washington Legal Foundation v. Massachusetts Bar Foundation*, 993 F. 2d 962 (1st Cir. 1993); *Cone v. State Bar of Florida*, 819 F.2d 1002 (11th Cir.) cert. denied 484 U.S. 917 (1987). However, the 5th Circuit ruled in *Washington Legal Foundation v. Texas Equal Access to Justice Foundation* that a trial should be permitted on this Fifth Amendment issue. 94 F.3d 996 (1996). The 5th Circuit decision will be reviewed by the U.S. Supreme Court sometime in 1998.

10. Jay Foonberg, "Saving Money on Phone Calls and Other Advice," *Lawyers Weekly USA*, 2 December 1996, B3. Also see J. Foonberg, "Client Trust Accounts: Disasters Waiting to Happen?" *Lawyers Weekly USA*, 9 September 1996, B9.

Part III
Mastering the Job

Chapter 9

Managing Assignments

When asked to cite the most important skills for any kind of paralegal work, most paralegals have three answers. Being well-organized is usually at the top of the list. Making the most of available resources is another essential. And finally, knowing how to get answers to your questions is a must. These three themes—becoming well-organized, using all available resources, and getting answers—are the focus of this chapter. In keeping with these themes, specific strategies are offered for getting started on your first assignments, for getting good results as experience grows, and for gradually becoming your own teacher as you progress through your internship.

 ## GETTING STARTED

New interns are sometimes a bit intimidated by their first assignments on the job. Questions that typically run through their minds are: How do I get started? Where do I begin? Taking four basic steps will quell that anxiety and get you off to a confident, productive start. The four steps are (1) clarify the instructions, (2) systematize your work, (3) find samples of the work you are doing, and (4) submit a rough draft. The following sections provide detailed guidance on how to proceed with each of these steps.

Clarify Instructions

Assignments generally come in one of two forms. Sometimes they arrive in a written memo. For most paralegal interns, however, assignments are conveyed orally, in person.

Although written instructions may seem less personal, they have many advantages. For example, there can be no dispute about what the instructions contained or what they omitted. You can read and reread written instructions slowly to get a good understanding of them. With everything on paper, informational gaps are usually obvious enough to be quickly identified and followed-up. And the memo provides a permanent record of instructions to refer back to as your work progresses.

However, few attorneys have time to write out detailed instructions for every assignment. Instead, many assignments are delivered orally under rushed circumstances. Rapidly delivered oral instructions can be confusing and difficult to remember. That is why smart interns try to get spoken instructions in writing, even as they are being delivered.

To gain the advantages of written instructions, interns should take notes of all assignments that are made orally. Here are a few pointers on how to do that.

- Use your customized personal planner or calendar for this purpose, if you have created one.
- Alternatively, buy an inexpensive steno notebook for keeping all instructions together in one place.
- Bring this notebook or your planner with you to all meetings where work may be assigned to you.
- Write all oral instructions in this book, in detail.
- To save time, often use abbreviations and symbols in your notes. Choose abbreviations you will recognize later.
- Identify each new set of instructions with the name of the client and the date at the top. Draw a line across the page between assignments.
- Note deadlines and completion dates. Underline them. Add these deadlines and completion dates to your personal calendar to help coordinate multiple assignments.
- After the instructions have been completed, draw a large "x" across those instructions but do not rip them out of the book.
- Keep past instructions as a reference in case questions arise later about what you were told.

Besides providing all the advantages of a memo from your supervisor, taking quick notes gives you the chance to ask a few questions and verify your understanding. It also shows a serious approach to your work, and that impresses supervisors.

Whether an assignment is delivered in writing or orally, questions frequently arise. Some of the terms being used may not be clear to you. For example, working in a municipal office for the first time, the difference between a *site plan* and a *subdivision plan* may not be immediately apparent. Understanding the legal and procedural differences between those terms might help avoid wasted time and effort.

The greatest risk of misunderstanding occurs when interns assume they know more than they really do. A smart intern is highly alert to possible unknowns. As instructions are being given, ask lots of questions. Do not wait—ask immediately.

Even after the instructions have been given, additional questions will sometimes come to mind. Act on lingering questions. *Make a list of the terms, procedures, or legal issues that are not 100 percent clear to you.* Then begin finding out about them, using the following strategies:

- Ask more questions! Start with whoever gave you the assignment. If that person is unavailable, leave a short memo listing your questions— perhaps noting your home phone number on the memo. Alternatively, ask others in the office who are familiar with the subject area.

THE STUDENT'S PERSPECTIVE 9.1: JULIO
Getting It on Paper

"I know just what you're talking about!" Julio sympathized with Bernadette, another intern at school. "Attorney Welch used to do the same thing to me—he'd stop by my office on his way to court or something and hand me a couple of files he wanted me to work on. He'd rush through a set of instructions and then he'd be gone. Later, I'd look over the papers and questions would occur to me but, by then, it would be too late to ask about them. As a result, I misunderstood several things and my first few projects were a mess. Eventually, I tried a slightly different approach."

"What did you do—quit?"

"Of course not," Julio laughed. "I just started jotting down the essentials of his instructions every time he came into my office with something new. I write quickly to avoid slowing him down too much, but it has really helped. It forces both of us to get focused. Plus, it gives me a chance to grasp some of the questions involved before he leaves for the rest of the day.

"Now, he actually expects me to write down the key points of his instructions. In fact, if I'm not writing, he sometimes says, 'Be sure to put that down' or 'don't forget to include this.' He's even beginning to anticipate the questions I'm likely to have.

"Explain to your boss that, even if this technique slows her down momentarily, it will save a whole lot of time later on—for both of you."

- Consult a legal dictionary, a legal thesaurus, *Words and Phrases*, or one of your textbooks at school.
- Get background on unfamiliar principles in a legal encyclopedia.
- You may know other interns and paralegals from other offices who work in that area of law; try consulting them. However, guard clients' privacy by not disclosing details that would reveal a client's identity.
- Check with the paralegal instructor at your school who teaches a related subject. Here, too, client confidentiality must be guarded.

When the assignment involves legal research or original drafting, many paralegals also find it helpful to do some preliminary "thinking on paper," jotting down legal and factual questions that come to mind while reviewing the matter. This helps them gain better focus, uncover issues that may have been overlooked, and put aside issues that are irrelevant.

When all the terms, issues, and procedures involved in your assignment are clear, you can begin working with confidence.

Systematize Your Work

Having reached a solid understanding of what an assignment requires, break the assignment down into several steps and create a checklist of the steps required to complete the assignment. For example, updating a lease agreement might be broken down into four steps: study the existing lease, contact the client to verify changes, research new lease clauses, and write a review draft. Then *set a personal deadline for each step and add these steps to your personal calendar.*

As you set a deadline for each step, estimate the amount of time needed for each one. Take these time estimates into account as you determine each interim deadline. Schedule these step in the light of other ongoing work.

QUICK TIP 9.1

Questions are *not* a sign of stupidity. On the contrary, good questions signal intelligence and an active, multidimensional mind. Never hesitate to ask questions.

> ## THE STUDENT'S PERSPECTIVE 9.2: MELANIE
> ## The Most Useful Skill
>
> Melanie thought long and hard before beginning her final internship report for her school. "More and more each day, I realize how important it is to stay organized, especially with large, complex assignments. Sitting down and figuring out the steps involved is the only thing that makes it possible for me to complete a project on time. I use lists every day. There are too many things to do to ever keep them all in your head.
>
> "If I didn't start by creating a plan for completing a project, I would be guessing most of the time about what was needed and when. I found out fast that guessing doesn't work.
>
> "It made me feel great when my supervisor commented, recently, on how organized I was. By the end of the internship, she was just leaving files on my desk with a few short notes, confident that I would know what to do and that I would handle things correctly. My ability to organize and plan is something that will stay with me forever, no matter where I work."

The checklist of steps can be kept inside the front of the file you are working on, or temporarily clipped to the file cover. Each time a step is completed, cross it off the list. That way, you will always know exactly where you left off, even if you have not seen the file in days. If the flu strikes and you cannot be at the office, anyone covering for you will see the list of steps and know immediately what remains to be done.

Systemizing your work brings order to what might otherwise be chaos. Breaking an assignment down into its component steps makes the project less intimidating and more manageable. As each step is finished, you can see real progress being made.

Use Samples

Rarely is a legal document drafted as a complete original from beginning to end. The format of law office documents—and much of the content as well—is often taken from earlier documents. The office has many resources that are copied and reused, again and again. Paralegals save a great deal of time by using this same approach whenever they can.

Not only documents, but also procedural checklists and legal research memoranda may already exist in your own office, providing a convenient starting point for assignments. Sometimes the person giving you your assignment will not think of these things, so you may have to inquire about them.

Here are several suggestions for finding material that may be partly copied or referred to as you complete assignments.

- Ask whether the office maintains a *forms file.* If so, see whether it contains forms similar to what you are drafting.
- Find out whether *document-assembly software* is available at your office for the kind of document you are creating. Wills, contracts, real estate forms, and bankruptcy forms are examples of documents for which special software exists, containing ready-made formats and clauses.
- Ask for an *earlier client file* in which similar work was done. Use documents in that file as samples.

- Check *forms books* in the law library for sample materials. Often these contain procedural checklists as well.
- Check the *Practice and Procedure volumes* for your jurisdiction for sample court forms and related materials.
- Try to find a recent *Continuing Legal Education (CLE) manual* on the subject you are working with. These manuals often contain very good sample materials.
- If all else fails, check with other interns, paralegals, or instructors at your school who are working in the same subject area. They might even have samples of their work.

Although such resources are great time-savers, copying must be done with caution and great care. When adopting material from forms books and other sources, there are two mistakes interns should make every effort to avoid.

The first mistake is adopting material that is wrong for your client's situation. Forms books, for example, may contain clauses covering every eventuality, but some may go too far. Documents in the office's forms file, drafted years ago, may include provisions that are outdated or wrong for the current situation. To avoid creating documents that could harm a client, read every word of the sample material you are considering. Constantly ask yourself: does this language do what we want it to do? Omit or carefully modify any material that does not clearly serve the client's objectives.

The second mistake is failing to copy the adopted language correctly. Simple errors can have surprisingly disastrous consequences. For example, changing *or* to *and* in a list of options can create dramatic, unintended changes in how a will, trust, or contract is structured. Where only one beneficiary or remedy was intended, there may suddenly be two or more. Copying punctuation incorrectly—such as changing a colon to a semicolon—also creates changes in meaning. If the language or format of a sample form is right for the current client, be sure to copy it flawlessly, right down to the punctuation.

Submit a Rough Draft

At least during the first weeks of your internship, supervisors are likely to make several changes to any document you submit. A savvy intern welcomes this review process as a valuable learning experience.

To encourage thorough review, *mark your submissions with the words "Rough Draft" or "Review Draft"* at the top. This makes it clear that you anticipate detailed suggestions from your supervisor. Only after sufficient experience should you try producing a final draft on the first attempt.

Even though your work is being reviewed, never waste your supervisor's time with correcting your spelling and punctuation errors. Carefully proofread all work before submitting it so that the supervisor can focus on content rather than your English. Proofread again each time your draft is edited or changed. If your word processor has spell-checking and grammar-checking features, use them, but know that these features are not foolproof. For example, the word *of*—typed incorrectly as *or*—would not be detected as an error. Make proofreading the final step to every project you ever have.

GETTING RESULTS

As your internship progresses and your workload increases, keeping track of upcoming tasks becomes more challenging. You will need to find ways to stay on top of it all. Several methods for doing that are offered in the following section. Following that are easy, timesaving tips on creating your own reference files and databases. Avoiding a chaotic, overloaded desk may also become crucial, and the last section shows how this, too, is not easy to do.

Keeping Assignments on Track

Whether you are juggling a dozen assignments or coordinating only one or two cases that are very complex, the competing demands on your time can have you headed in twenty directions at once. Unless you are well-organized, tasks get overlooked and details get lost in the frenzy. Experienced paralegals get control over a multiplicity of tasks by bringing predictable systems and routines to their work. Four such strategies are

- Keeping a to-do list
- Periodically reviewing client files
- Keeping notes on client-related conversations
- Identifying questions before meetings with the supervisor

First, most professionals keep a to-do list running from day to day. Your to-do list can be made a part of your daily internship calendar or planner as shown in Table 8.6 in Chapter 8. Alternatively, you can keep a running to-do list in a separate section of your personal calendar or planner. Your to-do list is updated by crossing off completed items and adding new ones throughout the day.

A second routine that helps you stay on track is periodically reviewing each client file that has been assigned to you. A good time to do this is at the end or at the beginning of each week, because most work has either wound down or not yet begun at that point. Done faithfully, a weekly review of all your current client files will help you to keep track of important aspects of your work, including

- *Legal and procedural issues* you may have temporarily overlooked, which still need to be resolved
- Upcoming *deadlines and follow-up steps* on your file checklists, for adding to your current to-do list
- *New developments* that have occurred since the last time you checked the file such as incoming correspondence, opponents' motions or answers, and recent phone messages
- New *procedural steps* for a file's checklist
- *Questions and reminders* for your supervisor

A third routine used by successful paralegals is writing down, often in abbreviated form, the substance of all conversations related to a client's matter. When you call clients and outside offices to gather details, jot down important information as you speak. If you cannot get everything on paper while talking, add missing details when the conversation ends.

The steno book you use for writing down your assignments can also be used to take notes on other important conversations. This includes conversations with clients, witnesses, outside offices, or anyone providing information regarding a client matter. Always have your steno book handy so that when the phone rings or an unexpected meeting takes place, you can ensure that nothing in the conversation is lost. Draw a line between each conversation. Identify each with the date and the client's name.

As with your notes on supervisors' instructions, keeping notes on client-related conversations together in one book prevents them from getting scattered and lost. Later, important details from these conversations can be transferred from your steno book to a clearer, more legible memo, either for placing in the file or for delivering to your supervisor. Cross out the handwritten entries after they are rewritten in another form.

However, do not discard these notes—even after you have transcribed them or completed your follow-up. Weeks after a conversation took place, questions may arise about what someone actually said. Old notes can suddenly become valuable, so keep all past entries in the steno book for future reference. Many paralegals keep their steno books for years, hesitant ever to throw away such potentially useful records.

Because they contain details of conversations about client matters, these notes are highly confidential. *Protect clients' privacy by guarding the whereabouts of the steno book containing these notes.* Always be aware of who may have access to it, and take appropriate precautions. When your internship ends, offer to leave these notes with the office for their records or else have the notes destroyed. Keep for yourself only whatever nonconfidential information you need to prepare a good résumé or to report internship activities to your school.

A fourth strategy for getting great results is to take a few minutes to prepare in advance for meetings with your supervisor. Do a quick review of each working file before the meeting. As you glance through each file, jot down the following things to be sure each of them gets covered in your meeting:

- What has or has not been done on each file you have been assigned (your checklist of steps facilitates this)
- Questions you have about each client matter and issues you need your supervisor to resolve
- Reminders for your supervisor's follow-up

By conducting a premeeting review, you come into the meeting "knowing your files," up-to-date and knowledgeable about each one. You will prevent embarrassing moments of flipping through countless documents for answers to basic questions. A premeeting review also eliminates the need to hunt down your supervisor later with questions you forgot to ask. Instead, your supervisor will be impressed with your knowledgeable approach and grateful for the time you have saved.

Creating Your Own Reference Files

Another way to streamline your work is to create reference files of frequently used items. After several different projects have been completed, the reusable portions of past projects can be kept together for future reference. When a similar project comes up later, you will save time by incorporating reusable portions of the old project into the new one. The same principle applies to information from past or current work that may be useful in the future. You can speed future work by creating reference files, on paper or on computer disk, for many of the following items.

- Forms used in the past
- Original clauses you drafted for pleadings, motions, contracts, wills, leases, and other transactions
- Often-used clauses copied from forms books
- Information on frequent contacts such as doctors, process servers, investigators, title companies, social workers, expert witnesses, or court reporters
- Timesaving comments about outside professionals you deal with such as their rates, restrictions on their availability, and particular expertise
- Research findings from past client matters
- Copies of key statutes or court opinions
- In complex litigation, data on all parties and witnesses involved including names, addresses, phone and fax numbers, their relationship to the case, and so on

Creating reference files requires an initial investment of time but pays huge dividends later. For instance, when you need the citation for a statute encountered weeks ago, checking a reference file marked "Past Research," will produce the needed law in a few seconds. And why search through interrogatories every time you need a witness's address when it could be found instantly on a list?

Some of these reference files—your forms file, for example—may be useful to you even after your internship ends. *As long as you are not departing with confidential client information and assuming you get permission regarding anything that might be considered attorney work product,[1] you may want to keep some of your reference files permanently.* For instance, your forms file and research file may be useful to your future job search, demonstrating the kind of documents you have drafted or the depth of research you have done. However, communicate your intentions about any material you plan to keep and get your supervisor's approval.

An intern's reference files may also be useful to other workers in the office. Leaving copies behind after you leave helps ensure that you will be remembered positively for future employment recommendations.

Preventing a Paper Avalanche

This section could be subtitled with many paralegals' complaint: "Help, I can't find my desk!" As assignments mount up and the pace quickens, real organization is needed to avoid mountains of papers and files. The more papers there are on your desk, the more difficult it becomes to find what you need. Documents, notes, and papers can disappear and chaos takes over.

The best way to prevent such problems is to keep as many things as possible off your desk. Paralegals often prefer to keep current client files stacked elsewhere—in an expandable file folder on a nearby shelf, for example, or even in a large carton on the floor. The only file on their desk is the one they are working on at the moment, so there is no risk of confusing papers from different files.

What remains on your desk can then be organized for easy identification. Try some of the following suggestions.

- Keep related items—such as research findings for a certain case—stacked together.
- Use stacking trays, if those are available.
- Connect related subfiles with a large rubber band.
- Tag urgent papers or files with a self-stick note containing short instructions such as "Call Back," "Alert Attorney," or "Check Court Rule."
- Ask the secretary to leave incoming items in a designated place—never on top of work in progress.

- Clear your desk at the end of each workday. Return loose documents to their respective files.
- Leave the next day's work in the center of the desk where you will be certain to find it when you arrive.

By keeping your desk organized, reviewing your client files regularly, creating reference files, and maintaining a to-do list, you will always be on top of your work. Instead of worrying about what to do next, your mind will be free to focus on doing an outstanding job and learning as much as possible from the experience.

 # BECOMING YOUR OWN TEACHER

In school, you relied on your teachers for many things: structuring your work, pointing you in the right direction, correcting your mistakes, and providing answers to your questions. Then, when your internship began, you looked to your supervisor and coworkers for those things. If your internship is like most others, you soon discovered that *supervisors and coworkers cannot be counted on to provide the same level of guidance as your regular teachers.*

For most coworkers and most supervisors, teaching takes a back seat to the pressing demands of their work. You probably found that sometimes you have to play the role of teacher to yourself, by yourself. By the end of your internship, you will understand how enormously valuable this process is.

Indeed, learning how to "teach yourself" is one of the primary purposes of internships. Becoming self-reliant in this way may be the most indispensable job skill anyone can acquire. The following sections help you to strengthen and solidify your ability to "teach yourself."

Mistakes as a Learning Opportunity

Nobody enjoys making mistakes. If you are accustomed to getting "As" in school, having mistakes pointed out to you can be quite painful at first. Nevertheless, the mistakes you make on the job have enormous hidden value. Something useful can be learned from every one of them. Becoming your own teacher means developing the habit of noticing mistakes in a positive way and taking advantage of the instruction they provide.

If you follow supervisors' instructions closely, use samples and other resources, and proofread your work carefully, then the mistakes you make will not be silly or embarrassing. They will be honest misunderstandings or oversights caused by lack of experience. Everyone expects that you will make such mistakes because the job is new to you.

As an intern, your job is not to avoid all mistakes at all costs. That is impossible to do. Your job is to learn all you can from the honest mistakes you could not foresee.

Even after checking a legal dictionary, Jennie misunderstood the subtle differences between "proximate cause" and "actual cause" in a personal injury case. As a result, a misstatement appeared in the pleadings she drafted. Her supervising attorney returned her draft with a big circle around the misstated paragraph, along with an article from the local bar journal on actual and proximate cause.

Some interns might have been annoyed that the article was not shown to them before the pleadings were drafted. But Jennie read the article and gratefully made a copy for her reference file. Using the guidance she now

QUICK TIP 9.2

The people who never make mistakes are people who never try anything new. Honest mistakes are often a sign that learning is taking place. Rather than being embarrassed by an honest mistake, learn all you can from it.

had, she revised the pleadings and sent them to her supervisor with a note saying "Thanks, the article really helped. Next time, I'll be able to draft such pleadings easily."

Her upbeat comments showed she was making the most of the learning opportunity she just had been given. Her comments also encouraged her busy supervisor to continue providing helpful materials when he thought of them.

When you are asked to do something again but differently, make a mental note of what you have learned as a result. Keep track of these incidents over time and work at never making the same mistake twice. Notice when a pattern develops, such as an abundance of writing errors as opposed to research errors. Repetitive errors may indicate the need to brush up in a certain subject, which you can do by finding a book about it or attending a seminar.

Finding Your Own Answers

Because supervisors and coworkers are not always available, they cannot possibly answer every question and solve every problem an intern might have. Often, you must be resourceful, finding answers and solutions on your own. Here are several strategies to try.

- Let everyone you talk to know you are looking for the answer to a certain question. Without revealing confidential details, mention the problem to other students and professionals. Some may have useful leads.
- Use e-mail and the Internet. Put your question out on NALANet at *www.nala.org*, on NFPA's List Serve at *www.paralegals.org*, or on an electronic bulletin board at your school. Take advantage of hyperlinks available at these sites for additional resources.
- Take questions to the next meeting of your local paralegal association.
- Scout resources in the law library that are new to you but might be related to the subject area of your question or problem.
- Take time occasionally to explore unfamiliar resources—even when no questions are pressing. You may stumble onto something that will help you in the future.
- Do not give up; be doggedly persistent in your search.

Lawyers and paralegals pride themselves—not on knowing the answer to every question—but knowing how to *find* every answer they might need. Because law and procedures are constantly changing, this skill may be more valuable than any other. What you memorize this year may soon become obsolete. But knowing how to find out about any given law or procedure is a skill that never goes out of date.

Learning to find your own answers is key to your development as a successful professional. Experiment with this process at every opportunity. With practice, you will expand your repertoire of resources. You will become increasingly nimble at finding answers. And you will gain a deep-seated confidence that time can never erase.

EXERCISES

1. The following practice exercises begin with the cooperation of another intern. One intern relays instructions that he or she recently received at

the office, imitating the pace and manner in which those instructions were actually given. The second intern does the following:

a. Takes notes on the instructions as they are being given.

b. Gently interrupts with important questions.

c. When the speaker is finished with the instructions, reviews the notes and makes a list of any additional questions or issues to be resolved.

d. Makes a list of resources that could be checked to find answers to any remaining questions or unresolved issues.

e. Breaks the assignment down into its component steps and creates a checklist of these steps. (Both interns may do this together.)

2. When you have completed all the items listed above, have the intern who relayed the assignment to you review your lists and compare them with what he or she actually did in the office. How different are your lists from those of the intern who actually had the assignment? How alike? Did either of you get any useful ideas as a result of this exercise?

3. For more varied practice, repeat the above exercises with various interns.

4. Imagine that your supervisor has asked for a meeting, first thing tomorrow, to update your current projects. Would you be ready? How much do you know right now about the following?

a. What has been done during the past week on each client matter?

b. What remains to be done on each client matter?

c. What questions do you currently have about each project?

d. What reminders do you have for your supervisor's follow-up?

5. Decide which of the reference files will be most useful to you in your internship:

a. Forms file: _____

b. Research file: _____

c. Phone/address list for: _____

d. Phone/address list for: _____

e. Other: _____

f. Other: _____

g. Other: _____

6. Decide which of the above reference files will contain material that you want to keep after your internship ends. Calendar a note to yourself to get permission, before the internship ends, to keep such information.

7. Decide which of the above reference files may also be useful to others in the office. Let coworkers know that you are creating such files.

8. Identify one or two subject areas in which you do a lot of drafting. Check the *ABA Journal*, your state bar journal, and your state bar newspaper for ads or information about document-assembly software for that kind of drafting work. Ask other interns whether they use document-assembly software for that kind of drafting. Contact the software manufacturer to request information about it. Ask the manufacturer for names of local users and check with them to see what they like or dislike about the software. Then decide whether the software is worth recommending to your office.

9. Take inventory of everything on top of your desk. Make a list of items that do not need to be there and decide where else they might be kept.

10. Write down, in detail, all the questions you currently have about the cases and projects you are working on. Then review the list, identifying questions you might find answers to on your own. Note possible

resources next to the questions you have identified in this way. Then try getting answers on your own to those questions.

ENDNOTE

1. Court rules in most jurisdictions define "attorney work product" to include memoranda and notes prepared by a paralegal, secretary, stenographer, or clerk in preparation for trial. The value of the "attorney work product" classification is that such material is not subject to discovery. However, this protection may be waived if due diligence and reasonable care are not taken to protect the confidentiality of the work. See, for example, *Clark- Fitzpatrick, Inc. v. Long Island R.R. Co.*, 556 N.Y.S.2d 763 (1990).

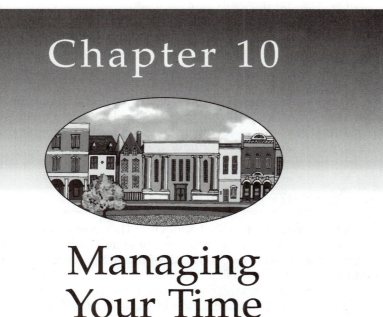

Chapter 10

Managing Your Time

Nothing sends stress levels spiraling like a deadline that suddenly becomes impossible to meet. This all-too-common phenomenon shows how time management is closely linked to stress management. When time is managed well, job stress is greatly reduced. This chapter outlines some practical strategies for managing your time well and—as a direct result—keeping stress to a minimum.

 ## MAKE GENEROUS TIME ESTIMATES

Accurately estimating the amount of time needed to complete various tasks comes with experience, which the average intern does not yet have. As they plan their work schedule, newcomers understandably tend to overestimate or underestimate the time they will need for each project. Of those two tendencies, *underestimating* how long a project will take is by far the more dangerous mistake.

To avoid the terror of suddenly facing a deadline you cannot meet, allow a cushion of extra time to cover unexpected interruptions or obstacles that may develop. Lean toward *overestimating* rather than underestimating the time you will need to complete a project.

Begin each assignment by asking for an estimate of the amount of time probably needed to complete it. If you cannot get such an estimate, make your own best guess based on experience with school projects or other things you have done so far on the job. Then add additional time for your own estimate, if you can. For example, if your supervisor says, "I think this probably will take two or three hours to do," then allow perhaps up to four hours—just in case there are problems with the assignment.

Let your supervisor know if assignments often take more time than what the supervisor estimated. Explore possible reasons for the discrepancy. Perhaps you need a different approach to your work, or maybe the supervisor

QUICK TIP 10.1

When a new assignment is given, ask how many hours you should need to complete it. If it is a task you have never done before, allow even more time in case the estimate is slightly off or in case the assignment gives you trouble.

needs to have more realistic expectations. Discuss what adjustments might be made to prevent the problem from happening again.

As you break an assignment down into its component steps and schedule each step in your personal calendar or planner, you can do one of two things with your built-in "cushion" of time. Either divide the extra time evenly among each of your assignment's component steps, or calendar in the full amount of extra time near the completion date.

With experience, you will most likely see the original time estimates becoming more accurate. Planning extra time for a project will be necessary less and less often. For assignments that are unusually complex, larger than normal, or new and untried, continue using this technique.

MINIMIZE INTERRUPTIONS

Interruptions are more than just annoying. They cost us time. They force us to refocus again and again on what we are doing. Worst of all, they can lead to genuine confusion in our work. All of this increases stress as well, so it is wise to keep interruptions to a minimum.

Interruptions commonly come from three sources: the office phone, coworkers wanting to chat, and calls or requests from family or friends.

Tame the Phone

If your responsibilities include handling incoming office calls, you gain from experiencing frequent client contact. Nevertheless, you may have difficulty concentrating on a project with the constant interruption of a ringing telephone. Good time management often means keeping written projects and telephone work as separate as circumstances allow.

To balance between the competing demands of telephone and ongoing projects, try this strategy. Set aside a period of time each day for working without telephone interruptions. If your supervisor agrees, have incoming messages taken by a secretary or recorded on an answering machine during that time as you work on your most challenging projects. Even one hour, set aside in this way, can help you work more calmly and productively.

Similarly, you can set aside a time just for phone work. Keep a list of all the calls you have to make and, when you are ready, take care of them all during "phone time." This helps reduce the number of interruptions you will have during the rest of the day. If you always make your return calls around the same time of day, soon clients will expect to hear from you at that time. They will be less likely to bother you at other times of the day.

Subdue Chatty Coworkers

Socializing with coworkers helps form friendships and professional alliances for years to come. So, friendly conversations should take place often, but not at the risk of sloppy work or missed deadlines. A line does have to be drawn, sometimes, between lighthearted chatter and serious work.

Every intern should create a personal policy about when and under what circumstances office socializing can comfortably be pursued. Some interns need more social contact than others; every individual is unique in this way. Know your own threshold of tolerance for chatty interruptions and have strategies ready for discouraging the ones you cannot handle. When social interruptions become a problem, communicate that fact in a professional manner. Here are a few strategies you can try.

- When someone stops by your desk with unimportant chitchat, smile and let the coworker know you are under pressure. For example, say, "I'd love to talk but this is a bad time; can I touch base with you around noon?"
- If you have an office with a door, signal your unavailability by keeping the door nearly closed when you need to work alone for a while. Coworkers will soon recognize the intended meaning.
- If the office environment is fairly casual, consider displaying a friendly sign during times you would rather not be disturbed. However, avoid sarcasm or antiwork sentiments.
- If someone is unthinking enough to interrupt you during a telephone conversation, avoid responding while also listening to a caller. Most people cannot do both. Smile, shake your head "no," and wave the coworker away for the moment. Check with the coworker right after the phone call, in case the interruption was about something important.

Social interaction is an important part of office life. Many coworkers will assume you welcome it, so sending the right signals is your responsibility. Just be sure they are friendly signals and that you are still available for a bit of office socializing at appropriate times.

Keep Personal Life in Tow

As you undertake the pivotal transition from student to professional, you may be simultaneously struggling with the demands of parenthood, a lack of financial resources, and perhaps also the unrealistic expectations of friends or family members. Working with a clear head is hard to do when pressures come from home as well as from the office. Sometimes, success is possible only by insisting on the cooperation and assistance of the important people in your life.

Convey to your spouse, parents, teenage children, siblings, friends, neighbors, and roommate the importance of the transition you are going through. Tell them that this internship will make it possible for you to land a well-paying job some day soon. Enlist their support. Be as specific as you can about the kind of help you need. For example, ask the people in your life to help in some of the following ways:

- Not contacting you at the office except for genuine emergencies
- Understanding that you may not be able to handle all of the household and social responsibilities you assumed in the past
- Providing backup transportation if the car breaks down
- Providing backup child care when your child is sick or the sitter lets you down
- Helping with personal errands, laundry, or shopping
- Assisting with the care of an elderly family member
- Helping you through an unpaid internship with a short-term loan
- Beginning meal preparation before you get home

Offer to return these favors. For example, you might offer reciprocal child care or household help on weekends. But do ask for the cooperation and support you need during this important time. You are worth it—and so is this internship.

 **ADDITIONAL SANITY SAVERS**

The following are additional strategies you can try to make the job go more smoothly.

- Arrive at the office a few minutes early to survey the day's work, reestablish priorities on your to-do list, and plan whatever schedule works best for the needs of each new day.
- To spend less time redrafting documents, try outlining them first, listing the points you need to cover.
- When possible, save trips to the courthouse or other work-related locations by combining errands, making two or more stops in a single trip.
- Take advantage of every automation feature and computer technique that is available. Time spent learning these techniques saves even greater time later—and adds impressive new skills to your résumé.
- If the workload becomes unusually heavy for a short time, see whether some work can be done on your own time, either at home or at your school's law library. Be sure to guard client confidentiality in these nonoffice settings.
- Above all, communicate workload problems to your supervisor. The following section advises you on how and when to do this.

CONFRONT PROJECT OVERLOAD

An important aspect of good time management is recognizing work overload when it occurs and conveying the problem to the appropriate person. Even experienced paralegals are sometimes faced with a task that simply cannot be completed by the requested date. An assignment may turn out to be more complex than anticipated. A paralegal may have unwittingly assumed responsibility for too many assignments. Or, the unexpected happens—illness strikes or a hearing date is suddenly moved forward and the most careful plans are completely undone.

Eager to please their supervisors, some interns struggle onward in silence, even when the workload is clearly getting out of hand. The more conscientious you are, the harder it may be to put on the brakes. But *there are times when project overload must be addressed.* Failure to address it can cause missed deadlines and possible disaster to everyone concerned—the client, the office, and you.

The trick, of course, is to address project overload in a way that jeopardizes no one's reputation—neither yours nor the office's. To do that successfully, you must consider three things. The first is to decide whether speaking up is really necessary. Call this the "should I?" analysis. The second is to find a positive way to communicate the problem. Label this the "how?" analysis. The "solution" analysis then requires exploring alternatives for getting the job done.

The "Should I?" Analysis

An inexperienced intern may have difficulty judging how much work is too much. To determine whether your workload is on target for the time you have available, add up the number of hours you expect you will need for all current projects. Compare the total to the due dates you have. Do you have enough time slots available in your personal calendar or planner for everything you are doing? When your estimated completion time for all current projects, taken together, add up to more than the hours available before the due dates—you need to speak up right away.

Often, our viscera have an uncanny way of knowing when enough is enough, even before our brain gets the message. If your stomach begins churning and your palms start sweating when you learn of yet another assignment, no "should I?" analysis is needed. Your body is already telling you: It is time to speak up.

The "How?" Analysis

Once you have decided you must do something about project overload, you then need to think about two things. Who needs to be informed of the problem and what is the best way to convey it?

The project's supervisor is the best person to inform immediately, if possible. If the supervisor is unavailable, decide whether you can safely wait until later or whether the problem is so urgent that it must be addressed right away. If a court deadline is at risk, then, obviously, you cannot wait. The problem *must* be conveyed to someone else in charge.

THE STUDENT'S PERSPECTIVE 10.1: ADAM
Sending Up an SOS

Having just completed a two-day trial, Adam's attorney-supervisor came through the door like a victorious warrior. "Congratulate me, everybody! Verdict for the plaintiff—a hundred thousand dollars! So, what's been happening around here for the last two days?"

Adam looked up. "Congratulations, Jim! I know how worried you were about that case—glad it went well. We had a close call yesterday. Good thing you weren't here. It wasn't pretty."

"What happened?" Jim wanted to know. Adam sighed, "Well, you remember the interrogatories for the Draper case? Today was the deadline for our responses. I was still working on them yesterday when it became obvious that certain information was missing. So I called the client to get what we needed, and guess what. She's vacationing somewhere in Mexico. Completely unreachable. Great, huh? I had no idea what to do."

"You didn't find out about this until the day before the responses were due? Adam, that's not how we do things."

"I know, I know. But the Stiller contract was needed right away, plus you wanted the research memo on the Stanley case by tomorrow. It all piled up at the same time. I was working at top speed trying to get it all done for you—honest."

Jim was trying not to lose his patience. "What happened with the interrogatories?"

"I went to Attorney Hendry for help. He called opposing counsel and got them to agree to an extension of time. He used your trial as the basis for the request."

"Good. You were right to go to Hendry. But we have to talk about your letting things get ahead of you. Why didn't you say something long before things got so bad—like last week, before my trial started?"

"I thought if I just pushed hard enough, I'd be able to pull it all off on time. I never imagined our client would be out of the country! I'm sorry."

"Adam, haven't you heard the saying, 'If there's anything that can go wrong, it will'?" *Always* assume that something can go wrong. Allow yourself enough time so that when things do go wrong, you're covered.

"And for heaven's sake, let somebody around here know when your workload is getting so heavy you're approaching meltdown, Adam. Don't struggle alone in silence. Send up an SOS, okay? Give us a chance to help you prevent disaster!"

During your office orientation, you checked to see who could provide assistance in your supervisor's absence and who would be responsible for emergencies when the supervisor is unavailable. Now is the time to seek out that person and explain the situation to her or him. As embarrassing as all this may seem, remember that you are protecting the integrity of the office's work.

After deciding whom to tell, you need to find the right words. The most important thing (and sometimes the most difficult) is to avoid blaming anyone. Avoid even using anyone's name. Explain your situation in as neutral, purely factual a way as possible. For example, "It seems I have two big assignments due on the same date; unfortunately, it's going to be impossible to finish both of them at the same time." Never mind who assigned them to you or how rushed and unthinking they may have been—that is not the problem you are addressing right now.

Emphasize that you are not looking for a way out. You are looking for a way to make sure the work gets done. You are protecting the interests of your clients.

The "Solution" Analysis

Having communicated your difficulty, your task is now to help find a solution. Explore the following options with your supervisor or with whoever is in charge in your supervisor's absence:

- Can priorities be clarified for competing assignments? Which is most urgent and which can be delayed?
- Can someone else take some portion of a major assignment to speed things up and lighten your workload?
- Can one of your assignments be given to another paralegal altogether?
- Can the client's matter be postponed somewhat to allow you more time to complete the project?
- Is there another way to creatively resolve the problem?

After a solution has been found, use the occasion to help prevent similar problems in the future. Lead the way with a tactful suggestion, phrased as a question to your supervisor. For example: "In the future, could we take a minute to check the deadline for a new assignment against deadlines we already have coming up, and make needed adjustments early on?" Later, make the same suggestion to others who have assigned you work.

POINT OF ETHICS
Timeliness

Reducing stress and working effectively are not the only reasons for good time management. The ultimate goal of everything that occurs in the office—and therefore the ultimate goal of time management—is to serve clients well. Perhaps more than anything else, the key to good client service is *timeliness*.

Comments following Rule 1.3 on "Diligence" in the ABA Model Code perfectly summarize this principle, as follows:

> A client's interests often can be adversely affected by the passage of time or the change of conditions; in extreme instances, as when a lawyer overlooks a statute of limitations, the client's legal position may be destroyed. Even when the client's interests are not affected in substance, however, unreasonable delay can cause a client needless anxiety and undermine confidence in the lawyer's trustworthiness.

Even when no immediate financial harm is caused, delays breed suspicions in clients' minds. Some clients may take their business to another law office in exasperation. Others become prone to filing a formal complaint against the office as soon as anything goes even slightly wrong with their case or transaction.

When delays harm a client's interests, the consequences can be devastating. Rules governing the conduct of lawyers may be breached, the responsible lawyer may be sanctioned, and the law office may be liable to the client. Paralegal association codes of ethics and professional responsibility also emphasize the paralegal's responsibility to ensure the competent, timely completion of clients' work. Specific provisions are provided in Appendix 3.

EXERCISES

1. If you have not been estimating needed time for each internship project, begin doing so now. List each project you currently have. Next to each project, write the number of hours you think you will need to complete it. Be sure to add a cushion of time for projects that you have never done before. Then check your personal calendar or planner to see whether ample time has been scheduled for each project.

2. Make a list of the personal chores and social obligations you have outside of the office. Is the list longer than you expected? If so, circle items that someone might be able to help you with. Ask for help with those items.

3. Imagine the following situation: you discover that you have more internship work than you can complete on time. An important deadline may be missed. Develop a plan for handling this. Whom will you approach and what will you say?

4. Imagine that you are working hard to complete a project that is due the next day. You are worried about finishing it on time. Now imagine that a coworker stops by to tell you all about her upcoming wedding, which she is understandably very excited about. How will you handle this situation? What will you say to her?

5. Check the *West's Digest* for your state under the heading, "Attorney and Client." How many cases are there involving the delay of client matters? What kinds of delays are described?

6. Check the Rules of Professional Conduct for attorneys in your state. Is there a rule on "Diligence"? What does it say?

7. Ask attorneys and paralegals in your office if they have ever been faced with a deadline they could not meet. If the answer is yes, ask what they were able to do about it. What strategies do they now use to prevent such problems?

8. Ask attorneys and paralegals in your office to share with you any shortcuts or time-savers they have picked up over the years. Make a permanent list of these. Add to this list any shortcuts or time-savers that you have found useful on your own.

Chapter 11

"Managing" Your Boss

"**M**anaging" someone whose job it is to manage *you* may sound strange at first—perhaps even defiant. But the concept is not rooted in rebelliousness at all. Properly conceived, it facilitates cooperation in the truest sense. "Managing" one's boss assumes that effective management is a two-way street in which common goals are supported on *both* sides. *To serve clients well and to make the most of your internship experience, you must often be a positive participant in your own supervision.*

For example, supervisors are not likely to know how you are doing, or even if you are learning anything, without input from you. Supervisors cannot resolve problems they know nothing about. And with no insight on how things are progressing from your point of view, evaluations and grade recommendations can sometimes be out of step with reality.

This chapter addresses the reciprocal nature of effective supervision and your role in it. In the sections that follow, you will learn how to be a participant in the supervisory process so that you can (a) get feedback on your performance, (b) benefit from both praise and criticism, (c) get better assignments, (d) prevent problems during a supervisor's extended absence, and (e) make sound decisions about a supervisor's unethical conduct, if it occurs.

GETTING FEEDBACK ON YOUR PERFORMANCE

When it comes to knowing how your performance measures up, ignorance is definitely not bliss. Just as students need frequent suggestions from instructors in order to learn and improve their work, interns similarly benefit from the review and comments of their supervisors and coworkers. Instructional feedback in the office heightens your skills. It helps you gauge your progress toward the level of professionalism you want.

Supervisors, on the other hand, are busy people, focused mainly on their own work. Weekly review sessions with your supervisor are ideal but not all supervisors can meet with an intern that often. You may have to devise creative alternatives—things that can be done whenever your supervisor has a free moment. Here are a few ways to create opportunities for feedback from your supervisor and coworkers and then make it as easy as possible for them to respond.

- Buy a brightly colored, plastic file cover and mark it in large letters with your name and the words "For Review." Use this to leave a copy of newly drafted letters, forms, or documents on your supervisor's desk, to be reviewed at the supervisor's convenience.
- Leave more than just a naked draft for review. Highlight the sections you want comments on. Include questions or comments of your own.
- When your work involves projects other than drafting, leave written questions instead. Keep questions legible, brief, and to the point.
- If you include a list of questions, try leaving a large blank space after each question for your supervisor's answer.
- If a project deadline is coming up soon, attach a self-stick note that says "Hearing on: _____" (or "closing" or "filing deadline" or whatever the event may be) with the upcoming date.
- If the matter is truly urgent, write "URGENT!" in large letters on a note attached to the outside of the file.
- Include information about when you will be available in the office and when you can be telephoned at home.

Flexibility on your part is crucial to getting good feedback. Remember that internship supervisors are providing a valuable educational service for which they are not being paid, and that your services may or may not compensate entirely for their investment in you. Your availability for a review session during noninternship hours, either in person or at least by telephone, is a small price to pay for valuable advice and comments.

> ### QUICK TIP 11.1
> The old adage, "The squeaky wheel gets the grease" applies to your need for feedback. So, speak up! Ask for comments and suggestions. Create opportunities for others to see and critique your work and make it convenient for them to do so.

 ## RESPONDING TO CRITICISM AND PRAISE

Being a participant in your own supervision means you are more than just a repository of whatever comments anyone happens to send your way. It means you share responsibility for the instruction you receive. Rather than passively waiting for praise or criticism to be offered, interns should actively seek and respond to both.

Getting Comfortable with Criticism

Student interns, like employees everywhere, tend to be so fearful of criticism that they sometimes go to irrational lengths to avoid it. Some pretend confidence in actions about which they are actually very doubtful. Others ignore or downplay mistakes, foolishly hoping no one will notice them. Both these approaches raise stress levels tremendously and can bring great embarrassment later.

Even more troublesome, some students divert useful criticism by blaming someone else for their error or misjudgment. Habitually resorting to blame signals an unwillingness to learn anything new from the experience—an attitude most supervisors regard with deep disdain.

QUICK TIP 11.2

Positive criticism focuses on your work product, suggesting useful improvements. Negative criticism, on the other hand, is an attack on your personality. If your supervisor does not know the difference, assertively shift the focus back to the work you are doing.

The honest mistakes of a conscientious intern are no cause for shame. Smart interns realize they do not know everything. They understand that mistakes are often a sign of growth and learning. Having mistakes pointed out and learning from them is precisely what internships are designed to do for you.

Constructive criticism is not "blame" but a form of evaluative comment or judgment that you learn from—a potentially helpful critique or analysis of your work. Encourage your supervisor and coworkers to use criticism in this positive way by freely sharing problems and difficulties. Ask coworkers to critique your work, too. Try using words such as these:

- "Would you mind looking at this for me; have I missed anything here?"
- "Here's what I've come up with so far; tell me what you think."
- "Am I headed in the right direction with this?"
- "Is there another approach I could try?"
- "How would you suggest handling this?"
- "If you could improve on this somehow, what would you do?"

How you respond to suggested improvements is also important. Saying "thank you" may be difficult when you have been told that what you did was not quite right. But "thank you" is the appropriate response to helpful criticism. An appreciative reaction tells everyone your goals are to produce the best work possible and to learn all you can.

Many students intuitively sense the difference between constructive criticism on the one hand and destructive criticism on the other. Constructive criticism consists of an instructive critique of your work and should always be welcomed. Destructive criticism, on the other hand, consists of name-calling, blaming, and verbal abuse—none of which should be tolerated. Sweeping condemnations such as "This is stupid!" are a form of character attack, not constructive criticism. Such hurtful remarks are counterproductive. Fortunately, they are also very rare.

If you find yourself dealing with a supervisor who does not understand the difference between objectively critiquing your work and attacking you personally, then you may need to address the problem. Calmly and gently identify the offending remark for what it is. Then direct your supervisor's attention back to the work product.

For example, an intern who is told that something she wrote is "stupid" might look her supervisor in the eye and calmly say, "I assure you that I am not stupid, and I can see you're not happy with this draft. Tell me what improvement you're looking for and I will do that." Usually, a calm, factual response puts an end to personal insults and directs the focus back to the work issue, where it belongs. Often, such a response also brings an apology.

If you are extremely uncomfortable speaking this way or if you have addressed the matter but without lasting success, then ask for help from the internship director at your school. Intervention may be needed.

Interns who can overcome their fear of constructive criticism soon understand what a valuable component it is to the internship experience. By actively seeking positive criticism from your supervisor and from coworkers, you take your learning to the maximum. By getting frequent comments on your work, you take advantage of others' greater skill and experience, and make it your own.

Accepting Praise

Although everyone hopes for praise, many of us become oddly embarrassed or apologetic when praise finally comes our way. Instead of graciously

> ## THE STUDENT'S PERSPECTIVE 11.1: TANIA
> ## Coping with Corrections
>
> Although she did her best, Tania's grades at school were far from outstanding, so she began her internship worried about meeting the office's expectations. For the first two weeks, every assignment came back with suggestions for further work. The suggestions were made kindly and without personal criticisms, but they caused Tania to doubt her abilities. "I'm disappointing these people—I just know it," she thought.
>
> At the end of an especially busy day, her boss stopped by and found her alone, in tears. Surprised, she asked, "Tania, what's wrong?"
>
> Tania wiped her nose. "Oh, I'm sorry. It's nothing. I was just feeling badly about disappointing you all. I'll be okay."
>
> Her boss shook her head in confusion. "Disappointing us? Tania, you're one of the best, most hardworking interns we've had! What made you think we were disappointed?"
>
> "Well, you know, all the suggestions you have to make every time I turn in an assignment. I just can't seem to get it right, can I?" Tania asked sardonically.
>
> "Tania, listen to me," her supervisor responded. "You're an intern—a student, still. You've only been here two weeks. You never spent a single day in a law office, until now. So, of course there are going to be suggestions and corrections along the way. You're expected to make mistakes at this stage!
>
> "The truth is," she continued, "we haven't had to correct your work as much as we did for the last intern we had. Your work is actually better than most. Did you know that?"
>
> "No—I had no idea." Tania brightened a little.
>
> "Well, then I'm sorry I didn't tell you. I probably should have. But I never dreamed you were taking my suggestions so personally.
>
> "Maybe you need to look at the whole process a little differently. We all correct each other's work around here—all the time. We're constantly looking out for each other, spotting errors, and trying for improvements.
>
> "Pretty soon, Tania, you'll be correcting us, too—you wait and see. Our best interns always do, sooner or later."

accepting a verbal pat on the back, students too often minimize their accomplishments, pointing out imagined flaws or insisting that "anyone could have done it." Humility is a wonderful thing, but not when it discourages accurate evaluation of a job well-done or gives the impression that you lack confidence in your work.

When praise comes your way, smile! No one wants you to brag or lord it over others, but do let go of any tendency toward feigned humility or self-doubt. Instead, strive for genuine graciousness. The phrases below are examples of how you might convey an upbeat response.

- "Thank you! It was my first attempt at a project like this. I'm so glad it turned out well."
- "I appreciate the encouragement. This project was challenging for me. I really learned a lot doing it."
- "Thank you for saying so! Actually, I had fun working on this project. I look forward to the next one even more."
- "Well, thank you! You know, I'm kind of proud of these results myself."

Praise is given to make you feel good about your work. Let the giver know that it does. You just may improve your chances of receiving it again and again in the future.

GETTING BETTER ASSIGNMENTS

Sometimes, interns complain of boredom on the job. An intern may be doing the same kind of assignments over and over. Worse, an intern may have nothing to do. When these problems occur, the question must be asked: what has the intern done about it? If the intern has done nothing to improve the situation, then the problem is partly of his or her own making.

Supervisors do not automatically know what kind of work you want to do. Often, they are not even aware of what you *can* do. Rightly or wrongly, it is your responsibility to tell them.

If you are faced with these problems, you must calmly explain the situation to your supervisor. Begin by citing the goals you and your supervisor agreed upon in your learning contract. Remind your supervisor that learning goals must be met in order to warrant academic credit. Then, point out which goals are being met and which ones are not. Politely ask for assignments that address the unmet goals. If necessary, ask whether others in the office might assign you work, to facilitate more varied or challenging experience.

Usually, the direct but courteous approach is extremely effective and, once addressed, the problem is quickly resolved. If not, then the final step is to bring the matter to the attention of the internship director at your school. Be prepared to justify the director's intervention by explaining the steps you have already taken to resolve the problem on your own.

Alternatively, you may be able to avoid a confrontation with your supervisor by using indirect tactics, instead. Often dubbed the show-and-tell approach, this involves demonstrating, on your own initiative, the kind of work you can do and then suggesting opportunities to do more of the same. The show-and-tell method for getting better assignments includes these strategies:

- Check client files and identify additional steps needed on current projects. Try doing some of the tasks you have identified. Take the results to your supervisor as an example of what you can do.
- Suggest *specific* projects to your supervisor. Describe in some detail how you would proceed with them.
- Describe to coworkers the kind of work you are looking for. Ask whether they need help with something of that nature.

For the bored and underchallenged intern, speaking up is crucial to changing the situation, and very likely to get the desired results. This is probably the only paralegal internship you will have. You have the right—even the obligation—to help steer it in the right direction.

WHEN THE BOSS IS AWAY

Lawyers and other supervisors often have obligations outside the office, so their temporary absence is commonplace. Most interns learn to handle this situation without serious difficulty. The smart intern determined early on who should be consulted for questions and guidance when the supervisor is temporarily unavailable.[1] If this eventuality has not already been resolved, then it should be addressed right away—before serious difficulties develop.

More problematic is the plight of the intern whose boss announces an unexpected two-week vacation or is suddenly called away for an extended period. When paralegals risk unethical conduct such as the unauthorized practice of law, it is most often because of the supervising attorney's chronic unavailability. The lengthier the supervisor's absence, the more heightened the risk. For interns working in a solo practice, the risk becomes overwhelming.

When a supervisor is going to be completely unavailable for a week or two, immediate planning is needed to protect yourself from insufficient supervision and ensure the continuing value of your internship experience. When you learn that your supervisor will be out of town for several days, act quickly to resolve the following issues:

- Who will be available to handle matters requiring immediate legal judgment? To avoid any hint of the unauthorized practice of law, you *must* have an answer to this. If you are not given a satisfactory answer, consult the director at your school without delay.
- Whose responsibility will it be to review and approve your work in the supervisor's absence? Will this person also contribute to your final evaluation?
- What steps have to be taken on client matters while the boss is out of town, and which of these require the supervisor's action or approval? Review current files and list upcoming steps that may cause concern. Be sure your supervisor sees this list before leaving.
- If litigation documents have to be filed in your supervisor's absence, what are the local rules on who may—or may not—sign court documents? Do not be left in the position of putting a signature to document that court rules may prohibit you from signing.
- Will you have enough assignments to keep you learning productively while the boss is away? Agree in advance on additional projects, just in case.
- Can your supervisor be contacted if an emergency arises? You will be much more relaxed knowing how to reach this person if you really need to. Ask for a phone number for reaching your supervisor if urgent problems develop.

Because supervisors may not be conscious of all the implications from an intern's viewpoint, you must assume partial responsibility for protecting your interests while the boss is away. Initiate the planning process yourself if your supervisor does not. He or she will be grateful for your intelligent foresight. With good planning, your boss can enjoy a much-needed vacation or take depositions two thousand miles away, with no loss either to clients or to your internship experience.

Point of Ethics
The Unethical Boss

An office willing to expose its operations to the scrutiny of a local paralegal program is not likely to be involved in criminal conduct or unethical behavior. Many of your school's internship offices have already established a very positive track record. If ethical problems had been noticed, the offending office would undoubtedly have been removed from consideration. Most offices operate ethically in any event. So, chances are slim that you will ever find yourself at the center of an ethics storm.

Nevertheless, the actions of a lawyer or other coworkers sometimes raise doubts in an intern's mind. Questionable practices do occur, and every intern should be prepared to deal appropriately with such things if they become worrisome.

Unethical conduct can take many forms. The following list includes some of the most serious examples:

- Deceiving (deliberately misinforming) clients
- Deceiving (deliberately misinforming) third parties such as creditors, mortgage companies, a court, or opposing counsel
- Using client funds for personal or office use
- Revealing confidential client information to outsiders without the client's consent
- Neglecting a client's case in a manner that puts that client's interests at risk
- Neglecting upcoming deadlines
- Accepting a personal, perhaps financial, interest in a client's business, transaction, estate, or court case
- Direct, personal solicitation of a client's business
- Fraudulent client-billing practices
- Discrimination against employees or clients on the basis of race, sex, religion, national origin, marital status, and in some jurisdictions, sexual preference
- Sexual harassment of a client, coworker, or other professional
- Facilitating another person's ongoing illegal conduct.[2]

If you suspect unethical conduct on the part of your supervisor, take the following steps. If you follow these steps in the order they are given, then the third, most drastic, step may never have to be taken. The three steps are (1) discreetly verify what you think you heard or observed, (2) articulate your concern to the most appropriate person, and (3) decide whether you should change your internship setting.

Verification: Is This What I Think It Is?

One intern saw her lawyer-supervisor notarize a document without checking the signer's identification. Also noticing an aura of secrecy surrounding the matter, the intern believed the lawyer might be facilitating a forgery. Another intern suspected her supervisor of using funds from the client trust account to bribe a city official.

In both situations, the interns' impressions were entirely wrong. The first supervisor knew the signer of the document he was notarizing from previous transactions, and he was respecting the signer's demand for utmost privacy. The second supervisor was paying the official money owed by a client who had deposited that money with the lawyer precisely for that purpose.

Not everything is as it first appears. Fortunately, both these interns discreetly asked their supervisors about what they observed. Each knew to *ask the supervisor general questions conveying no assumptions whatsoever*—realizing they may have misunderstood what they saw. The interns also knew to phrase the question as a search for better understanding of legal procedures—not as an accusation of any kind.

For example, the first intern approached her boss sometime later and said, "I've never completely understood all the rules about notarizing documents, so I was hoping you could shed some light on this for me. When can documents be notarized without identification? I'm thinking, for example, of the gentleman you saw this afternoon." Her supervisor laughed, "Watching out for me, are you? Well, good for you! It can be critically important later whether a document was notarized properly." Then he explained what he did and why. The intern's suspicions were completely dispelled.

The second intern used a similar approach. She explained that she wanted to understand how client trust funds work—what they can or cannot be used for—so that when she works in a solo office some day, she will know what to do. "For example," she added, "I noticed the check going to the building inspector this morning, and I didn't understand what was happening." As in the first scenario, this supervisor also took some pride in her intern's professional curiosity. She explained the transaction that occurred that day. She also recommended reviewing a key section of the Rules of Professional Conduct for lawyers in her state so that her intern could learn more.

Consider what might have happened if these interns failed to check out their suspicions. Imagine that, instead of speaking to their supervisors first, they reported their unfounded suspicions to their school, to others in the law office, or to the state's ethics committee. At best, these interns would have experienced severe embarrassment on discovering their error. They certainly would have jeopardized their internship. They could have caused their school embarrassment throughout the local legal community, making internships difficult to arrange in the future. Worst of all, they could have been accused of slander. So they were smart to use the verification technique described here *before* taking their suspicions any further.

On the other hand, what if these supervisors had become defensive about even very general questions? What if the supervisors had become accusatory themselves, even though no accusations were being made toward them? What if they flatly refused to discuss the matter? That kind of behavior would tend to confirm an intern's suspicions. Met with such behavior, an intern would probably progress to step two, described below.

Articulating Your Concerns

If a neutral question—phrased merely as a search for better understanding of law office procedures—fails to bring a satisfactory response, then it may be time to share your concerns with someone you trust. You need the advice of someone who understands your interests as a student and who can help you make the best decision in the light of your long-term interests.

Start by discussing the matter with your school's internship director. An office supervisor's misconduct affects the integrity of the school's internship program, so your director needs to know about it.

Your director will want details showing how certain you are about what you observed. Your director will also help you evaluate the seriousness of the suspected offense. If it is very serious, your director may even want to consult the school's legal counsel for advice. After considering all factors, the two of you can decide whether the matter should be reported to appropriate authorities.

Explore with your director the risks and benefits of the following strategies:

- Reporting the matter to higher management in your internship office for possible in-house discipline. Usually, this also puts the responsibility on management to report the matter to the state's ethics committee or to other relevant authorities, if that is appropriate.
- Reporting the alleged violation directly to the ethics committee or similar authorities in your state if there is no higher law office management *and* if you are prepared to substantiate the alleged misconduct.

> ## QUICK TIP 11.4
> Face-to-face accusations rarely accomplish anything. If the accusation proves unwarranted, you have needlessly offended your supervisor. If the accusation is correct, no supervisor is likely to admit it. Instead, get confidential advice from someone you trust.

- Reporting it to law enforcement authorities, such as the county attorney or state attorney general, if the matter involves criminal conduct such as fraud or theft of client funds *and* your suspicions have a sound basis.
- Taking no action at all in cases in which (1) the suspected offense is very minor and no one has been harmed, (2) your suspicions are impossible to corroborate, or (3) reporting the matter risks disclosure of information protected by attorney-client privilege.[3]

Reporting the matter to outside authorities can have repercussions on the program's reputation and possibly on your own as well, so the decision should be a joint one. It should be thoroughly explored in all its ramifications before any action is taken.

Students need to remember that laws on slander and libel make it risky to officially report violations that you are uncertain about or that you cannot hope to substantiate. Neither you nor your school wants to invite lawsuits for unwarranted defamation of character.

Before assuming the need to report a lawyer's misconduct, check the Rules of Professional Conduct for lawyers in your state. They differ from one state to the next. Lawyers codes of professional conduct normally impose a reporting obligation only on lawyers—not on paralegals or support staff. A few states, such as California, impose no such obligation at all.[4]

Moreover, most such codes only impose this obligation on lawyers actually "having knowledge" (Rule 8.3 of the ABA Model Rules) or having unprivileged knowledge of conduct "which he believes clearly" (EC 1-4 of the ABA Code) to be in violation of the rules. Mere suspicions may not amount to "knowledge," much less something one "believes clearly" to be a violation. Given the language of these rules, anyone reporting unethical conduct should try to verify the nature of such conduct before reporting it to authorities. Always consult the school director before proceeding further.

The ethics rules of paralegal organizations also address this issue. For example, Canon 9 of NALA's Code of Ethics and Professional Responsibility refers its paralegal members to local bar associations' codes of ethics and professional responsibility governing the attorneys who employ—and are therefore responsible for—law office paralegals. Because local lawyers' codes sometimes differ regarding a lawyer's obligation to report the unethical conduct of other lawyers, NALA's Code seems to suggest that NALA members inform their supervising attorney, or perhaps a managing partner, of suspected ethics violations so that management may make an official report if that is deemed legally appropriate. NALA's approach has the advantage of ensuring that its members will not take action that is inconsistent with the reporting obligations legally imposed on the lawyers that employ them or risk interpreting the fine points of client confidentiality, lawyer-client privilege, or past and future criminal conduct on their own.

NFPA's approach, on the other hand, appears to place a reporting obligation directly on the paralegal. EC-1.2(f) of NFPA's Model Code of Ethics and Professional Responsibility requires NFPA members to "advise the proper authority of nonconfidential knowledge of any dishonest or fraudulent acts by any person pertaining to the handling of the funds, securities, or other assets of a client." Another provision of the NFPA Code similarly requires members to advise proper authorities of nonconfidential knowledge of actions clearly demonstrating fraud, deceit, dishonesty, or misrepresentation; and still another provision requires the immediate reporting to appropriate authorities knowledge of *future* criminal activity.

These provisions of NFPA's Code wisely recognize important (but often complex) distinctions between confidential and nonconfidential information, and between future and past criminal activity. However, the NFPA Code does not address the possibility of acting beyond what may be required, or perhaps even allowed, under lawyers' court-enforced codes of ethics and professional responsibility in any given jurisdiction.[5]

Whatever the reporting obligations for professional paralegals may be in your jurisdiction, enrolled students most often consider their reporting obligation fulfilled by reporting their suspicions to the school's internship director. If the internship is an academic undertaking, many see the sponsoring school as the first (though perhaps not final) authority over ethics issues arising in that context. On receiving reports of unethical conduct in an internship office, the school becomes responsible for determining whether the matter should be reported further. As uncredentialed learners, interns are wise to defer to their school's best judgment on this issue.

Sadly, the possibility of professional retaliation is another concern that affects one's decision to report a lawyer's misconduct to outside authorities. Continuing your internship with a lawyer against whom you have filed a formal ethics complaint is not a pleasant prospect.

In many states, so-called whistle-blower's-statutes give employees the right to recover losses caused by an employer's retaliation against them for reporting misconduct to authorities. These statutes may also allow employees to seek an injunction against being fired. However, *whistle-blower's statutes do not always protect unpaid interns.*

When all is said and done, only you know what your personal moral values require of you—and what it takes to bring you peace of mind. The very few students who face these choices must ultimately listen to their own hearts.

Your Ethics or Your Internship

In those rare instances in which serious misconduct is clearly apparent, an intern may have to make hard choices—and make them quickly.

An intern working for a solo real estate practitioner suspected questionable dealings between her supervising attorney and a local mortgage company with whom the attorney frequently worked. As the intern processed mortgage applications, she noticed that reports on applicants' income and assets had been inflated, making unqualified home buyers appear qualified on paper. Extravagant purchases and odd comments from her supervisor suggested that he might be receiving kickbacks from the mortgage company. Understandably, she became frightened. She went to her school's internship director and asked to be placed in a different office, immediately.

The school's director gave her two options: be placed right away in another office that might not be the best match for the intern's career goals, or wait and begin a new internship search the following semester. The intern opted for the latter, eventually interviewing for a fresh internship and mentioning nothing of the last one. A year after the incident, local newspapers were full of reports about the first internship supervisor, who was suddenly being indicted on multiple counts of fraud.

This was an extremely unusual situation, but the intern instinctively took the best possible action. *If you are reasonably certain that serious ethics problems exist in your internship office, do what you can to get out immediately.* Particularly if the misconduct is an ongoing pattern of activity, it will be discovered eventually—with or without your reporting it. You do not want your professional reputation tainted by association with unethical or criminal conduct.

Students facing serious unethical conduct in a supervisor should do the following:

- Get help from the internship director at your school.
- Quietly but quickly disassociate yourself from this internship office.
- Seek another internship office immediately, if that is possible, or begin a new internship search the following school term.
- Do not mention the troublesome internship experience to other offices. When interviewing for permanent employment, use your second internship experience as the basis of discussion.
- Cooperate fully with any law enforcement or investigative body that becomes concerned about the supervisor's conduct.
- Take pride in your own ethical conduct and in maintaining high standards in the paralegal profession.

EXERCISES

1. Review the list of methods for getting more frequent feedback. Select two or three of these methods and try them with your supervisor. Decide which was most helpful, and repeat it as often as needed.
2. Make a list of the suggestions or criticisms of your work that you have received in the last week (or longer, if you have not received any in that time). Next to each item, note the new information or skill you acquired as a result.
3. Keep a running list of the suggestions and comments you have received regarding your work throughout your internship. Add this list to your personal internship notebook for drawing on later when listing job skills on your résumé or in interviews.
4. Referring to the list of techniques for getting comments and suggestions from supervisors and coworkers, prepare a list of your own questions, phrased in a way that is comfortable for you. Try using them in the office.
5. Using the list of suggested responses to praise, prepare a list of possible responses to praise, phrased in a way that is comfortable for you. Use one of them the next time you are complimented on your work.
6. Review the suggestions on getting better assignments and devise a proposal for a new assignment. Deliver this proposal to your supervisor in the form of a memo. Follow up on your memo with a personal discussion.
7. Imagine that your supervisor is being called away from the office on a family emergency for several days. Make a list of the steps you would take to ensure that needed work will continue to get done and to ensure that your internship will continue to be a good learning experience in your boss's absence.
8. Check the Rules of Professional Conduct for lawyers in your state for the following information: (a) whether a reporting requirement exists, (b) what kinds of unethical behavior must be reported, (c) to whom it should be reported, and (d) what category of professionals have this reporting obligation.
9. Check the ethics rules for your local paralegal organization and also for your national paralegal organization (NFPA or NALA, in Appendix 3) to see what kind of reporting requirement exists for members, what kind of unethical behavior must be reported, and to whom. Evaluate these in the light of the Rules of Professional Conduct for lawyers in your state.
10. At your next paralegal association meeting, ask whether members have ever encountered unethical conduct in a supervisor and, if so, what they

did about it. Ask what they recommend others do if unethical conduct is discovered in the office. Evaluate these comments in the light of the Rules of Professional Conduct for lawyers in your state.

ENDNOTES

1. See "Orientation Meeting with Your Supervisor" in Chapter 5.
2. A distinction must be made between the past conduct and the future conduct of clients and others. Lawyers are not generally required to report the past illegal conduct of criminal defendants if doing so would undermine client confidentiality, privileged attorney-client communications, or effective legal representation. In most jurisdictions, however, lawyers *are* required to report threatened future conduct involving serious harm to others. And under no circumstances are lawyers or their staff permitted to participate in, encourage, or facilitate another person's ongoing illegal behavior. The NFPA Code of Ethics and Professional Responsibility also recognizes these distinctions (see Appendix 3).
3. If the knowledge the intern has is privileged information under applicable rules of evidence, then there may be no obligation to report it unless it has to do with the commission of a crime. Reporting client's information may also violate separate rules on client confidentiality. The specifics of all these rules vary from state to state and should be checked.
4. Deborah K. Orlik, *Ethics for the Legal Assistant* (Encino, CA: Marlen Hill Publishing, 1994), 17.
5. In addition to these codes, state and local paralegal organizations may have their own rules on this subject.

Chapter 12

Managing
Client Relationships

Strategies for effectively relating to clients are difficult for supervisors and coworkers to explain. Because the subject is not often discussed on the job, this chapter addresses in detail the relational side of client dealings. In the following sections, you will learn how to emphasize client service, define the boundaries of client relationships, encourage clients' trust in you, and communicate productively even with difficult clients.

 ## EMPHASIZING SERVICE

Successful offices realize they are in a service industry in which customer relations are crucially important. Some law offices seem to have forgotten this. You will make yourself invaluable by imitating the best service people in your experience—even if "the best" are not necessarily found in your current internship office.

Addressing clients by name when speaking to them implies that you recognize their individuality. "Thank you, Mrs. Perry," sounds a great deal more personable than a curt "Thank you." Using clients' names also draws their attention more closely to what you are saying.

When speaking to clients, use words that convey respect and let clients know you are doing something for them. For example, *do say:*

- "Let me see what I can find out and get right back to you."
- "Where can I or Attorney So-and-So reach you with the answer?"
- "Do you mind if I put you on hold for a moment while I check that?"
- "Let me relate this to Attorney So-and-So; I know she will be interested in hearing it."
- "We appreciate your cooperation with this request."
- "Let me see whether there's a way to resolve this scheduling conflict (or other procedural glitch) for you."

- "Although Attorney So-and-So is not here right now, I'll be glad to relate the problem to him just as soon as he gets in."
- "It will be helpful to your case if you can tell me . . . . "

Unfortunately, the statements in the list below have actually been heard at some offices. The following list contains "avoidance" phrases used to get rid of someone or to delay dealing with a problem. They are sheer poison to client relationships. Even if you hear others using these words, avoid using them yourself.

When speaking to clients, *do not say:*

- "You shouldn't feel that way."
- "You're wrong."
- "I can't do anything about that."
- "That's not my problem (not my job, etc.)."
- "I'm putting you on hold."
- "I don't have any idea when Attorney So-and-So will be back."
- "There's nobody here to talk to you."
- "I can't help you if you don't cooperate."
- "Don't be . . . (stubborn, pigheaded, stupid, etc.)."

Also, bear in mind that words can be used either to inform or to impress, and avoid legal jargon when speaking to clients. Choose words that convey useful information rather than words that merely display technical expertise.

For example, an intern who relates well to clients might ask when a certain client "wants to sign his will." Another intern, eager to show off extensive legal knowledge, might ask when the client "wishes to execute his testamentary instruments." The first question informs the client, simply and directly. The second question is certainly impressive but fails to inform the client, who may now wonder just who is being executed and for what crime!

Legal jargon effectively displays your technical expertise, but at the expense of genuine understanding among clients. Instead, explain legal matters in plain English using simple, direct terms.

DEFINING EACH RELATIONSHIP

Clients are often unsure about how to work with paralegals or why they should do so at all. For that reason, *part of your job is to help clients understand what you will do for them—and also what you cannot do.*

Ideally, your supervising attorney will explain your role to a client even before you and the client meet. If you are asked to sit in on the initial interview with a client, your role will be clarified at that time. However, prior explanations by the supervising attorney are not always possible. Sometimes you may have to explain your role to a client yourself. Even if someone else has already explained your role, you still need to make sure the client completely understands the arrangement and is comfortable with it.

When meeting alone with a client for the first time, greet this person with a firm handshake and a smile, and see that he or she is comfortably settled. Begin the business at hand by verifying your paralegal role—*before* discussing the case or transaction. An example of such a conversation appears in Table 12.1. Take these same steps when speaking with a client on the phone for the first time.

To be able to explain these issues, you yourself must have a good understanding of whatever role you will be assuming. Try to determine exactly what tasks you will be performing before meeting with a new client. That way, you will be able to explain your role fully and with confidence.

Table 12.1

Introductory Conversation with a Client

Client:	(Answering the phone) Hello?
Intern:	Hello, is this Mrs. Johnston?
Client:	Yes.
Intern:	Good morning, Mrs. Johnston. I'm calling for Attorney Mark Haverhill. My name is Pam Stockbridge. I'm Attorney Haverhill's paralegal intern.
Client:	Oh?
Intern:	Yes. I'm assisting Attorney Haverhill with your late husband's estate, and he's asked me to check with you to make sure we've correctly identified all the estate assets.
Client:	Oh, okay—I guess. Actually, I assumed I'd be hearing from Mr. Haverhill on that.
Intern:	Well, let me assure you that your expectation was correct. Attorney Haverhill remains fully in charge of your case and you certainly will continue to hear from him. As Mr. Haverhill's paralegal, I'll often serve as a liaison between you and him regarding routine procedural details. I'll also be completing many of the forms that we'll file with the Probate Court. Mr. Haverhill reviews them carefully before they're filed, of course. This is the process we normally follow with all our probate clients. My work frees Attorney Haverhill to spend his time on more complex legal issues. It also helps keep clients' legal fees down to a reasonable level.
Client:	I see. You must be a law student, then?
Intern:	No, I'm not studying to be a lawyer. I've nearly finished my degree in Paralegal Studies, which means I am trained as a lawyer's assistant. I work with clients in many ways, and I like to think I'm pretty helpful to them. But I'm not the one who advises you on your legal rights and responsibilities—that will always be Attorney Haverhill's job. What Mr. Haverhill and I do have in common, though, is the obligation to keep your legal matters confidential, Mrs. Johnston. The information you give me is for Mr. Haverhill's ears only.
Client:	Well, that's fine with me. What do we need to do?
Intern:	Assuming you're comfortable working with me, Mrs. Johnston (and it sounds as though you are), I just need a more detailed description of a few items. Depending on what you tell me, we may need to have those items formally appraised and insured. Could I meet with you soon to go over that?
Client:	Yes, of course. You sound quite knowledgeable, by the way. Evidently, Mr. Haverhill has found himself a very capable assistant!

Here are the preliminary issues you need to review with any client who is new to you.

- You are a paralegal intern, which means you are not an attorney but you are specially trained to assist with various aspects of the client's case or transaction.
- Your assistance frees the attorney for work that requires a law school background. Your work keeps the client's costs down while still providing skilled legal services.
- You will assist the client with many of the procedural aspects of the matter, but you rely on the attorney for questions requiring legal judgment.
- Describe in some detail the specific tasks you will be performing for the client.
- Tell clients that you share the lawyer's obligation to protect client confidentiality. Assure them that nothing said to you will be repeated outside the office without their consent and the attorney's approval.
- Does the client have any questions about your role in this matter? Ask.
- Make a note of questions you cannot answer and bring them to the attorney later. Assure the client you will relay the attorney's answers soon.
- Is the client essentially comfortable with the understanding he or she now has? Invariably, the client will say yes. If not, you are better off knowing this at the outset so the attorney can quickly intervene.

ESTABLISHING TRUST

As you learned in your paralegal courses, the *fiduciary*, or trusting, nature of attorney-client relationships is more than a legal technicality. Clients rely on the law office to protect their livelihoods, their financial security—perhaps even their freedom to carry on a normal life. Although clients do not always understand the fine points of fiduciary relationships, they instinctively know they need to trust the office on which they depend. Assuring them of complete confidentiality lets them know that you are someone with whom they can speak freely.

There are three additional steps you must take to create a trusting, client-paralegal relationship. The first requires conveying an appropriate degree of authority. The second involves tolerance for clients' idiosyncrasies, perhaps also developing a sense of empathy or rapport with the client. The third is something that is not conveyed with words—only with actions. That is the creation of lasting confidence by proving your reliability again and again over time.

> **QUICK TIP 12.1**
>
> To avoid offending your supervisor, do not hold yourself out as an office employee unless you are actually on the payroll. Be sure to indicate your status as a paralegal *intern*—particularly in correspondence.

Conveying Authority

More than anything else, clients expect professional expertise. You may find it hard to think of yourself as an "expert" at this stage in your career, but that is how you are perceived by clients. Consequently, clients expect a confident, somewhat authoritative demeanor.

Conveying authority does not mean being arrogant, flippant, or snobbish. It means speaking with calm assuredness about what you know to be so. It means remaining composed when tensions rise. Sometimes it means confidently admitting what you *do not* know but can find out easily enough.

Certain mannerisms help convey to clients the authority of specialized training and expertise. To convey professional authority, paralegals often do the following things:

- Speak "low and slow"—avoid rushed speech, mumbling, or high-pitched, childlike tones that betray nervousness.
- Sit tall—never slump—when meeting with a client.
- Look at the client when speaking or listening.
- Lean slightly forward to show interest.
- Maintain a serious voice and facial expression when serious subjects are discussed.
- Smile or laugh when something humorous is mentioned (but never laugh *at* a client).
- Never giggle, twirl hair, or cover portions of the face with fidgety hands.
- Remain fairly still throughout the conversation.
- Respond confidently and fully to questions when the answer is certain.
- Offer to get back to the client later when answers are not certain.
- Defer to the attorney in charge when legal judgment is needed.

In this way, you diplomatically take charge of the conversation. At the same time, you subtly proclaim your expertise in the matter. These two qualities—your professionalism and your expertise—are two of the most important bases for a client's faith in you.

QUICK TIP 12.2

When talking to clients on the phone, pretend you are conversing in person. Use the same posture, facial expressions, and body language you would use if speaking face-to-face. You will be surprised how professional and authoritative your voice becomes.

Developing Acceptance, Empathy, and Rapport

Acceptance, empathy, and rapport are degrees of relatedness to the clients you serve, with rapport being the strongest and acceptance being the minimum that is needed.

Acceptance

Acceptance refers to taking clients as you find them and working with them as they are—warts and all. It means expecting that clients will not always share your values in life and knowing that this does not threaten your own value system in any way. It means pursuing social reform efforts *outside* the office only. It means continuing to cherish deeply held opinions but, for the most part, leaving those opinions at home. *In short, "acceptance" means not passing personal judgment on clients* because, in the legal profession, that job belongs to judges and juries.

In some fields such as criminal defense, family law, or social services, clients' priorities in life become abundantly clear. Occasionally, you may find those priorities incomprehensible or even repugnant. At such times, maintaining objectivity can be difficult, but every intern must try. Here are a few thoughts that often help paralegals remain objective and tolerant of clients' idiosyncrasies:

- We are not our clients. We do not have to share their view of the world, and they do not have to share ours.
- Someone made a conscious decision to accept this client. That person may have insights into the case that you do not have.
- Technically, paralegals do not work for clients; they work for attorneys. The attorney may bear responsibility for clients' actions but, in a law office, you do not.
- As long as the client's objectives are fully within the law and consistent with your office's objectives, it is not a paralegal's job to discourage or dissuade clients.
- If a client's actions seem legally unwise, do convey your concern to the attorney in charge of the matter—but do *not* discuss it with the client.
- If a client appears to need some additional form of counseling or therapy, relate this observation to the attorney—but do *not* mention it to the client.
- When conflicting values are getting in the way of quality work, discuss your reservations with your supervisor.

Rarely does paralegal work create serious, personal moral conflict for an intern. When it does, the conflict usually relates to a major societal issue such as child abuse, abortion, or discrimination. A serious conflict in values may stand in the way of your best efforts, so give your boss the chance to let someone else take the assignment. Most supervisors have great respect for this kind of honesty.

As interns become attuned to the vast, human diversity that passes through many offices, the contrasts become less startling and the differences easier to tolerate. Many students report such experience as a major step toward growth and maturity.

Empathy

Unlike sympathy, empathy does not require your agreement with what someone is, has done, or wants to do. Empathy requires only your understanding of what someone is feeling. You may privately disapprove of what

---

THE STUDENT'S PERSPECTIVE 12.1: DARBY
Seeing Beyond the Clientele

At the end of her internship, Darby enthusiastically summarized her experience for her class. "Screening cases for the state office of the American Civil Liberties Union was not your average law office experience, but it left me convinced that I can now handle anything—and I do mean anything—with equanimity.

"I dealt with complainants from every point on the political spectrum, from neo-Nazis on the far right to pseudo-Communists on the far left, with civil servants, parents, schoolchildren, and even college professors somewhere in the middle. I interviewed a newly released inmate of what used to be called a hospital for the criminally insane. I helped a woman who spoke a language I never heard of before. I believe I've spoken to callers of every possible political, social, and sexual persuasion. And you know what? It was the most exciting, eye-opening experience I've ever had!

"I learned that I can actually enjoy helping people with whom I might never agree and wouldn't socialize with on a bet. The trick is to believe in something bigger than any one of these people. For some, that might be saving the environment, protecting consumers, or making the justice system work the way it should. For me, it's the Bill of Rights. Sorry if it sounds corny to some of you but that's what I believe my work was really about.

"To me, that's what objectivity is: serving something that may be bigger and even more important than any single client. A larger goal can make a client's peculiar ideas seem pretty insignificant."

---

a client has done (as lawyers and paralegals sometimes do) and still feel empathy for what the client is experiencing. Even if you lack genuine rapport with a client, you can almost always find in yourself some degree of empathy for the client's situation and feelings.

In a human service industry, being able to empathize with all kinds of clients is essential. Unfortunately, some professionals fail to see the delivery of legal services in that light. But the practice of law is a human service industry above all else, particularly in the neighborhood and solo offices where many paralegals begin their careers.

Clients trust professionals who show sensitivity to their feelings and who treat them as people—not as just another file to be processed. Clients who sense empathy from you will usually be more cooperative and willing to disclose full information.

You might demonstrate empathy in the following ways:

- Taking occasional breaks from note taking to look up at the client and really listen
- Nodding affirmatively when a client shares personal feelings
- Modulating your voice to keep it lively, avoiding a flat monotone
- Offering a tissue and a smile to a tearful client
- Gently touching the arm of a distraught client and saying "I'm so sorry for your loss" (or "for the trouble you've had")
- Laughing at the client's humorous portrayal of a situation, if humor was intended
- Responding encouragingly to the client's triumphs with words like "Good for you!"

- Asking if an emotionally upset client would like to take a break, perhaps offering coffee or a cold drink

Rapport

Rapport is a sense of affinity or connectedness between people. Rapport most often comes when people discover something in common between them—something they both relate to well. When you share rapport with someone, you tend to be more relaxed and trusting with that person than you are with others. Whenever some link between you and a client becomes apparent, cultivate that sense of rapport to bring greater trust to the relationship.

By staying alert and open to possibilities, you will occasionally find something that you and your client share. An older client may remind you of an aunt or uncle you always admired. You may discover that you and a client share the same passion for a certain kind of music, sport, pastime, or humanitarian cause. Or, you may share an intense dislike of some kind and can laugh about it together. If you notice such a commonality, mention it to the client. A degree of rapport can suddenly be created. Greater client trust usually follows.

Proving Reliability

Think back to when you have relied on the promise of someone whose help you needed—a family member, another student, or an instructor. Was it someone who had already come through for you several times in the past? If so, the promise undoubtedly brought complete peace of mind. You knew from past experience that the promise would be kept. Clients tend to see things the same way.

Trust is built gradually. It becomes stronger every time you follow through on your word to a client—doing *what* you said you were going to do, *when* you said you were going to do it. For example, when you tell a client you will "call tomorrow morning" to report the attorney's response to a legal question, much more is at stake than just the response you promised to convey. Also at stake is your credibility with that client, who may literally be afraid to leave the house for fear of missing your call. You *must* follow through.

An important counterpart to keeping promises is being careful about what promises you make. Many times, the hardest promises to keep are ones that were made glibly, without thinking. Before promising anything to a client, stop and think: am I really going to be able to do this? As the saying goes, never promise more than you can deliver. You may want to build flexibility into your agreement or not make any assurance at all.

If you are careful about what you agree to do for a client, and do everything you agree to do, then clients will come to see you as someone on whom they can truly depend. Many of them will carry grateful praise to your office supervisor—bringing you the ever-deepening reputation of a paralegal to be valued in any setting.

 ## THE "PROBLEM" CLIENT

Clients typically seek law-related services at dramatic points in their lives when emotions are intense. Many clients are under a great deal of stress. Personal weaknesses—invisible in ordinary situations—sometimes surface strongly under the pressure. What may be a kindly Dr. Jekyll outside your office can become a raging Mr. Hyde during his conversation with you, unless you know how to tame him.

This section introduces you to concrete strategies for bridging clients' emotional difficulties. You will learn how to deal with (1) the nonstop talker, (2) the "takeover" client, (3) the troubled client whose anger or sadness must be soothed, (4) the evasive client who may be concealing needed information, and (5) the client who is physically or culturally different from you.

The Nonstop Talker

Most of us have known someone who talks so much, so fast, that listeners cannot seem to break through the monologue long enough to respond, add a thought, or change the subject. The flood of words comes so fast that the only response a listener can interject is a quick "uh-huh." Sometimes nonstop talking is the client's way of handling nervousness. This is particularly true in legal settings, where clients often feel out of place and apprehensive.

The nonstop talker is a challenge when time is limited and certain subjects must be addressed. Here are several tactics you can use to slow down your nonstop talker and get the client focused on what you need to discuss.

- Understand the human drama that is unfolding before you. Silently see the humor in it. Also, appreciate the discomfort your client may be experiencing.
- *Do* let the client ramble for a few minutes while you listen attentively. This gives the client a sense of control and lets a nervous client get acclimated to you and the office setting.
- After a few minutes, smile and interrupt a bit forcefully. Say "excuse me," and address some detail of the client's discussion. Start with a specific question about something the client just said, such as "At what time of day did that happen?" Now you are leading the discussion.
- Follow up with more questions. For example, "So this happened in broad daylight, then? Did you have a clear view?" Keep at it.
- Alternatively, you can explain that you are running out of time and there are many details you need to get on paper. Explain that you are now going to lead him or her straight through a fairly long series of questions. Invariably, the client will comply.

Dealing with the nonstop talker involves a delicate balance between control on the one hand, and absolute cordiality on the other. Interrupt you must—but in a kindly tone. Also, a client's emotions must always be respected and given a reasonable chance of expression.

The Takeover Client

Among "takeover" clients, there are two common variations. On one hand, the "field marshal" tends to give legal directives that may contradict even the attorney's best judgment. The "nitpicker" or skeptic, on the other hand, repeatedly quizzes professionals on how and at what speed their work is being performed. Both types of takeover clients can cause great consternation for the unwary intern. However, they can easily be dealt with if you know what strategies to use.

The Field Marshal

Occasionally, you may have a client who is more comfortable *giving* directions than taking them—an independent entrepreneur, for example. Other

> ### QUICK TIP 12.3
> For interns taught from childhood never to interrupt or "talk over" others, cutting off a nonstop talker can be unsettling. Reconcile your good manners with the need to interrupt by beginning with "excuse me"—loudly enough to be heard and firmly enough to be believed.

times, a client is just a bit bossy by nature. Meanwhile, interns are so often told what to do and how to do it that taking directions from others may seem normal in any context. But it is not normal here. Taking legal instructions from a client can lead to devastating mistakes.

Not being trained or experienced in the law, clients are unaware of all the options available to them. They may have read or heard enough to *sound* knowledgeable about a few concepts, but they lack the broad, detailed view that an experienced lawyer (and many paralegals) would have. For example, the worried, middle-aged child of a terminally ill parent may insist that a guardianship is needed immediately, not realizing that easier, less costly options also exist.

When clients give you legal instructions, a red flag should go up in your mind. Allowing clients to dictate their own legal remedy is like allowing patients to dictate their own medical treatment. Because clients lack a lawyer's training and experience, the odds are against their knowing what is best.

When clients insist on certain legal procedures, assure them that you want to see their interests fully protected. Tell them that what they are suggesting may or may not be the best choice. Inform them that there is often more to the situation than either you or they are aware of and only the attorney can explain these things fully. Insist that they discuss the matter with the lawyer in charge of their case. If necessary, arrange the appointment yourself to ensure adequate follow-up.

The Nitpicker

The nitpicker accepts recommended procedures well enough but constantly questions whether, when, and how those procedures are being carried out. This is the client you hear from almost daily, with questions on the progress of his or her case.

When a client constantly questions your work, a yellow flag of caution should go up in your mind. This is a client who, at some level, lacks trust. Although annoying, this client is entitled to have all questions answered fully and courteously. The key is to discreetly cut down on the frequency of those questions. Keep this client fully informed, but in a way that is more convenient to your own schedule.

Restore this client's trust by using some of the following strategies.

- Never say "good-bye" without telling the client two things: (1) *what* happens next, and (2) approximately *when* there will be news of it. This reduces the client's worries—and the number of calls to the office.
- When a client has waited hours for your return call, thank the client for being patient, no matter how commonplace such waits may be.
- Explore the possibility of some broad, underlying anxiety. Is there something about this case in general that has the client worried? If you can identify what it is, maybe you or the supervising attorney can resolve the client's fears and end the disruptiveness.
- Offer to regularly send copies of documents prepared or received on the client's behalf. (If this is *not* standard procedure, get prior approval from the attorney in charge.)
- Offer to provide weekly or biweekly progress reports to the client—in writing or by telephone.
- For long discussions, suggest a telephone appointment at a time that's convenient for you.

What these clients usually fear is having their legal matter overlooked in the office's pursuit of bigger, more "important" cases. The more information you can periodically provide these clients, the more reassured they will be and the less often they will quiz you. A methodical system for doing so drastically reduces disruptive calls and questions.

The Troubled Client

Troubled clients are the ones who are overwhelmed by emotions—sadness over a loss, anger at whoever caused their problems, or fear of what might become of them financially or physically. Because of intense feelings, these clients may not see things as clearly as they would under ordinary circumstances. Grasping information, understanding legal maneuvers, or responding fully to questions often becomes a struggle for them.

Communicating with a highly emotional client can be a huge challenge, because they are not usually focused on the business at hand. The behavior of an angry client can be downright frightening. So every intern should have a ready arsenal of strategies. When you are dealing with an overwrought client, try some of the following techniques.

- Create different settings for different clients. An older, angry man might best be reminded of your professional status facing you across a well-appointed desk. A child or anxious adult, on the other hand, might be more at ease seated on a comfortable couch in a private area, away from reminders of legal activity.
- Defuse anger by voicing empathy for the client's situation. Then guide the conversation to a more productive vein. For example: "You've been through a lot, haven't you!" or "I'd be concerned, too, if that happened to me." Then: "Let's get the details we need to set things right for you."
- Do not meet a client alone outside the office unless it is someone known to be reasonable and the setting is not isolated.
- When meeting a client who is prone toward outbursts, leave the door ajar so coworkers can hear any trouble that develops and step in, if needed.
- Before a troublesome client arrives, arrange to have a coworker on standby in case you need help.
- If a client behaves physically in a way that alarms you (such as slamming objects or throwing things), stand up and move toward the door. Announce that you are leaving the room unless the behavior stops. If the behavior continues, leave, and get help.
- Legal jargon puts distance between you and a fearful client. Avoid legal jargon with clients who may be needlessly intimidated by it. Instead, explain upcoming legal procedures in ordinary language, using sensible terms that anyone can understand.
- With fearful clients, take the mystery out of the legal system. Explain not only the procedures being followed but also the reasons for them.

When emotions make it completely impossible for a client to focus productively, your only recourse may be to end the discussion—at least temporarily. Give the client a break from the conversation. If anger is the problem, *insist* on taking a break, giving the client a chance to cool down. Continue the discussion only after the client has regained composure—perhaps on another day.

Understand that clients' emotions are rarely directed at you personally—although it may sometimes seem that they are. Normally, clients' emotions are created by things that happened long before you entered the picture. Reminding yourself of this may help you keep your composure even when clients cannot.

THE STUDENT'S PERSPECTIVE 12.2: HEATHER
Angry at the Boss But Yelling at You

When asked to describe the most frustrating experience interns had on the job, one student responded impatiently. "My supervisor is so busy that he forgets to return clients' calls. Several times, I've had clients absolutely furious with me because Attorney Cardozo failed to call them back."

"Was it really *you* they were furious with?" the internship director asked.

"Well, no. But I was the one who had to listen to their tirades and try to calm them down. I'm getting really tired of making excuses for him."

Having had a similar experience herself, Heather joined in. "The same thing happened to me a few times, but I've stopped offering excuses for my boss. Instead, I offer to get clients' questions answered and call them back myself."

The first student was annoyed. "Don't you think that's the attorney's job?" he asked insistently.

Now Heather was annoyed. "We're legal assistants. It's our job to assist the attorney, right? That's what I'm doing."

The instructor asked for an example and Heather responded. "Let's say a client shouts 'How come that so-and-so has kept me waiting—doesn't he know what's at stake in this case?' and so on. Well, I don't even respond to that. Instead, I calmly ask the client what information he or she was waiting for. I write it down and tell the client I'll check it out. I say that either Attorney Jans or I will get back to them within some definite period of time—usually no longer than one day.

"Now the client knows *two* people are on it. The tirade always stops at that point.

"Then I check the file, check with Attorney Jans or the secretary or whoever has the answer to the question, and if Jans can't call them back, I do.

"I'm careful to avoid giving legal advice on my own. I'm passing along Attorney Jan's advice—not deciding myself what that advice should be.

"The point is: I've found that this approach really works. I've stopped listening to tirades about client's unanswered questions. Instead, I get those questions answered for them."

The Evasive Client

Certain kinds of behavior suggest that a client may be withholding information. Such behaviors include contradictory statements, avoidance of eye contact, and repeatedly answering "I don't know" to questions the client clearly has reason to know. Vague responses may be another indicator. When a client continually qualifies answers with "maybe" or "I think" in situations in which most people would be quite specific, then the client could be revealing less than he or she knows.

When clients conceal information from you, it is typically due to fear or embarrassment and it always *signals a lack of trust*. It is those negative feelings—not the concealment of information—that you must focus on first.

For example, a paralegal working on a bankruptcy case sensed that a client was holding back information on the actual amount of indebtedness the client had. As the intern pursued a checklist of assets and liabilities, the client's answers became increasingly vague. Suspecting evasiveness, the intern did two things. First, she explored the client's emotional viewpoint. Then she explained the importance of full disclosure, suggesting what could happen if disclosure is not made.

The paralegal mentioned how she knew, from past cases, that bankruptcy clients are sometimes embarrassed about their debts. She said this was surprising because bankruptcy is not particularly unusual, even among smart and successful people. (Notice that the intern never suggested that *this* client was embarrassed.) The client responded immediately to the intern's tactful statement and admitted that, in fact, she was deeply embarrassed about her unpaid debts.

Then the paralegal spoke of a bankruptcy petitioner who multiplied his problems greatly by failing to report all of his outstanding debts. "Really?" was the client's worried reaction. Full and detailed information then flowed freely. In fact, she disclosed double the amount of debt previously disclosed to the supervising attorney!

When concealment of information is suspected, reaffirm your assurances of confidentiality and of serving the client's interests. Explain that *all* information—the bad along with the good—is essential to fully protecting that client. Most of the time, this restores the client's trust and, consequently, the client's cooperation. If it does not, then doubts about the client's truthfulness should be reported promptly to the attorney in charge.

The "Different" Client: Overcoming Barriers

Interns must be prepared to meet needs that may seem unusual at first. For example, you may have to anticipate the difficulties of a client who is wheelchair-bound, visually or hearing impaired, or suffering from speech difficulties. You may need to accommodate a client who speaks little or no English. You may have to help a client whose cultural background attaches unforeseen meanings to certain terms, procedures, or customs. You may even have to work with a client whose physical appearance startles you.

A good rule of thumb for interns having extensive client contact is this: expect the unexpected—and treat the unexpected as if it were commonplace. There is no safe way to predict what kinds of "different" clients will appear in any office. For example, firms specializing in personal injury or medical malpractice often represent clients having extensive injuries, some of which may be hard to face calmly. Clients with physical limitations are also common in offices serving the elderly. Where immigration law is a principal focus, an intern may face different languages and cultural expectations. In a general law practice, any of these situations may be encountered at any time.

Behind even the most startling differences, there is an ordinary human being like yourself. All clients are apprehensive about legal or governmental processes and all of them want things to go well. And all clients expect to be treated with kindness and respect.

Here are additional guidelines for gracefully accommodating unusual client needs.

- When you are assigned a new client, ask whether the client has special needs.
- If you know in advance of a client's physical limitations, check the office for obstacles that may create problems. Are there stairs that should be avoided? Will a wheelchair get through the door of your office or should you conduct the interview elsewhere?
- If you know in advance of language difficulties, see about bringing in an interpreter—perhaps one of the client's family members. Be sure your interpreter understands the need for complete confidentiality.
- Do not respond to language difficulties by shouting. The language is the problem—not the client's hearing.

- Never let yourself appear shocked by a client's appearance. Minimize any embarrassment the client already feels by smiling, shaking hands (if physically possible), and speaking to her or him the same way you would to any client.
- Remember that clients with a physical impairment are not helpless or stupid. Do not assume everything must be done for them. Instead, ask whether the client would like assistance with other than the most obvious obstacles.
- Do not assume you know how to help a physically challenged client. Ask the client about his or her preferences. For example, a visually impaired client may prefer to be led by the elbow—not by the hand.
- With clients from a different culture, consider apologizing for your lack of familiarity with the client's customs. Show respect for the client's culture and for his or her unusual garb.

Try to remember a time when you felt extremely different from those around you and how painful that may have felt. How grateful you would have been (and perhaps were) to anyone who made you feel welcomed in spite of whatever set you apart. Do the same for clients.

There are also legal reasons for respecting others' differences. The federal *Americans with Disabilities Act* requires places of public accommodation to make reasonable efforts to accommodate people with physical disabilities. Failure to do so can result in serious penalties. In addition, discrimination in a place of public accommodation on the basis of race, sex, religion, ethnic background, age, or physical handicap is prohibited by the laws of virtually every state.

Graciously meeting clients' special needs does more than avoid causing offense to valued clients. It also helps your internship office avoid breaking the law.

EXERCISES

1. Imagine that you are meeting a new client to obtain factual information about the client's case. Also imagine that your supervising attorney had no opportunity to explain to the client your role in the client's legal representation. Plan, in detail, how you will accomplish the following:
   a. Introducing yourself
   b. Explaining your role in the client's legal work
   c. Making the client comfortable about working with you
2. As stated in this chapter, you are perceived by clients as an expert. To bolster your sense of personal expertise, make a list of the characteristics you have that justify this perception. Make this list as long as you reasonably can. When you have finished, compare your list to that of other interns to see whether you have overlooked any significant items.
3. Before beginning this exercise, review the list of professional mannerisms in this chapter. Then, with another intern, take turns presenting the introduction and explanation you wrote in Exercise 1. Read your statements as if you were speaking to a client, using as professional a voice and manner as possible. As each reads, the other should observe and take notes on the performance. After each of you finishes, the other will then describe what was best about the speaker's voice and manner and what still needs improvement.
4. This exercise helps you to analyze and improve your ability to build rapport. First, identify five people at your school with whom you currently share a sense of rapport. Then, identify what it is you have in common with each of these people that led to the rapport you feel. Third, try to remember *how* and *when* you first realized what you have in common

with each of these people. Next, consider whether there is anything you could have done to discover these commonalities earlier in the relationship. Last, consider what steps might help you to develop greater rapport with clients or others in the office.

5. Read the following descriptions of various, fictitious clients. For each, devise a conversational statement that would convey empathy for the client's situation without causing further embarrassment to the client. After you have finished, compare your responses with those of other interns for insights on various ways to respond.

   a. A very anxious, middle-aged couple who are having wills drafted to safeguard the future of a disabled, adult child

   b. A juvenile charged with shoplifting, who believes that the charges are unfair and that the legal system has no tolerance or understanding of young people

   c. A former executive who is putting her life savings into an exciting new business of her own

   d. A bankruptcy client who feels he is a financial failure

   e. An accident victim who has lost the use of one arm and feels intense frustration at the slowness of the legal system

   f. A confused parent—abused throughout childhood by her own parents—who is now accused of abusing her daughter

   g. A single mother whose landlord has threatened to evict her and her children

6. This exercise helps you analyze and improve your reliability. Try to remember at least three things you have recently volunteered to do for a client, a friend, or a colleague. What was the outcome of each incident? Did you perform exactly as promised? If so, you are already very reliable. If not, answer the following questions:

   a. What prevented you from coming through exactly as promised? Were you thwarted by something you might have foreseen if you had first thought things through?

   b. Could the situation have been handled differently—not volunteering exactly as you did but helping the person in some other way?

   c. Can the same principles be applied to your work at your internship office?

7. With another intern, role-play a conversation with each of the following client types. Take turns playing the client and the interviewer. The student playing "client" will have to make up his or her own fact pattern and be prepared to talk for two or three minutes about it, improvising as needed to create the situation indicated in each scenario. The student playing "interviewer" must respond to the "client" in a way that promotes productive communication.

   a. The client is a nonstop talker. The interviewer must break through the client's talkativeness and lead the conversation into productive fact finding.

   b. The client is a "field marshal" type, instructing the paralegal interviewer on what legal steps are needed. The interviewer must gently but firmly explain the need for the attorney's expertise in making such decisions.

   c. The client (a plaintiff) is angry at your office for not responding quickly enough to her calls and her questions. The interviewer must defuse the client's anger and lead the discussion into productive fact finding and resolution of the client's complaint.

   d. The client (a defendant) is a nitpicker with many questions about what is being done in his case. The interviewer must address the client's insecurities and offer positive alternatives to the client's nitpicking.

e. The client (a bereaved, elderly widow) frequently breaks into tears over the recent death of her husband. The interviewer must convey empathy and gently try to bring focus to the interview about the deceased's estate.

f. Fearful that he may have contributed to the injuries he suffered in an accident, the client is concealing information about how the accident occurred. The interviewer must establish trust in the relationship to achieve full disclosure of the facts.

8. Ask the lawyers and paralegals you work with to describe the most shocking or difficult client they ever met. Then ask how they handled the situation. Privately evaluate the usefulness of the lawyers' or paralegals' reported behavior toward the client. Consider whether you would have behaved the same way, or differently, and why.

Part IV
Staging the Transition

Chapter 13

Why Document Your Learning: An Introduction

Caught up in the exciting demands of their internships, students are often reluctant to spend additional time documenting what the experience teaches them. Those who do take time to document their learning find that it greatly enhances their education as well their careers.

First, by documenting your learning as you go, you engage in the important process of self-monitoring, ensuring that learning objectives are being met as the internship progresses. Second, the documentation you create becomes an effective, practical resource in your job search. Your records provide details for strengthening your résumé and for leading the discussion in interviews. Third, documentation facilitates the assembly of an impressive portfolio for submitting to prospective employers.

Finally, a record of internship learning gives your school specific insights into the quality of your experience. It verifies the academic value of your program, perhaps ensuring continued accreditation as a degree-granting institution. In paralegal programs that are ABA-approved, documented learning may also facilitate qualification as a "legal specialty" course under ABA guidelines.

ARE YOU ACHIEVING YOUR GOALS?

At the beginning of your internship, you developed a list of specific learning objectives—work habits and skills you wanted to develop, procedures you wanted to master, and practice areas you wanted to experience firsthand. The success of your internship depends on how many of those goals you achieve.

During their internships, few students realize every single learning objective. But by identifying learning as it takes place, you increase the likelihood that goals will be achieved. *By periodically evaluating what you are or are not learning, you can request adjustments along the way and ensure that your internship indeed serves your education and your career.*

For example, on seeing your ability to summarize medical information effectively, a supervisor might be tempted to have you repeat the same procedure for a large number of clients. After performing a string of nearly identical assignments, you could find that you are learning nothing from the repetition. With the help of documented learning, the need for new assignments becomes crystal clear to everyone involved. Your documentation can be shown to those in charge as ready proof of the need for change.

The methods that best allow ongoing documentation and evaluation throughout your internship include

- Keeping a reflective journal
- Submitting periodic reports to your school's director describing new skills, experiences, and professional insights
- Making periodic oral reports to your internship class or seminar, describing recent learning experiences
- Using "preview" evaluation forms early in the internship
- Periodically reviewing your own list of learning objectives

One or more of these methods may already be required by your school. If not, then consider pursuing at least one of these documentation methods on your own.

Another reason exists for bringing focused awareness to your learning on the job. Unforeseen learning opportunities often arise as the internship progresses. New interests may develop. As a result, interns sometimes find their learning objectives shifting to unexpected areas.

When this happens, some thoughtful evaluation should accompany the shift. Be sure that changes in your learning objectives are not being made haphazardly or simply because of office pressure. Also evaluate the potential loss of original goals when new ones are added. If the achievement of learning objectives is continually monitored, then the decision to add new goals or to drop old ones can be made in an informed manner—better protecting your long-term career interests.

Whichever documentation method you choose, carry it out consistently throughout your internship. When the internship ends, you will have concrete evidence of all you have gained from the experience. Detailed on paper over many weeks' time, the depth and breadth of your on-the-job learning is guaranteed to surprise and gratify you.

STRENGTHEN YOUR JOB SEARCH

You already know the advantages of the functional or achievements-style résumé,[1] listing specific skills and accomplishments rather than mundane job titles. When the time comes to prepare a serious résumé, unaided memory may not serve you well. But if you have consistently documented your learning, you can draw on the skills and experiences noted throughout the course of your internship. *Details for updating and expanding your résumé will be readily available.* You will have generous amounts of material from which to choose, for adding to the "Qualifications" or "Professional Achievements" section of your résumé.

Keeping a good record of your learning throughout the internship also increases the flexibility of your job search. By surveying all that you have learned, you will be able to select the appropriate details for different job openings. For example, when preparing your résumé for a position in the claims department of an insurance company, you might add specifics about the personal injury litigation skills your documentation shows that you acquired. On the other hand, when applying for a job with a solo general practitioner, you may prefer to emphasize newly acquired skills in client relations and office systems, instead.

You will also have the advantage of being able to *review the record of your learning as part of your preparation for job interviews.* If internship learning has been systematically documented, you can use that material to refresh your memory about each new skill, each professional insight, and each proud accomplishment—including those not listed on your résumé. You will be thoroughly prepared even for the most impromptu questions about your experience.

Keeping your morale high is crucial during a job search. Documented learning helps you there, too. Having concrete evidence of all you learned and

---

AN EMPLOYER'S PERSPECTIVE 13.1
Only the Experienced Need Apply

"When this office needs a new paralegal, our ads always specify 'minimum of two years experience.' For us, simply having attended the 'XYZ Paralegal Program' does not stand out. We get far too many résumés of that kind, and we can't afford to spend hours pouring over them all, hoping to spot something useful. We need someone with certain well-defined skills. The two-year experience requirement helps ensure applicants with that focus.

"So, I was genuinely surprised when I realized that one of our most impressive résumés came from someone right out of school. Almost all of the right skills were listed, and in such knowledgeable detail that they appeared to come from someone who had been working for some time. Specific computer skills, specific documents, specific procedures—it was the specificity that got our attention. Clearly, this applicant understood the office's needs, and she responded to almost all of them in her résumé, with details that made her quite credible.

"So, even after noticing this year's graduation date near the end of her résumé, we called her in for an interview. When she explained that her experience was acquired during an internship, I became doubtful. I remember internships as being pretty worthless—simple, meaningless chores that merely gave me a chance to watch real work being done by others. But this applicant brought out a portfolio of several things she produced during that experience, and those documents painted a very different picture. She responded easily and very knowledgeably to questions about the nature of the work she did. She also provided a wonderful letter from her office supervisor, summarizing her work.

"The evidence of her skills was impressive. We decided to make an exception to the two-years-experience rule. We hired her on a trial basis, at a salary that is somewhat lower than what we might offer to someone more experienced but with a six-month salary review process built in. If she performs well, we might be able to increase her salary after that.

"I'm betting that anyone smart enough to find the kind of internship she did, perform the challenging work she performed, and then document her skills so thoroughly is probably going to serve us extremely well."

achieved can be a wonderful boost to your confidence during a challenging job hunt. When a few disappointments inevitably occur, a written record of all that you accomplished reassures you of your positive value in the marketplace.

THE PORTABLE PORTFOLIO

When you interviewed for internship positions, you probably had sample class projects available to demonstrate your abilities to prospective supervisors. Demonstrating new internship skills to prospective employers is accomplished in much the same manner, this time using a far more professional work product.

A collection of carefully selected, high-quality work samples, the portfolio represents your best internship efforts. Ideally, it demonstrates how a broad combination of skills—research, writing, organization, and technical knowledge, for example—has been applied to specific projects. Unlike the capsule summaries that appear on your résumé, the portfolio provides direct proof of what you can do.

Many law offices expect job candidates to offer a portfolio of sample work. Schools also sometimes require a portfolio of internship work samples as a prerequisite for academic credit. Whether assembled for prospective employers, your school, or both, the portfolio is an unbeatable method for documenting your new skills.

The portfolio is a documentation technique that every intern should use, regardless of what additional methods may also be used. No other method is so valuable to your job search.

SUPPORT YOUR SCHOOL'S ASSESSMENT PROCESS

For most interns, the internship is an academic undertaking. If academic credit is being granted, schools are obliged to record and evaluate your performance in some way. Because internship work does not lend itself to uniform quizzes or exams, individualized methods are normally used to evaluate an intern's performance. Consequently, you may find that some of the methods suggested here and in later chapters are also required by your school.

The documentation of many interns, taken together, tells your school in what ways the internship program is successful and also where changes might be needed in the future. By keeping good records of your learning, you may be providing a valuable service to your school as well as to yourself.

If procedures are in place for evaluating interns' on-the-job learning for academic credit, you must follow your school's instructions carefully. If your school allows flexibility in your choice of documentation procedures, subsequent chapters may provide useful ideas. In addition, consider supplementing your school's procedures with one or two methods of your own to strengthen your job search.

POINT OF ETHICS
Creating Credibility

When your internship ends, serious judgments will be made about the experience you had. Those judgments can affect your career for years to come. For example, your internship grade will be greatly influenced by your direc-

THE STUDENT'S PERSPECTIVE 13.2: RITA

The Accuracy Lawyers Love

"What happened with that job interview last week?" Rita's internship director asked. "Any news?"

"Yes!" Rita beamed. "I can hardly believe it. I'm going to be working for Tom Reilly, one of the most well-known criminal defense lawyers in this area!

"I was kind of surprised when I got the news because he was not easy to interview with, believe me. I felt like I was on the witness stand or something. He wanted so many details.

"For example, he asked me if I had ever drafted a Motion in Limine. Well, I drafted a lot of motions as an intern at the Pubic Defender's Office, but I couldn't remember if this was one I did. So I explained about the record I kept of new skills I acquired during my internship. I told him I wanted to check, just to be sure, and promised to get back to him the next morning.

"Well, I couldn't find a Motion in Limine on my list, but I did find several other technical motions I had worked on, so I mentioned those. And he offered me the job!

"It turns out that he only asked about the Motion in Limine to see whether I knew what I was talking about. And the motions list I came back with impressed him more than whether I knew about that particular motion. He was also impressed that I didn't try to bluff him. I'm someone he can trust to be 'thorough and accurate,' he says. How about that?"

The director smiled. "That's what a lot of these people look for. Obviously they found it in you, Rita."

tor's perception about what you learned and how you performed. Career advice may be shaped by your advisor's perception of your experience as an intern. Perhaps most importantly, prospective employers will be quick to draw conclusions about your internship experiences.

If no documentation is available, some of those conclusions may be the result of inaccurate notions about you—or about internships in general— rather than a reaction to the experience you actually had. You will want to be sure these crucial judgments are based on accurate, firsthand information. Documented learning ensures accuracy and fairness in such evaluations.

Documenting your learning also helps you assess your own career strengths and weaknesses. By documenting new skills and learning experiences, you *can accurately identify your strengths and promote them effectively to future employers.* As a result, no one is misled about what you can or can not do—not even you.

With good documentation, a real estate paralegal intern can quickly list specific transactions he or she has become familiar with, the procedural obstacles that surrounded their completion, and the success that nevertheless followed. A student who interned with a collections attorney can list specific procedural skills and knowledge to impress the billing department of a Health Maintenance Organization (HMO). Taking advantage of good documentation throughout their internship, both these interns are maximizing their job prospects and perhaps also their internship grades. And neither intern is likely to mislead anyone—even inadvertently—by overstating the skills they acquired.

Employers respect candidates who thoroughly know themselves. Legal professionals especially appreciate having proof of the work you can do, either in a portfolio or through other forms of documentation. They value the candid, well-informed self-evaluation a candidate can provide when skills and experience have been documented.

With a detailed record of skills and learning experiences to refer to whenever the need arises, you bring an informed honesty to all career decisions. You help ensure that the judgments being made by others are based on facts, not assumptions. You can *tailor future claims about your skills and experience to the record you have*—ensuring accuracy, honesty, and even written proof, if called for. In short, you will be able to present yourself as a job candidate whose credibility cannot be doubted.

EXERCISES

1. Review the list of learning objectives you created in response to Exercise 8 in Chapter 1, including general employment skills, law school skills (if any), and skills in the practice area of your choice. Check off the objectives that you have achieved so far. Circle the objectives you have not yet achieved.
2. Create a plan for achieving the circled, unmet objectives during the time remaining in your internship. Consult with others for suggestions: your office supervisor, your school's internship director, and other student interns, if you wish.
3. Think about whether your learning objectives have changed since your internship began. What skills or experiences have you identified as desirable that were not on your original list? Add them to your list of learning objectives.
4. Discuss your revised list of learning objectives with others, such as your office supervisor and the internship director at your school. Ask other student interns whether they have had experience in the areas you are adding.
5. Create a plan for achieving the new learning objectives identified in Exercise 4, again consulting with others for suggestions: your office supervisor, your school's internship director, and other student interns.

ENDNOTE

1. See Chapter 4.

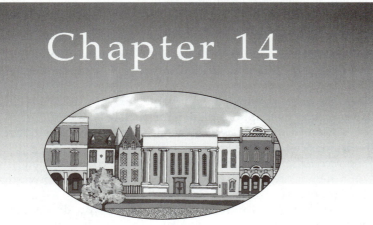

Chapter 14

What to Document: Identifying New Skills

L ike students everywhere, you may have learned to rely heavily on teachers to document your learning for you. Using exams, quizzes, reports, and class projects, instructors traditionally assume all responsibility for identifying what students have learned. Because of instructors' advanced knowledge and experience, this approach usually works well. Unfortunately, it relegates students to a mostly passive role in the evaluative process. After a lifetime of depending on teachers to do it for you, identifying your own learning may feel strange and uncomfortable, at first.

Nevertheless, identifying your own learning is not the mysterious process it seems. If you have followed the suggestions in Chapters 8 and 9 on record keeping for your internship work, then *many records already exist from which you can develop detailed documentation* of internship learning. The first section of this chapter helps you use existing records effectively.

Focusing on distinct areas of learning then makes the identification process manageable. Following the suggestions in the second section, identify general work skills for broad application in many future employment settings. The third section then helps you identify technical, law-related areas of learning. In addition, no intern should overlook the expanding network of professional contacts that internships facilitate. The fourth section shows you how to track that learning area for future development. And finally, the last section guides you through the whys and hows of documenting internship cases and clients to avoid conflicts of interest in future employment settings.

 ## BEGIN WITH EXISTING RECORDS

Evidence is everywhere of new skills you have learned on the job. Your personal internship records reflect countless achievements. Records kept by your office also provide many good indicators.

Listed below are several kinds of records you can review to find abundant examples of internship learning.

- Your *pocket calendar or personal planner* contains information on the assignments you were given. Using that information, think about both general work skills and specialized, legal skills that were involved.
- Your *old to-do lists* and written instructions provide even more details about projects you performed.
- The *time sheets* or time slips prepared for your office's billing functions contain brief descriptions of all your billable activities.
- The *total amount of the billable hours* you produced may be an impressive indicator of your skills level in itself.
- The *checklist or tickler sheet* inside the front cover of client files may jog your memory regarding the documents, research, and investigative work you completed.
- Review *client files* to locate the documents you drafted. Ask for your office's permission to copy and keep these documents—or at least your original portions of them.
- Also review client files to identify examples of new case management skills, client liaison work, and organizational abilities.
- Your *personal reference file* is another source of work samples that testify to your internship learning.

GENERAL WORK SKILLS

In identifying their internship learning, students have a tendency to overlook general work skills, believing they are somehow unimportant. The truth is that general work skills are sometimes the most valuable skills of all, because they transfer to a wide variety of work settings both in and outside of the conventional law office. For many students, these are the skills that should be heavily emphasized on résumés and in job interviews.

As you review records of your internship activities, try to identify examples of the following general work skills. They are listed roughly in the same order in which many employers seem to value them.

- *Working on your own initiative.* Example: Noticing—without being told—that several additional steps were needed on a certain project and completing those steps with little or no assistance.
- *Organizational ability.* Examples: Monitoring the progress of a complex client matter including the coordination of others' work; also, bringing order and clarity to a large, disorganized client file.
- *Handling multiple tasks.* Example: Maintaining progress on several projects or client matters simultaneously.
- *Computer expertise.* Examples: Document assembly, (preferably using macros), database management, spreadsheets, Westlaw or Lexis, Internet research, automated office management systems (including time and billing systems), and specialized transactional software such as for real estate transfers, probate, or estate planning.
- *Writing and drafting skills.* Example: Virtually anything one full page or longer that involved organizing detailed information and conveying it clearly.
- *Legal research skills.* Examples: A research memorandum to your supervisor. Alternatively, you might list legal questions you researched and the legal resources used.

- *Factual investigation skills.* Examples: Any information gathering you may have performed by phone (such as to governmental agencies), by mail (such as for Freedom of Information Act requests), in personal interviews, at courthouses, at registries of deeds or probate, on the Internet, or by other means.
- *Interpersonal skills.* Example: Instances in which you had to communicate effectively with clients or others, particularly in difficult situations.
- *Problem-solving ability.* Example: Quickly thinking of a solution in a crisis situation.
- *Effective follow-up.* Example: Being able to follow directions without a hitch and complete the assignment on time. This is a basic requirement in every office. Be prepared to cite examples of this key skill.

In addition to the items just listed, you may have some unusual achievement you could include as an indicator of serious learning during your internship. For example, maybe you assisted with a stressful, high-profile case, working effectively in spite of media attention. Or, perhaps you organized a major project for your state paralegal organization, developing sophisticated organizational and communications skills in the process. Such achievements are also worth documenting.

The key is to consider every internship activity with this question in mind: What useful things did it teach me? Internship learning goes far beyond technical, law office procedures. To maximize your career prospects both in and out of conventional law office settings, recognize examples of the broader, general work skills outlined here and be ready to cite examples of them in reports to your school and especially in your job search.

TECHNICAL, LAW-RELATED SKILLS

After identifying general work skills, you then need to identify the skills that relate specifically to legal work and to the specialty areas of your choice. The technical skills sought by one employer may be somewhat different from the skills sought by another, and you want to maximize your options. To ensure the widest possible variety of career choices, document as large an inventory of technical skills as possible.

This section divides technical skills into three major areas. The first skills area is that of office systems—important in a wide range of employment settings. The second skills area covers litigation-support skills, which are useful in a majority of law office settings. And finally, the third skills area includes specialized skills in transactional work such as contracts, corporate law, and real estate.

Skills in Office Systems

A working knowledge of law office systems is especially valuable in solo practices, where paralegals not only assist with client matters but typically help manage the office's day-to-day operations as well. Your knowledge of office systems is also useful in corporate and nonprofit settings. Because these categories probably offer the greatest number of opportunities for conventional, entry-level paralegal employment, documenting your skills in this area can be highly beneficial.

Use the following list as a starting point in identifying what systems have become familiar to you. Then inventory all the systems in which you now have expertise, noting examples of experience you have had with each system.

Also, note whether the system you experienced was manual or automated. If it was automated, record the name of the computer program you used.

Try to document experience in several of the following:

- Filing systems
- Timekeeping and billing systems
- Docketing or tickler systems
- Conflicts-checking systems
- Client trust accounts
- Law office operating accounts
- In-house communications, including memoranda, notices, e-mail, and document exchange on a computer network

Experience with computerized systems is especially important. Increasingly, offices want paralegals with sophisticated computer skills. In fact, offices that are poorly automated may seek your expertise in implementing better systems. Even if the networking and software programs you worked with in your internship office are different from what is used elsewhere, your general familiarity with such programs is of value. For example, the steps needed to work with one time-and-billing software program are usually very similar to the steps needed to work with another. Learning a slightly different version usually takes only a few minutes, so generic familiarity with such systems should always be emphasized.

Litigation-Support Skills

Law offices often see litigation as falling into narrow areas of specialization. Plaintiffs' personal injury work, medical malpractice defense, and debt collection are three examples of this narrow view. Although that view may be appropriate for very experienced paralegals, the entry-level intern is smart to look at litigation-support skills from a much broader perspective.

Litigation formalities may be structured differently in different courts, but all civil court actions have certain basics in common. Interns who are not routinely involved in litigation may find that some assignments nevertheless develop litigation-like skills. Identify skills you are developing in each of the following categories for possible use in your job search.

- *Investigation and fact gathering:* This category covers a wide range of activities including, for example, interviewing witnesses, gathering medical and employment information, and verifying financial data.
- *Legal research:* This includes statutes, case law, government regulations, and court rules.
- *Drafting and filing pleadings:* This normally includes complaints or answers.
- *Service of process:* This includes, for example, drafting the necessary documents, making arrangements with a process server, and verifying that service was made.
- *Formal discovery procedures:* Examples include drafting interrogatories, requesting admissions, arranging depositions, and summarizing deposition transcripts.
- *Drafting and filing motions:* This may also include the drafting of supporting affidavits and memoranda of law.
- *Trial preparation:* Examples include organizing a trial notebook, lining up witnesses, and preparing exhibits.
- *Enforcing judgments:* Typically, this involves preparing documents for effecting liens, attachments, wage garnishments, and so on.

Try grouping your litigation skills under these general categories for later reference (see Table 14.1 for an example).

When interviewing at an office where the area of specialization is *different* from that of your internship, emphasize your skills and experience in terms of the basic litigation steps listed above. You might make a convincing case for easy transfer of your litigation skills from one area of specialization to another.

For example, good fact-gathering skills are extremely valuable in virtually any law-related service, from divorces to the administration of public benefits. And although filing procedures may vary greatly from one court to another, proven skill in drafting, rules checking, and independent follow-up may make you a "quick study" in a new litigation area.

Specialized Transactional Work

As your paralegal courses undoubtedly taught you, not all legal work involves litigation. Much of it involves the legalities of doing some sort of business: buying, selling, leasing, building, making applications, seeking approvals, and creating or dissolving businesses themselves. Even giving things away often involves complex legal procedures as in creating a will or providing charitable services. Most governmental activities also require legal knowledge.

As you review the following list, *be alert to "overlap areas" where work in one area of practice takes you into others areas as well.* For example, the intern of a busy

Table 14.1

Sample List of Litigation Skills

Fact Gathering and Investigation
- Processed medical releases
- Collected medical records (doctors, hospitals, etc.)
- Summarized medical losses
- Conducted asset checks (bank records, deeds, mortgages, liens, etc.)
- Obtained employment histories

Legal Research
- Checked court rules on new appellate procedures
- Found all state statutes applying to wetlands easements (for municipal board hearing on subdivision)

Pleadings
- Drafted summons and complaints for several personal injury cases, including one with multiple defendants
- Reviewed answers and summarized them (personal injury)

Discovery
- Prepared interrogatories for opponent (personal injury)
- Prepared answers to interrogatories (personal injury)
- Requested admissions (personal injury)
- Summarized deposition transcripts (personal injury)

Trial Preparation
- Prepared exhibits (municipal board hearing on subdivision)
- Prepared trial notebook (personal injury case)
- Issued subpoenas (personal injury case)

divorce lawyer may be asked to check the history of deeds and mortgages at the local registry. So, in addition to litigation-like divorce practice skills, this intern also learned to conduct title searches—a real estate skill. Similarly, a paralegal working in an insurance office may be exposed to contracts law (affecting insurance policies), regulatory law (state insurance commission regulations), and litigation-support skills (investigating and defending claims).

No matter what your area of internship work, you are likely to have many incidents of overlap into other specialized areas. Review your internship records in the light of the following list and note all examples of such overlap. The more overlapping skills you can identify, the broader your career prospects become.

- *Business formation:* preparing documents for creating partnerships, corporations, limited liability entities, proprietorships, and mergers and acquisitions
- *Corporate maintenance:* preparing minutes of shareholders and stockholders meetings, complying with blue-sky laws, and preparing for stock issuance and redemptions
- *Contracts:* drafting or reviewing agreements for services, products, real estate, and credit transactions
- *Real estate:* preparing for purchase, sale, leasing, mortgaging, building and development, or foreclosure; also real estate management, and researching and abstracting titles
- *Employment law:* preparing the paperwork for hiring, dismissal, or administering employment benefits; also assisting with governmental compliance procedures
- *Regulatory law:* researching and assisting with carrying out environmental, land use, workplace safety, product safety, consumer protection, and taxation rules
- *Benefits law:* providing procedural assistance with unemployment compensation, Social Security, Aid to Families with Dependent Children, Medicaid, Medicare
- *Estate planning and probate:* drafting wills, trusts, and health care directives; also probating decedents' estates
- *Intellectual property:* assisting in acquiring and protecting patents, copyrights, and trademarks
- *Bankruptcy and collections:* assisting debtors' or creditors' attorneys in resolving debt matters

Transactional work does more than create expertise in specialized areas of the law. It may also lead to skills not readily acquired in a litigation practice. Because transactional work focuses mainly on finding solutions and bringing people together (rather than turning them into adversaries), it may take communications and interpersonal skills to a higher level than litigation work alone might achieve. For example, an intern might develop strong mediation skills in a consumer protection agency or other government office. In an office that represents a real estate developer, the intern may have to balance the competing demands of many subcontractors. Useful in a multitude of work settings, these skills are well worth documenting.

YOUR CAREER NETWORK

Most likely, you have made many professional contacts during your internship. The number and nature of these contacts may have little importance academically, but they have tremendous significance to you personally.

Every professional contact represents someone who may be able to help in your search for employment.

Some day, one of these individuals might be a source of job referrals or letters of recommendation. Others may be a source of guidance or assistance in carrying out a future assignment. You might need their advice on unfamiliar procedures or needed resources.

Remembering who these people are, what they do, and where you can find them could be important to you in the future. Consequently, identifying these people and their areas of expertise is a significant aspect of internship learning. Such documentation should be preserved for future reference.

To ensure that you can reestablish contact with anyone who might be helpful, compile a permanent list of your professional contacts (see Table 14.2). Along with each person's name, also record each one's office affiliation, title or position, address, phone number, fax number, and e-mail address (if available). Because professionals change jobs from time to time, putting a date on each entry helps you recognize when an address and phone number may need updating.

THE STUDENT'S PERSPECTIVE 14.1: TRACY
If Only I Could Remember His Name . . .

Addressing a group of students on career development strategies, Tracy shared what she thought was one of the most useful tactics she had tried.

"I was always one of those people who could never remember names. It became a serious professional handicap that caused me quite a lot of embarrassment. I'd run into familiar faces at paralegal society functions or at the courthouse, for example, and I'd have no idea who some of those people were. I bluffed my way through many awkward conversations, earnestly hoping the other person wouldn't notice how clueless I was.

"One of the worst incidents was at the clerk's office at the Superior Court. I was dropping off some papers for filing—in a rush as usual. A tall, skinny guy in a sweater walked by and hit me with that dreaded, "Hi, Tracy! How are you?" Vaguely thinking he might be an errand-runner from a local law office, I was a little curt in my response.

"Well, he was *not* a mere errand-runner. I later found out it was the newly appointed Clerk of the Superior Court. My secretary reminded me that I had met this man a few times when he was an associate in a nearby office. Now he oversees the processing of every document we file with that court! He has become someone on whom my office depends heavily—definitely not someone I want to offend.

"Because of that incident, I vowed to overcome this 'handicap' of mine and really work at knowing who people are. I started keeping a list of my professional acquaintances, including where they are and what they do. Just the simple act of writing these things down helps me remember them better, and I review the list now and then to refresh my memory.

"I also try to update the whereabouts of people on my list as often as possible. For instance, when law partners I know have split up to start their own practices, I add that change to my list, noting two prospective employers where before there was only one. I do the same thing with the paralegals on my list when they change jobs. And if someone I know becomes a judge or an official of some kind, you can be sure I make a note of it!

"I find people are flattered—and a great deal more helpful to you—when you enthusiastically remember who they are."

Use the following categories as a starting point. Write the name of each professional acquaintance you can think of who corresponds to each category.

- Lawyers
- Paralegals
- Secretaries
- Elected officials
- Government agency personnel
- Courthouse personnel
- Clerks and officials at registries of deeds and probate
- Law enforcement personnel
- Banking professionals
- Insurance professionals
- Real estate professionals
- Personnel at nonprofit human service organizations

Organizing your list of professional contacts according to areas of expertise or occupation makes forgotten contacts easier to locate than listing them

---

Table 14.2

Sample List of Professional Contacts

Lawyers
- *Henry Z. Brocken* (partner)   Brocken & Laufer, P.A.
- *Marilyn X. Laufer* (partner)   987 Lawyers Row
- *Michael Y. Bison* (associate)   Anytown, NH 12345
                                    Phone: (206) 555-4567
                                    Fax: (206) 555-8910

> *NOTES:* Henry is former president of county bar. Civil litigation (mostly environmental). Marilyn does mainly municipal work. Michael is developing a practice mostly in real estate. Supportive of paralegals.

- *Chester Q. Finney*
  979 Lawyers Row
  Anytown, NH 12345
  Phone: (206) 555-2435
  Fax: (206) 555-1324
  e-mail: finneyq@funlaw.com
  NOTES: Chester is big on computerization—knows everything. Former engineer, now patent attorney.

Paralegals
- *Geri D. Larimer*—Brocken & Laufer
  Very experienced in environmental litigation, municipal procedures, and real estate.

- *Bernie V. Shedd*—works for Chester Finney
  Very knowledgeable about computer systems and patent procedures.

Elected Officials
- *Gertrude F. Stein,* Register of Deeds, Anytown County
  County Office Building
  Anytown, NH 12345
  Phone: (206) 555-0001
  Very helpful when needed. Does not tolerate noise or chatter at the registry.

- *Mavin P. O'Boise,* Chair, Anytown Planning Board
  Anytown City Hall
  12 S. Main Street
  Anytown, NH 12345
  Phone: (206) 555-2223
  Insists rules be followed to the letter. Has a son, Brad, attending my college, majoring in geology.

all alphabetically. Specialty practice areas might also provide additional categories for you. When many names appear under one category, arrange the names within that category alphabetically, if you wish.

Make a permanent record of this list. Leave room for additional names and data in the future. As you conduct your job search in the months to come, your network of professional contacts will surely expand.

Your growing list of professional contacts can be kept by any of several methods: in a computer database, in an address book kept only for this purpose, on file cards in a file box, or on a Rolodex. Use whichever method seems most convenient to you.

POINT OF ETHICS

Future Conflicts Checks

Your documentation is not complete until you also make a list of the clients for whom you have done any confidential legal work. This list will enable you to check for conflicts of interest in the future (see Table 14.3).

In other paralegal courses, you may have learned that conflicts of interest most often occur when a lawyer changes jobs. If the client of a lawyer's new office is in an adversarial position to a client that the lawyer represented in the past, then that lawyer may have a conflict of interest. The newly hired lawyer—and possibly the entire office—could be disqualified from involvement in the current case.

This rule exists because lawyers usually know confidential information about their clients. It would be unfair for that knowledge later to be used to a client's disadvantage. Allowing that to happen, even inadvertently, would destroy the possibility of a trusting relationship between clients and their lawyers. Allowing the misuse of information about former clients would also motivate law firms to hire lawyers who once represented the firm's

Table 14.3

Sample Client List

Office:	Attorney Barbara T. Lazaras (1997 Internship)
1. **CLIENT:**	WWW Wonderful Widgets Corporation, Inc.
	34 Industrial Highway
	Anytown, Kansas
Related parties:	Wally W. Widget, President, Director, and 50% Shareholder
	Wanda Widget, Treasurer, Director, and 50% Shareholder
Case:	*Anytown Neighborhood Association v. WWW Wonderful Widgets*
Date:	Filed June 1997 in Anytown County Superior Court, Docket No. ASC6-12ANA-97
Cause of action:	Nuisance
2. **CLIENT:**	Ronald Landowner, Plaintiff
	1234 Pleasant Street
	Anytown, Missouri
Related parties:	Mrs. Ronald Landowner (client's wife and co-owner of subject property, in joint tenancy)
Case:	*Ronald Landowner v. Anytown Board of Zoning and Adjustment*
Date:	Filed July 1997 in Anytown County Superior Court, Docket No. ASC7-7RL-97
Cause of action:	Seeking reversal of zoning decision; violation of state constitution

opponents and pick their brains for damaging information. Such a practice could never be tolerated in our justice system.

If the newly hired lawyer's conflict of interest is known at the outset, then the situation can often be managed with no harm to anyone involved. But if the conflict is not discovered until the office is well into the case, then irreparable harm may be done to that case and to the law firm involved.

To prevent these problems, law offices require newly hired lawyers to provide a list of the cases on which they have worked in the past. This information is checked against the office's own list of clients to see whether any conflicts appear. In most offices, the checking process is repeated each time a new client is accepted by the firm.[1]

In many jurisdictions, a law firm can be disqualified from a case due to a paralegal's conflict of interest just as it can for a lawyer's conflict, so a paralegal's previous casework may have to be cross-checked, too. To protect themselves and their clients, growing numbers of offices are asking newly hired paralegals for the same kind of case list demanded of newly hired lawyers. As a job candidate, every paralegal intern should be prepared for this possibility.

Of course, the information on your client list is highly confidential. It is not compiled for your school's benefit. It certainly should never be shared with friends or family. It is provided only to future employers and only after you have been hired, so that continued confidentiality can be ensured.

Your list of cases should include the following information:

- The full name and address of your office's client
- The case name, date, docket number, and cause of action (nature of the case)
- The full names of related parties such as co-owners of disputed property or directors, officers, and major shareholders of a corporation

Even if a prospective employer does *not* inquire about former clients and cases, discovering that you have a list available can be an impressive factor in your favor. It shows you are keenly attuned to the ethical implications of law practice and prepared for all contingencies. Having such a list demonstrates your willingness to take responsibility for protecting the office's clients—in ways the office might not yet have considered.

You may change jobs several times in the years to come. Each time you do, this list may once again become critically important. Update your client list regularly, such as when you undergo a salary review, when your hiring contract is renewed, or on each anniversary of your hiring. And never leave a law office position without making sure your list is up to date.

EXERCISES

1. In preparation for the documentation techniques outlined in the next chapter, do the following things:
   a. Review your internship records as follows:
      (1) Your personal calendar or planner
      (2) Your old to-do lists
      (3) Your time sheets or time slips
      (4) The checklist or tickler sheet in client files
      (5) The contents of client files
      (6) Your reference file, if you have one

b. As you review these records, note instances in which you have demonstrated the following general work skills:
  (1) Working on your own initiative
  (2) Organizational ability
  (3) Handling multiple tasks
  (4) Computer expertise
  (5) Writing and drafting
  (6) Legal research
  (7) Factual investigation
  (8) Interpersonal skills
  (9) Problem-solving ability
  (10) Effective follow-up
  (11) Other skills or special achievements
c. In reviewing your records, also make a list of examples of the technical, law-related skills you have developed, including
  (1) Expertise in law office systems
  (2) Litigation-support skills
  (3) Specialized transactional work
2. Make a list of your professional contacts. Keep this list for use in your job search and for further development throughout your career.
3. Make a list of the clients for whom you have performed work. Keep this list to check for conflicts of interest in future employment.

ENDNOTE

1. Chapter 8 (on "Filing Systems") discusses conflicts-checking systems in further detail.

Chapter 15

How to Document: Instructions and Samples

Several methods are commonly used to document internship learning. Each of these techniques is covered in a separate section of this chapter. They include (a) the reflective journal, (b) periodic reports, (c) a portfolio of selected work samples, (d) self-evaluation forms or checklists, (e) testimonial letters from your supervisors or coworkers, (f) supervisors' evaluation forms, (g) an hourly log, and (h) a capstone report combining several of the foregoing documentation methods.

Some of the methods discussed in this chapter may be required by your school; others may not. The descriptions contained here will help you understand the rationale behind commonly used documentation methods, including the advantages and difficulties of each. These descriptions will also help you maximize the effectiveness of each method you use.

Schools use these documentation methods for many purposes: advising interns on career options, recommending future course selections, assessing and reporting internship content for school accreditation and approval processes, and—most important from the intern's point of view—grading each intern's performance. So, of course, *you should follow your school's instructions precisely for any documentation methods that your school requires,* even if those instructions are somewhat different from the descriptions and samples provided here.

You may also want to supplement your school's documentation procedures with one or two procedures of your own. For example, creating a portfolio of work samples or obtaining testimonial letters helps greatly in your job search, even though your school may not require them. Review and evaluate each method to determine its usefulness as a supplementary technique.

▣ THE REFLECTIVE JOURNAL

Journal keeping is a self-evaluation method often used by interns in other disciplines, such as business and psychology. It can be very beneficial to paralegal interns as well. A journal of this kind contains descriptions of each day's activities and the intern's thoughts and observations about them. A sample journal entry appears in Table 15.1.

What makes a journal different from other documentation methods is its *reflective component*, not only reporting but also evaluating the intern's experience. In an internship journal, the intern records such things as

- The dates and hours worked
- The tasks accomplished each day
- The skills developed in performing those tasks
- What the intern enjoyed or disliked about each day's activities
- What insights were gained regarding the work environment
- How new insights affect future career choices

Usually, a new journal entry is added with each workday. A single entry can be anywhere from a paragraph to a page or more in length, depending on the activities being reported and the intern's thoughts about them.

The main advantage of a journal is that your activities, thoughts, and observations are recorded daily, while they are fresh in your mind. Observations that would otherwise be quickly forgotten are committed to paper for later evaluation by you, your school's director, and perhaps your career advisor. Strengths and weaknesses are identified early in your internship. Patterns

Table 15.1

Sample Journal Entry

February 4, 1998
Five hours: 9–12 A.M., 1–3 P.M.

Today was even more exciting than yesterday. Juanita decided to let me handle my first dispute from beginning to end. I'm terribly nervous about it, but I've decided to just take it one step at a time. I called the consumer and got all the information I needed—that took over a half-hour. Then I composed a letter to the merchant following Consumer Division guidelines and using some of Juanita's letters as examples. I'll follow up with a phone call to the merchant next week. From what I've seen, merchants and business owners can be difficult to talk to. I can't wait to see how that goes.

I staffed the hotline for a short time. Next, I organized several big files that were a mess. This chore has become easier now that I know the sequence of the office's procedures. However, the best thing was sitting in on a mediation session for the first time. That was truly the high point of my day.

The session began with the consumer and the store manager not even speaking to each other. But Jim, the mediator, was good at keeping both sides calm and gradually drawing them out. By the time the session ended, the parties had agreed on two points: the product was still under warranty, and the store's normal practice is to exchange the defective item for the consumer. The parties will come back for one more session next week and decide how to resolve two things: (1) the fact that the customer eventually disposed of the defective item rather than taking it back, and (2) the fact that the customer still owes one or two payments.

I am learning so much from this. For example, I've learned that there is almost always some way to compromise. It just takes creativity and a lot of practice, I think. Persistence seems to accomplish a lot, too—slow, calm, repeated persistence. I also see how much can be accomplished when you "objectify" the dispute, as Juanita says—focus on solving the problem rather than finding fault. I can put these principles to use in so many ways, in so many different areas of life!

I'm beginning to think that I would really love to be a divorce mediator some day. Now, that would be challenging! Of course, I would need additional training for that. But this internship is a great start.

QUICK TIP 15.1

Show serious learning by writing legal terms correctly. If you are unsure about the capitalization of legal names and terms, do not guess. Check the rules before you write. Do the same for spelling, grammatical usage, and proper use of abbreviations.

emerge as your journal progresses, perhaps suggesting career directions you might not have considered.

Journal keeping usually works best when learning is most intense and there are many new things to absorb, such as in short-term internships (a month or less in duration) or during the first weeks of a longer internship. Thoughtful analysis of each day's activities helps the intern make sense of new challenges and identify rapidly developing skills as they emerge. After becoming comfortable with internship work, students sometimes prefer a less demanding form of documentation.

PERIODIC REPORTS

Many schools require interns to prepare periodic reports summarizing recent internship experience. Required content, length, and format vary widely from school to school. Nevertheless, periodic reports usually have certain basics in common. *Minimum requirements commonly include (1) an overview of tasks performed on the job and (2) an analysis of what was learned as a result—new skills, technical knowledge, and career insights.* When required in place of a journal, periodic reports are often accompanied by an hourly log (discussed later in this chapter) verifying the number of hours spent on internship work.

Written Reports

Periodic written reports differ from journal keeping in several ways. Journal entries are written every workday, but periodic reports are done on a weekly, biweekly, or monthly basis. Some schools require one written report at the midpoint of the internship and another when the internship ends.

Rather than analyzing each day's events, periodic reports function as a general summary of tasks the intern performed, highlighting experiences that led to significant learning. An example appears in Table 15.2.

Periodic written reports work best when the daily self-evaluation of journal keeping is not needed. Interns with several weeks on the job, for example, may no longer have dramatic new experiences to report every day. Periodic written reports may also be a more manageable method for directors to monitor many interns simultaneously.

At many schools, written reports are also taken as an important indicator of your writing ability. After all, a major goal for paralegal internships is to improve writing skills. So your school may put a great deal of emphasis on the writing proficiency shown in these reports.

As you write each report, begin by organizing your thoughts in a logical manner. Choose your words carefully, checking a dictionary often. Use legal terms correctly. Proofread for spelling, punctuation, and grammatical errors. And finally, let your report have the crisp, clean appearance of an office memo.

Oral Reports

In programs in which interns meet periodically in a class or seminar, oral reports may be required. Often, the oral report covers the same elements as the written report and may even be based on a written report prepared for the same class. However, oral reports achieve still broader career goals.

First, *oral, classroom reports allow each intern to vicariously experience the different work settings of other interns.* For example, your observations about life

Table 15.2

Sample Periodic Report

To: Edward Lead, Internship Director
From: Jeri Q. Goode
Date: February 13, 1998
Re: Internship Report #2

During this second two-week period, I continued many of the same tasks that I was involved with during the first two-week period: gathering medical information, answering interrogatories, and preparing other discovery documents. In response to my request for more varied assignments, Attorney Pagliani also gave me a trust to draft. It turned out to be a great deal more difficult than I expected. I've spent a good portion of the last two days on it. In addition, I covered for the receptionist one afternoon, which was an interesting change of pace for me.

I've learned several things. First, I've learned to speak up to lawyers! It may not sound like much to someone more experienced in legal work, but it was very hard for me to do. Mr. Pagliani is somewhat intimidating (even though he does not try to be), and I was apprehensive about his reaction to my request for different work. But he immediately understood and was actually very accommodating. I learned that if you explain your reasons, have a few specific suggestions to make, and appear calm and confident, they listen!

I think I have also resolved my confusion about using form books for drafting things. Mr. Pagliani says it is permissible to use them often. He does it himself, all the time. I just have to be selective about the language I am adopting, check several sources and use the best one, and modify the wording to meet the client's particular situation. It can be very time consuming, but obviously less so than if I tried to draft everything myself.

Surprisingly, filling in for the receptionist turned out to be a good learning experience. For phone calls I have made in the past to clients, hospitals, and others, I always planned in advance what I was going to say. Acting as receptionist, there was no chance to do that because I never knew who was calling or what it was about. This experience gave me a chance to practice responding to unforeseen questions and problems in a professional manner. I do not think I would want to do this every day, but I am glad I had that one afternoon of experience.

A major highlight may be coming up soon. Next week, I am hoping to accompany Attorney Pagliani to court and sit at counsel table to assist with locating documents, tracking exhibits, and taking notes. This is also in response to my request for more varied assignments. So, I am seeing real results from my new-found assertiveness and improved communications skills.

---

in a large law firm may be a fascinating eye-opener to students interning with a government agency. Similarly, someone's report about the nonprofit environment may be extremely enlightening to you. As employment opportunities for paralegals become more diverse, this informational exchange is increasingly valuable to all students.

Second, sharing oral reports allows you and your colleagues to understand how common some internship difficulties are and to collectively brainstorm for solutions. For example, after reporting an incident with an unreasonable client, other interns may be able to offer helpful advice based on similar experiences. To promote this collective approach, solicit listeners' questions and comments after presenting your report.

Third, delivering oral reports gives you the chance to develop professional speaking skills. As you relate your experiences, let your demeanor and your style of speech reflect the competence you have acquired at the office. Stand tall, speak clearly, and use complete sentences. Consider dressing professionally for the occasion to demonstrate the businesslike image you are acquiring.

Sharing oral reports with other interns does more than help you identify your own learning; it multiplies internship learning many times over. Consider trying this technique even if your school does not routinely require it. You and several colleagues might meet informally every week or two for this purpose. Alternatively, ask the paralegal club at your school to sponsor a few sessions of this kind. Invite newer students to attend for a realistic preview of internship experiences. With relatively little organizational effort, many will benefit from the verbal exchange.

THE WORK PORTFOLIO

Journal entries, written reports, evaluation forms, and testimonial letters always present some risk that the information they contain may be colored by personal biases. An overly critical supervisor, for example, might overlook some hard-earned skills. An unduly optimistic intern may unknowingly over-state them. School administrators and accrediting agencies are often aware of these possibilities. Future employers are especially skeptical about them.

A portfolio eliminates suspicions of biased reporting. It allows employers and others to draw their own conclusions about your skill level. Providing tangible evidence of reported achievements, a portfolio facilitates independent eval-uation by each reader. It may even indicate skills you did not know you had.

To create a work portfolio, begin by reviewing your reference file, if you have one.[1] If you do not have a reference file or if your reference file does not contain sufficient work samples, then review client files with which you were involved.

Identify all the documents you have drafted, choosing at least three that meet the criteria listed below. The shorter your documents, the more of them you should include. Keep the following elements in mind as you select sam-ples of written work:

- *Complexity.* Your best research memorandum, for example, is one that relies on several legal authorities. A civil complaint containing multiple claims or litigants is more impressive than a simple one. And a letter that addresses several different issues shows greater ability than a one-issue note to a client.
- *Flawlessness.* Use only samples that are typed or word processed, proof-read, and error free.
- *Length.* Longer documents usually demonstrate more impressive skills than short ones. Exceptions are documents containing mostly boilerplate language adopted completely from other sources without change; such documents are not the best choice.
- *Creativity.* Try to include drafting work that involved selecting and com-bining language from various forms books, including tailor-made modifi-cations of your own creation—or writing that shows skillful handling of a difficult issue.
- *Versatility.* Choose as wide a variety of work samples as possible. Let each one demonstrate a different kind of expertise.

Sometimes, writing samples alone are not indicative of an intern's best work. Interns in non-law-office settings may have drafted very few docu-ments. Instead, they may have been mediating consumer disputes, screening and referring *pro bono* clients, or interviewing and investigating. Even con-ventional law office interns sometimes find that their proudest achievements had nothing to do with drafting. What if an intern implemented a litigation database and retrieval system for a major trial, or speeded up the office's forms work with significant changes in their document-assembly system? How can evidence of these achievements be included in a portfolio?

Where challenging internship work is not demonstrated by writing samples alone, other kinds of evidence can also be used. Here are several suggestions.

- Single-page *computer printouts* (accompanied by a brief, typed explanation) showing the templates you created, the index you wrote for a database, or other technological improvements you implemented

- *Step-by-step outlines* of the procedures you followed in dispute resolution, investigation, or other major processes
- *Copies of checklists* you created (or followed) for interviews, client follow-up, and similar work
- *Copies of forms used* in complex areas of your work, particularly if you helped create them
- *A one-page, narrative description* of a challenging case or assignment, outlining your involvement in it
- *Testimonial letters* from your supervisor or coworkers

After choosing items to include in your portfolio, you must then determine whether these items are protected by client confidentiality. Documents that are already a matter of public record (such as recorded deeds or mortgages and most pleadings) might be included in your portfolio without breaching client confidentiality. Others may be highly confidential in nature. Some documents may be sensitive enough to be withheld from distribution even though they do not technically fall within the rules of client confidentiality.

Never decide on your own whether a work sample is safe for inclusion in your portfolio. Instead, show each item to your office supervisor. If client confidentiality is an issue, see whether deleting names, addresses, and other identifying information is sufficient to remedy the problem. Major portions of a document can be omitted while impressive sections of your drafting work remain. Occasionally, a document will simply have to be replaced with something less sensitive.

When confidentiality issues have been resolved, the mechanics of assembling your portfolio are simple. Follow these guidelines:

- Use copies for all your documents—not originals. Keep extra copies for later use in your job search.
- Omit clients' names, addresses, and other identifying information as requested by your supervisor. Do this neatly with typewriter correction fluid. Check the entire document for hidden references to a client's identity.
- If your documents come in different sizes, copy them on a machine that adjusts their dimensions for uniform presentation.
- Purchase a slim, professional-looking binder for keeping your documents together.
- Prepare a cover page identifying your bound collection as "Work Portfolio."
- For prospective employers, mark the cover page with your name, address, telephone number, and the date on which the portfolio was completed.
- For your school, indicate the name of your internship supervisor and the course number, if required.

 ## SELF-EVALUATION FORMS

Schools often create self-evaluation forms for interns to use in reporting their learning on the job. Functionally similar to a checklist, self-evaluation forms list the characteristics and skills schools want their interns to develop. Often, these forms also require interns to rank their level of achievement for each item.

The exact contents of such forms vary from school to school, reflecting whatever characteristics and skills each school perceives as most essential. These forms commonly emphasize basic work skills such as dependability, thoroughness, and effective communications. They may also include specific, law-related skills and tasks. Table 15.3 shows a sample self-evaluation form.

Table 15.3

Sample Self-Evaluation Form

Intern's name _____ Date _____

1. Check each area of practice in which you gained experience.

_____ Civil litigation		_____ Business/corporate law
_____ Criminal litigation		_____ Environmental law
_____ Real estate		_____ Municipal law
_____ Divorce/family law		_____ Intellectual property
_____ Wills/estates		_____ Administrative law
_____ Other _____		

2. Check each law office system with which you had experience.

_____ Filing systems		_____ Library maintenance
_____ Timekeeping		_____ Computer network
_____ Client billing		_____ Document assembly
_____ Client trust accounts		_____ E-mail
_____ Docket control		_____ Litigation database
_____ Other _____		

3. Identify each software program with which you had experience.

a. _____

b. _____

c. _____

d. _____

e. _____

f. _____

4. Check each of the following tasks that you performed. If possible, also give a brief example or description.

_____ Manual legal research _____

_____ On-line legal research _____

_____ Drafting pleadings_____

_____ Drafting correspondence _____

_____ Interviewing _____

_____ Factual investigation _____

_____ Managing a file _____

_____ Answering/drafting interrogatories _____

_____ Other discovery tasks _____

_____ Summarizing/digesting _____

_____ Assisting at counsel table _____

_____ Other _____

5. Rate yourself either "E" or "I" on each of the following work characteristics. "E" means "Excellent." "I" means "Improvement needed." Wherever the response is "I", provide details.

_____ Arrives at work on time

_____ Follows instructions as given

_____ Completes assignments on schedule

_____ Requests help when needed

_____ Establishes pleasant working relationships

_____ Maintains a professional appearance

_____ Communicates effectively with coworkers and clients

_____ Demonstrates consistently good writing skills

_____ Guards client confidentiality

_____ Avoids the giving of legal advice

_____ Develops new contacts in the legal community

6. Identify six (or more) new skills, traits, or characteristics that you acquired during your internship.

_____

_____

_____

_____

_____

_____

7. Identify three (or more) skills, traits, or characteristics that you need to improve or acquire in the future.

_____

_____

_____

_____

_____

8. Describe your plan for improving or acquiring each of the skills, traits, or characteristics listed in number 7.

_____

_____

_____

9. Have your career goals changed as a result of your internship? If so, explain.

_____

_____

_____

_____

_____

Intern's signature	Date

Your school's self-evaluation forms call attention to objectives that were chosen long before your internship. Knowing from the outset what your school's expectations are, you can seek tasks and experiences that will help you achieve those objectives. Using forms prepared by your school also brings uniformity to the self-evaluation process, ensuring that all interns use the same criteria to evaluate and report their learning.

The list of learning objectives you prepared at the beginning of your internship represents a second, equally important, self-evaluation checklist. It has the added advantage of being uniquely tailored to your educational and career goals. If your school requires the completion of a standard self-evaluation form, complete it conscientiously—but also evaluate your learning on the basis of your own, original list of learning objectives. Review your learning objectives from time to time throughout your internship, noting which goals have been achieved and which still need to be pursued.

As you complete your school's self-evaluation form or your own goals checklist (or both), add as much detail as possible. Note concrete examples of each skill and characteristic. For a full and accurate assessment, also ask your supervisor and coworkers how well you met each goal. Their responses may pleasantly surprise you.

TESTIMONIAL LETTERS

A testimonial letter is written by a supervisor or a coworker, explaining the work you performed and describing the skills you demonstrated (see

Table 15.4). Testimonial letters differ from letters of recommendation in only one respect: testimonial letters are not addressed to any specific employer. Instead, they may be addressed to the internship director of your school or simply "To Whom It May Concern." These letters may verify internship learning for your program director at school. They can also be used in your job search. As noted earlier, testimonial letters make an impressive addition to your internship portfolio.

Most supervisors are happy to write such a letter for you in return for the work you have done. Key coworkers may also be delighted to help in this way. Make letter writing easy by giving your writers a short, written summary of your major projects or achievements on the job, along with a list of suggested skills areas for their comment. For example, you might remind them of certain cases on which you worked and list pertinent skills such as organization, writing, research, client communications, thoroughness, and timeliness.

Only invite comment on projects with which the writer has familiarity. Assure your writers that you only seek their comments on skills and qualities they are comfortable writing about. And give them at least one week's notice of your request.

Interns sometime feel uneasy about "feeding" letter writers information about the contents of their letter. But among professionals, no offense is taken to the availability of factual background and suggested topics of discussion. This information ensures appropriate focus. It saves your letter writers' time and helps ensure relevant, useful content. If the tables were

---

Table 15.4

Sample Testimonial Letter

Gnerkin & Pagliani P.A.
Attorneys at Law
1 Enterprise Way
Everytown, NM 00010
(302) 555-7100

April 3, 1998

To Whom It May Concern:

Jeri Q. Goode worked as a legal assistant intern with this office from January 19, 1998, to the current date. She was placed with this office by Enterprise Community College for a one-semester legal assistant internship. I served as her primary supervisor.

During her internship, Jeri very competently handled the following tasks: (1) file management, (2) gathering medical data for plaintiffs' personal injury cases, (3) preparing interrogatories and other discovery documents, (4) drafting pleadings and motions, (5) digesting deposition transcripts, (6) performing legal research, and (7) assisting me at counsel table in Superior Court. She also performed various nonlitigation work such as drafting a complex trust agreement and documents for corporate formation.

She is a quick learner whose skills developed very rapidly during her time with us. Her writing and drafting skills are excellent—on a par with many of the law students who have worked in this office after their first year of law school. Her dealings with coworkers, clients, witnesses, and even court staff are courteous and highly professional. She is someone who is always willing to go beyond immediate expectations, often doing far more than what is asked of her.

Jeri's work has been so helpful to this office that I wish it were possible for us to hire her. Indeed, I wish every new staff person came to us with her competence and commitment to her profession.

Sincerely yours,

Attorney Oscar X. Pagliani

turned, your letter writers would probably extend the same courtesy to someone writing a letter of recommendation for them. As long as you present your material in an unassuming manner, it will be taken for the efficient professionalism it represents.

THE SUPERVISOR'S EVALUATION FORM

This is probably one of the most frequently used methods for verifying an intern's learning and performance. At many schools, the supervisor's evaluation not only provides important data, but also figures heavily in the intern's final internship grade.

Structured much like the self-evaluation forms sometimes required of interns themselves, these forms ask office supervisors to rank the intern's level of achievement in various skills areas. In addition, blank spaces are often provided for the supervisor's detailed comments. As with interns' self-evaluation forms, the contents of these forms depend on what skills and professional characteristics have been identified as important, and this varies from school to school. A sample supervisor's evaluation form is shown in Table 15.5.

Table 15.5

Sample Supervisor's Evaluation Form

Intern _____   Office _____

Supervisor _____   Address _____

Number of hours covered by this evaluation _____   Phone _____

My intern worked in the following areas of practice:

_____ Civil litigation	_____ Business/corporate law
_____ Criminal litigation	_____ Environmental law
_____ Real estate	_____ Municipal law
_____ Divorce/family law	_____ Intellectual property
_____ Wills/estates	_____ Administrative law
_____ Other _____	

My intern had experience with the following office systems:

_____ Filing systems	_____ Library maintenance
_____ Timekeeping	_____ Computer network
_____ Client billing	_____ Document assembly
_____ Client trust accounts	_____ E-mail
_____ Docket control	_____ Litigation database
_____ Other _____	

My intern had experience with the following software programs:

_____

_____

_____

_____

My intern performed the following tasks. Give an example of each, if possible.

_____ Manual legal research

_____ On-line legal research

(Continued)

Table 15.5 (Continued)

_____ Drafting pleadings _____

_____ Drafting correspondence _____

_____ Interviewing _____

_____ Factual investigation _____

_____ Managing a client file _____

_____ Answering/drafting interrogatories _____

_____ Other discovery tasks _____

_____ Summarizing/digesting _____

_____ Assisting at counsel table _____

_____ Other _____

_____ Other _____

Rate your intern from "1" to "5" on the following characteristics. "1" equals "excellent," "2" equals "above average," "3" equals "fair or average," "4" equals "below average," and "5" equals "unacceptable."

_____ Arrives at work on time

_____ Follows instructions as given

_____ Accepts criticism and suggestions for improvement

_____ Requests help when needed

_____ Completes assignments on time

_____ Maintains a professional appearance

_____ Establishes pleasant working relationships

_____ Communicates effectively with coworkers and clients

_____ Demonstrates consistently good writing skills

_____ Guards client confidentiality

_____ Avoids the giving of legal advice

_____ Shows initiative (willingness to work beyond minimum requirements)

_____ Produces quality work

_____ Produces a sufficient volume of work

_____ Demonstrates good judgment in making decisions

_____ Can often solve problems without assistance

List your intern's greatest strengths.

_____

_____

_____

_____

List skills, traits, or subject areas most needing improvement.

_____

_____

_____

Your overall evaluation of this intern (excellent, above average, fair or average, below average, or unacceptable) is: _____
Are you willing to provide a reference for this intern for future employment? _____ yes _____ no _____ unsure
May we place another student intern with your office in the near future? _____ yes _____ no _____ if unsure, please contact us first.

_____   _____
Supervisor's signature   Date

_____   _____
Student's signature   Date

Thank you for your contribution to the success of our Paralegal Studies program in training and evaluating this intern.

To get the maximum benefit from a supervisor's evaluation, try to meet with your office supervisor to review the form together. Suggest treating this evaluation like an employee's annual performance review. In an employee's annual review, supervisor and employee interact together in the evaluation process. Each helps clarify the perceptions of the other as criteria are reviewed, item by item. As a result, a full understanding is achieved on both sides.

A major advantage of supervisors' evaluation forms is that they facilitate evaluation by the person best able to make such judgments. Knowing the requirements of the job and having personally observed the intern's performance, the supervisor is usually in a better position than anyone to assess the intern's learning. Schoolwide use of these forms also brings uniformity to the evaluative process, ensuring that all interns are judged on the same criteria.

Supervisors' evaluations also help identify an intern's shortcomings more readily than any other method. Supervisors are usually more alert than inexperienced interns to areas in which more learning is needed. Although no student enjoys hearing about professional weaknesses, this input is nevertheless extremely valuable.

Seemingly negative comments are useful to your long-term career planning. For example, a comment criticizing an intern's speaking skills may suggest the need for a course in public speaking or communications. When you know your shortcomings, you can take steps to correct them. Career prospects are enhanced as a result.

Ironically, the biggest advantage of this kind of evaluation form can also be its greatest disadvantage. Because supervisors typically report an intern's shortcomings as well as strengths, *this form probably should not be shared with prospective employers.* If your supervisor is blunt about occasional weaknesses, then this form is best used only for your school's purposes and for your own career planning. In your job search, focus instead on your work portfolio, testimonial letters, and other documentation strategies. Naturally, you will also work to correct any shortcomings noted in your supervisor's evaluation.

Some schools require supervisors to complete an evaluation form twice—once near the midpoint of the internship and again at the end. The "preview" evaluation gives the intern a chance to work toward improvement in areas in which the need is indicated. Having two successive evaluations also helps demonstrate progress over time.

THE HOURLY LOG

The hourly log is simply a list of the dates and times during which the intern worked. Although it does little to document new, on-the-job skills, an hourly log does show whether the intern completed the number of office hours required for academic credit. In many schools, this information is written on a form provided by the school. Alternatively, an intern might simply list this information on a sheet of paper (see Table 15.6).

The simplest of all documentation techniques, an hourly log's only challenge may be in ensuring its accuracy. To be certain your hours are reported honestly and fully, use the following strategies:

- Unless your hours are exactly the same every day, do not rely on memory. Jot down arrival and departure times each day in your personal calendar or planner, or use a rough copy of your hourly log to keep track.
- Assume that your school may contact the office to verify your hours. *Never* report inflated hours.

> **QUICK TIP 15.2**
>
> To help make the final evaluation a positive one, request a confidential preview halfway through the internship. Ask your supervisor what skills need extra attention and work on strengthening those weak spots.

Table 15.6

Sample Hourly Log

Paralegal Internship Log

Student's name _____

Course number _____

Internship requirement _____ total hours

Date	Times	General Description of Tasks
1.		
2.		
3.		
4.		
5.		
6.		
7.		
8.		
9.		
10.		

Supervisor's verification _____

Date _____

- Check your log against an ordinary calendar to be sure that no dates have been confused.
- As with any document prepared for your school, make the final version neat, legible, and professional looking.

You may be asked to include a one-line description of the tasks performed on each date. For example, "client interview, research, drafting" might be stated next to a certain date. Reporting these additional details requires diligent record keeping. If you keep your personal planner or calendar complete, these details will be easy to report.

Some schools require verification by your office supervisor of the times reported in your log. A signature line may be provided at the end of the form for this purpose. If you have more than one supervisor, you can add signature lines to your single log or prepare separate logs for each supervisor, noting the hours worked for one supervisor on one log and the hours worked for the other supervisor on the other.

CAPSTONE REPORTS

A capstone report requires many of the preceding documentation methods to be submitted simultaneously when the internship ends. For example, a daily journal or hourly log might be submitted along with a work portfolio, a completed supervisor's evaluation form, and perhaps also a completed self-evaluation form. The exact combination varies from school to school.

A final written report may also be included. In this case, however, the written report summarizes the entire internship, providing a broad overview of work experiences and the skills you acquired. It may also include recommendations on the value of your office to future interns and the office's availability for that purpose.

Because they bring together several different documentation methods, capstone reports provide a wonderfully detailed record of all you have achieved. They ensure ample documentation of internship learning for your school's accreditation and approval processes and also for you to use in your job search.

If there is a disadvantage to capstone reports, it is that they can be challenging to coordinate and prepare as a busy internship draws to a close. The longer the internship, the more there may be to report, so students should pace their preparations accordingly. For example, students whose internships are four to six weeks in duration should probably begin working on their capstone materials about ten days before the due date. Where internships are two or three months in duration, interns should begin their capstone reports even earlier. The following chronology will help you coordinate your preparation.

- Schedule a meeting with your supervisor to review evaluation forms—yours and the supervisor's. Give your supervisor adequate lead time to set this up.
- Preparing your portfolio may be the most time-consuming chore, so begin that next. Identify your best work samples and take steps to protect client confidentiality.
- The final written report also takes considerable thought, so do it in stages. Prepare an outline early. Return to it periodically to refine it and fill in details. Then write a rough draft. Proofread it and prepare the final version.
- Check your journal or your hourly log to be sure it is up to date. If not, glean the information you need for missing entries from your personal calendar or planner. Time sheets kept for your office's use may also help jog your memory.
- Shop for the binders or packaging your school prefers.
- Complete your self-evaluation form last so that it consistently reflects all the other information you have gathered.

The time it takes to create all the components of a capstone report is an investment in your future. When you are done, you will have before you concrete evidence of professional achievements you may never have imagined possible so early in your career. You will have a clear indication of what steps are needed to further improve your career prospects. Most importantly, you will have, on paper, a gold mine of details to draw on in your job search.

EXERCISES

1. If you do not yet know what documentation methods are required by your school, check with your internship director to determine the exact requirements. Then calendar the dates on which you will begin, develop, and complete each one.
2. If any of the following documentation methods are not required by your school, consider developing one, two, or more of them on your own. Refer to the instructions and samples provided in this chapter.

      a. A reflective journal

      b. A work portfolio

      c. A self-evaluation form

      d. Testimonial letters from supervisors or coworkers

      e. An evaluation form for your supervisor

      f. A final report summarizing your internship experience, including tasks performed, skills developed, and insights gained regarding your chosen work environment

3. Review the list of learning objectives that you developed at the beginning of your internship. With a colored marker, highlight each of the goals that you have achieved.

4. In preparation for Chapter 16, make a permanent file of all your documented, on-the-job learning. Label this file as "Job Skills." The material in this file will be used in your employment search (explained further in the next chapter). Include the following items in this file.

      a. Copies of all the documentation you prepared for your school

      b. The documentation you prepared in Exercises 2 and 3

      c. The list of professional contacts you prepared following the instructions in Chapter 14

ENDNOTE

1. See Chapter 9, "Creating Your Own Reference Files."

Chapter 16

Using Documented Skills in Your Job Search

This chapter shows you how to strengthen your job search, drawing on the evidence you have collected of new skills and knowledge. Using the documentation you brought together in a Job Skills file (as instructed in the last exercise of Chapter 15), you will learn to do the following four things.

First, you will be shown how to conduct a postinternship career review—deciding what direction to take, which skills to emphasize, and how to use your professional network wisely. Second, you will learn how to create an outstanding résumé using your Job Skills file. Third, you will be shown how to make the Jobs Skills file work for you in job interviews, as well. Finally, you will be shown why you need a long-term career plan and how to create one.

 ## THE POSTINTERNSHIP CAREER REVIEW

The purpose of a postinternship career review is to survey where you have been professionally and determine where you want to go next. Figuratively speaking, you may want to turn left, turn right, or proceed straight ahead. Whatever career route you choose, let it be the result of a thoughtful, informed decision.

Where Do I Go from Here?

First, identify your professional strengths. Delve into your Job Skills file, reviewing the tasks you have performed and the skills you acquired in the process.

In which tasks did you excel, perhaps earning praise from your supervisor? These are your individual strengths—some of which may be transferable to many different subject areas and work settings. For many interns, there will also be a number of tasks and skills that fall into certain practice areas, such as real estate or personal injury work. These are your subject matter strengths. Seeking employment in these or in closely related practice areas may be the easiest career route to pursue—though not necessarily the only one.

Now ask: do the strengths you have identified coincide with the tasks and practice areas you most enjoyed? If so, you are one of those lucky individuals whose career choice is clear. You know what you enjoy doing and you have now gained expertise in doing it. You can proceed straight ahead! Your task is simply to find offices needing your kind of know-how.

On the other hand, if the tasks you have *performed* most often are not necessarily the tasks you most *enjoyed*, then you may need to plot a turn in your career path, mainly emphasizing the individual strengths you have identified. Consider how your new skills and knowledge may be applied in distinctly different work settings. For example, knowledge acquired in performing plaintiffs' personal injury work might be equally useful in an insurance company. The skills developed in working on real estate foreclosures may also be useful in a municipal tax office or in the mortgage department of a bank—and so on.

Look for a wide range of uses for the strengths you have identified. Start with offices outside of but related to your internship work: the government entities, service organizations, corporations, businesses, and opponents with whom you interacted. Further broaden your view by talking to paralegal acquaintances, graduates from your school, and your career advisor.

Explore positions that differ from your internship setting but nevertheless require similar skills. For example, fact-gathering and communications skills developed in a litigation practice may be valuable for working in government agencies, health maintenance organizations, and nonprofit associations. Research and writing skills acquired while working on an appeal might prove valuable in the office of a legal publisher. Organizational skills and a knack for details are useful in many employment settings.

Which Skills Should I Emphasize?

Job candidates should emphasize the knowledge and skills most wanted by the employers they have targeted. To know what employers want, read want ads carefully for any buzzwords they contain. Use those words in your cover letter and résumé whenever you can do so truthfully.

Buzzwords may be specific to certain practice areas, such as *abstracting* (real estate) or *trial prep* (litigation). If a term is ambiguous, phone the employing office for clarification. For example, the term *file management* means different things to different people, so further explanation is essential to detailing your skills appropriately.

Often, buzzwords are of a more general nature. *Self-starter* and *works independently* are common examples. In your Job Skills file, look for instances in which you performed as the employer's buzzwords suggest. Use those same words wherever you can do so honestly and be prepared to back up your claims with specific examples.

In addition, try to phrase your descriptions in terms that are appropriate to the work you would like to do. If you are switching fields, some skills might be best described in generic rather than legal terms. For example, a litigation intern seeking employment in a public service agency might claim to have "indexed scores of documents" rather than "indexed pleadings, discoveries, and motions."

As you identify skills that prospective employers want, let your Job Skills file be your final reference point. Claim all the skills you can, looking for their broadest possible career application. But always *be sure there is evidence of the skills you say you have.* If no example can be cited, do not claim the skill.

How Do I Use My Professional Contacts?

Typically, prospective employers ask job candidates for professional references or comments from other professionals regarding the candidate's experience, skills, and suitability for a certain position. Most students see their internship supervisor and coworkers as their primary sources of such references. Other professionals with whom you had frequent contact may also be willing to provide a reference—limited, perhaps, to addressing the nature of their professional interaction with you.

Professional references are conveyed in a letter of recommendation addressed to the prospective employer or in a telephone call initiated by your potential employer. It is the employer's prerogative to decide which method is preferred. If the employer's preference is not clear, then you should ask, so you can let your reference providers know what to expect.

Job seekers need to know that something of a protocol surrounds the reference and recommendation process. *Job candidates should never give someone's name as a professional reference without permission from the person they have chosen.* Listing as references your supervisor, coworkers, or even the program director at your school without their knowledge is often considered professionally naive, if not downright presumptuous. You want your reference providers to say flattering things about you, so do not risk offending these people. Get their permission in advance.

A good approach is to ask your chosen professionals if they are comfortable about providing a job reference for you. This approach invites a discussion about any hesitation they may have so you can be aware of it *before* doubts are conveyed to prospective employers. If you sense reluctance on anyone's part, omit that person from your list, if you can, and ask someone else to provide the needed reference.

Most job candidates do not list the names of professional references on a résumé unless a prospective employer specifically requests this information. Instead, applicants usually include the phrase "References available upon request" at the bottom of their résumés. This strategy ensures that reference providers will not be contacted unless you are being seriously considered for a position.

There are other ways in which your professional contacts can help you in your job search. Some of these additional tactics may actually be more productive than job references. Consider asking knowledgeable professional acquaintances to help you in some of the following ways.

- Provide a half-hour *informational interview* about current job prospects in an unfamiliar specialty area and the skills needed for a career in that field
- Give you an informal *evaluation of your professional strengths and weaknesses,* identifying areas in which improvement would heighten your job prospects
- *Review your résumé* for suggestions regarding its content, format, and appearance
- Keep you informed of *job openings* as they become aware of them
- Provide opportunities for *part-time or freelance assignments*—or even *volunteer work*—to develop more marketable skills

An intern's professional contacts are often flattered to receive one of these requests and impressed by the seriousness these strategies imply. Continued

THE STUDENT'S PERSPECTIVE 16.1: KRISTEN
The Unwitting Job Reference

Kristen struggled to pull herself out of the shock she felt when she heard the news: the Superior Court Clerk's Office had decided on a different job candidate. And her interviews there had gone so well! As the caller thanked Kristen for her interest and her time, Kristen acted quickly to see whether she could determine what went wrong.

"If you wouldn't mind telling me," Kristen wisely inquired, "I'd like to ask what discouraged your office from hiring me. As I continue my job search, it would help to know what the problem was and what I might do differently next time."

The caller responded thoughtfully. "Most of your attributes are well-suited to this position, Kristen. We had one other candidate who appeared about equally qualified, and we had a tough time deciding between the two of you. What it came down to was a big difference in the references that each of you provided. The other candidate had much more positive references. I'm sorry."

Upset and somewhat angry, Kristen telephoned the paralegal program director at her school to ask about what now appeared to have been a negative job reference. Surprisingly, the director was a little angry, herself.

"Kristen, you gave me no warning that a call was coming from a prospective employer," the director began. "Don't forget that it's been a while since you graduated. I have taught hundreds of students—that's a lot of names and details to remember. In your graduating class alone, there were no less than three 'Kristens,' each with a different spelling to her name.

"If you had just let me know that a call was coming soon about a job reference, I could have refreshed my memory, checked my files, and planned several wonderful, very specific things to tell them about you. But you gave me no chance to do that. Instead, a surprise caller asked me to describe my experience with Kristen Something-or-Other, and I had to have him spell the name and give me time to check my records! Can you imagine what impression that made? I offered to call him back in an hour or two, but he seemed discouraged and said 'Don't bother.'

"Frankly, I think he realized you had not told me his call was coming. That may have figured into their evaluation of you as a candidate. Is it possible the same sort of thing happened when they called your other professional references?"

"Probably," Kristen admitted sorrowfully. "I was just so excited! I talked myself into thinking I really had this job and that the reference thing was just a silly formality."

The director shook her head. "It's not just a formality, Kristen. Employers often attach huge importance to the responses they get from professional references.

"Next time, let your job references know what's going on. Make sure they are fully with you before you count on them for something so crucial to your career."

interaction beyond your internship also keeps you in their thoughts, ensuring that you will be among the first to know when a job opening occurs.

Some of these strategies are especially useful to interns trying to break into a new field or different work setting. For example, an informational interview helps you become well-informed about alternative career choices. And volunteer work or freelance assignments allow you to test your internship skills in a new environment.

When making these requests, show respect for others' busy schedules. Avoid asking anyone for too many favors and try to accommodate the

Table 16.1

Sample Thank-You Letter

Jeri Q. Goode
123 West Street
Anytown, MN 00010

January 5, 1999

Dear Attorney Pagliani:

Thank you so much for agreeing to write a testimonial letter on my behalf and for all the kind words of praise that it contained.

Although it has only been a short time since your letter was written, it has already helped me immeasurably. It contributed heavily to the "A" I received as my internship grade. It has also been mentioned by two prospective employers as a reason for scheduling an interview with me. When I shared your letter with Attorney Bridges at Anytown's Legal Assistance Office and later with Attorney Carmine on Main Street, both said that they were quite impressed by it. Apparently, they know you well and they value your opinion very highly.

I count myself as fortunate, indeed, to have worked with you. You taught me skills that will be valuable throughout my career and now you are helping me to get that career underway. I am truly grateful for all the time and support you have given me.

Sincerely yours,

Jeri Q. Goode

---

scheduling needs of every person you contact. Tailor your requests to each professional's particular expertise. And, of course, always express gratitude for the help. For time-consuming favors such as informational interviews or an evaluation of your professional strengths, follow up immediately with a note of thanks, as shown in Table 16.1.

BUILD A BETTER RÉSUMÉ

One of the greatest advantages of an internship is that it gives you a wealth of material for creating a résumé that attracts favorable attention. Using your documentation of internship learning, you can now *replace the non-law-oriented, unskilled, or semiskilled experiences that originally appeared in your résumé with specific, up-to-date, career-related information.*

Begin with the résumé you prepared for prospective internship offices. Using a colored marker, strike out old information that is best replaced. Omitted items might include part-time jobs that helped you financially but had little or no career value: waiting on tables, pumping gas, or clerking in a department store, for example. Be cautious, however, about omitting non-career-related experience that nevertheless demonstrates important skills such as in communications, problem solving, organization, and supervisory responsibility.

Where nonparalegal experience may have relevance, do not describe it merely in terms of job titles. Instead, describe the actual responsibilities or skills it required. You may remember that the functional or achievements-style résumé in Table 4.5 provided several such descriptions. So does the new, updated version of that résumé, which appears in Table 16.2. Table 16.3 shows how the older résumé was updated and revised to emphasize internship experience.

Table 16.2

Achievements-Style Résumé—Updated

Chris Dumont
2345 Education Road
Paralegal City, North Dakota 02000
(701) 555-9340

Education
- North Dakota Paralegal College (ABA-approved; Paralegal Certificate completed in May, 1998)
- North Dakota University (B.A., History, 1997)
- Dean's List, Fall and Spring Semesters, 1996–1997
- Nominated to "Who's Who in American Colleges and Universities," 1997
- Winner of Legal Research Award, North Dakota Paralegal College, 1997

Qualifications
- Proficient in Westlaw, Lexis, WordPerfect, Windows, DOS, and Excel
- Experienced in all phases of pretrial investigation and discovery
- Produces quality drafting and writing (pleadings, motions, interrogatories, information requests, and client communications)
- Skilled in interviewing clients, witnesses, and others
- Summarizes depositions skillfully and concisely
- Can organize and manage a file independently, including calendaring and follow-up
- Experienced in organization and management of library systems
- Secures others' cooperation to coordinate large projects
- Works effectively in busy, high-pressure setting

Work History
Law Office of Attorney Meredith C. Botsworth, February 1998–present
Lambert & Botsworth, P.C.
Paralegal City, ND 02000
- Provided a wide range of pretrial litigation support
- Focused mainly on personal injury litigation
- Conducted pretrial investigation for criminal defense matters
- Frequently performed legal research (state statutes and case law)
- Earned high praise for skillful verbal communications, good organization, and attention to detail

Voorhees County Elderly Services Bureau, Spring 1998
Paralegal City, ND 02000
- Skillfully counseled needy, elderly clients seeking community services
- Secured the cooperation of many local agencies
- Managed dozens of the Bureau's cases from beginning to end

Voorhees County Community College Library, 1994–1995
Paralegal City, ND 02000
- As student library assistant, advised students on the location and use of various resources, including law library references
- Implemented a new system for computerization of law library records

Personal
- Self-supporting throughout college
- Has own transportation; can travel throughout the region

Available Upon Request
- Portfolio of law office work samples
- Letter of recommendation from Attorney Meredith C. Botsworth
- Other excellent references

Table 16.3

Résumé Revisions Explained

Regarding "Education"
- This topic heading is still appropriate, so it remains on the résumé.
- Only the highest degree earned is included now. The earlier Associate of Arts (A.A.) degree has been omitted to save space.
- Important scholastic honors are still included here, but without a subheading—again, to save space.
- The item regarding the winning of a Legal Research Award has been moved here. It was scholastic in nature and its original heading, "Professional Achievements," now has a more job-oriented focus.

Regarding "Qualifications"
- Repetitive items have been omitted, such as the early reference to "award-winning researcher."
- This list now emphasizes internship experience over classroom work. Numerous job-related skills are listed. Less-impressive, classroom-related items are omitted, except where course assignments might fill gaps left unfilled by internship work.

"Professional Accomplishments" has been renamed "Work History"
- This change allows the achievement-based résumé to also have some characteristics of a more conventional chronological résumé (explained in Chapter 4).
- The title "Work History" facilitates the listing of *unpaid* volunteer and internship work, where those are relevant, along with relevant paid positions. (Other titles, such as "Employment," would not provide this kind of flexibility.)
- Paid and unpaid jobs are listed in reverse chronological order—the most recent and most relevant (the internship) being listed first.
- This list emphasized mostly internship skills.
- Law office skills and tasks are described with some specificity.
- Non-law-office skills and experience are included only where they are relevant to the job being sought.

Regarding "Personal" Information
- The original items were highly relevant to the job being sought, so they are included here. If not relevant, they should be omitted.

Regarding "Available Upon Request" Line
- "Writing samples" now refers to genuine law office work.
- A new item refers to a testimonial letter written by the internship office supervisor.

Next, review the contents of your Job Skills file for examples of the skills and knowledge needed in the jobs you are seeking. Write brief, one- or two-line descriptions of the skills you find, as if for a résumé. Where possible, combine related skills into one succinct description. This helps you squeeze as much information as you can into a one-page résumé.

Fill two or three sheets of paper with as many résumé-style descriptions of law-related skills, achievements, and experience as you can—the more, the better! The goal is not to include every item in one résumé, but to give yourself as much material as possible to choose from for several, tailor-made résumés.

Then refine the descriptions you have created, keeping the following guidelines in mind:

- *Introduce each description with an action word,* such as *drafted, organized, pursued, completed, oversaw, achieved,* or *succeeded in.*
- *Avoid repeated use of the same words.* Check a thesaurus or a dictionary for interesting, accurate alternatives. For example, the words *responsible for* might later appear as *charged with* or *carried out.*
- Focus on *specifics—not generalities.* For instance, instead of claiming to have worked "efficiently," note that a project was completed "a week ahead of deadline."

- *Replace adjectives (descriptive words) with factual information, wherever possible.* For example, instead of saying you completed a *difficult* or *major* research memorandum, say you analyzed *six cases in one memorandum.*
- *Omit emphatic words* such as "very" and "extremely" from your descriptions. These words make it appear that you are exaggerating your achievements even when you are not.
- *Keep descriptions short and direct,* packing as much meaning as you can into as few words as possible. For example, in place of "Periodically handled most of the record keeping, purchases, billing, and business-related aspects of running a solo law practice," say you "Served as back-up office manager for solo law practice."
- *Consider writing alternate descriptions of the same skills and experience* for clear relevance to different employers. Technical legal terms might be used for targeting specialized law offices, general legal terms for a general practice, and nonlegal equivalents for nonprofit human service offices.

One, uniform résumé almost never works well for all employment settings. If you plan a diversified job search among different kinds of employers, then at least two or three somewhat different résumés are needed, each listing the skills and knowledge most appropriate for each kind of employer. Using a word processor, you can retain the same format and basic information for each résumé, changing some of your descriptions where needed. Your collection of one-line descriptions provides a handy basis for these substitutions.

You must also *research each office thoroughly before applying for employment there.* Use the same research techniques you used to find your internship[1] to find out as much as possible about the offices where you would like to work. Then shape each résumé and cover letter around the needs and the character of each office, using the same guidelines as for your internship search.

Prepare for Powerful Interviews

You gained considerable interviewing experience when you went in search of your internship. Now is the time to review that experience and build on it. Think back to your internship interviews with these questions in mind:

- What was your most successful internship interview? What made it a success?
- What was your most difficult internship interview? What made it difficult?
- What did you learn from those experiences about interviewing?

Put your previous experience to work for you. In upcoming interviews, try to imitate the attitude, behavior, and preinterview preparation that brought you good results during your internship search and avoid the mistakes that may have caused you difficulty. Also, review Chapter 4, "The Interview," before renewing the interview process to refresh your memory on what to expect, how to prepare, and what strategies to use.

There is, of course, a big difference between what you brought to interviews prior to your internship and what you bring to job interviews now. In the past, you had little or no paralegal experience to relate. This time, you have a great deal of relevant experience to report. And report it you must—confidently and in detail.

To recount your experience effectively, go into each interview thoroughly familiar with the work you have done. Be ready to report, sometimes in minute detail, the specifics of the work you performed. Most importantly, be prepared to show how your internship experience applies to the jobs you are seeking.

Refresh your memory prior to each job interview. Review your Job Skills file with these goals in mind:

- *Identify internship tasks* that are relevant to the position for which you are applying. For example, drafting pleadings would be relevant to a litigation support position; preparing for real estate closing would be relevant experience to a residential real estate practice.
- *Identify internship skills* that will be useful in the new job, even if you acquired those skills through seemingly unrelated tasks. Writing, fact gathering, investigation, client communications, computer database creation, and file management are just a few examples of skills that have wide application.
- *Practice describing the details* in an interesting, lively manner. Practice reporting some of the challenges you faced and how you overcame them.
- Practice explaining *how your internship skills relate* to the new job.
- *Prepare questions* about each job, focusing on opportunities to develop additional skills.

Get others' reactions to the oral descriptions you have formulated. Ask other professionals whether the descriptions are clear. What questions might your descriptions bring to an interviewer's mind? Plan appropriate answers. If videotaped practice interview sessions are available at your school's placement office, take advantage of the opportunity to see what your interviewer sees and, on that basis, fine-tune your interviewing techniques.

Also, review the contents of your work portfolio. Be sure it includes the samples most relevant for the job. Take additional copies of your résumé when you interview, along with the names, addresses, and phone numbers of your professional references. Dress professionally, smile, and feel confident! You have had good, professional experience, and you are now well-prepared.

DEVELOP A CAREER PLAN

Students often find it hard to think beyond their first job. But there are vast differences between a *job* and a *career*. A job is a form of employment and that is important. A career, on the other hand, is a continuing path involving a series of jobs or positions throughout your lifetime. A career suggests more than a job. It implies growth, new challenges, continual learning, increased skills, and the fulfillment of goals.

Undoubtedly, your first job will not be your last. Most likely, *your first paralegal job is merely one step on a long, intriguing path that has yet to unfold.* The question is: Where would you like that path to lead? To a large extent, you help determine the direction of that path by the choices you make—both before and after that all-important first job.

Take charge of your career by thinking hard about where you would like to be in, say, five years. The exact number of years is not crucial; what matters is acknowledging the dream. Would you like to be in (or perhaps headed toward) a supervisory position? Maybe you imagine becoming a leading paralegal specialist in a certain field. Or, perhaps you picture yourself running for office one day.

Whatever your vision, try to choose your initial employment with that dream in mind. The following strategies may help.

- Try for a job that allows you to pursue your long-term interests in some way. For example, if you choose a general practice employer, let it be one that gives you occasional exposure to your favorite specialty area.

- Ask prospective employers about their willingness to help with the expenses of continuing legal education seminars, workshops, or the completion of a degree.
- Volunteer work is a great way to acquire additional experience doing work you love if your regular job does not give you that chance. Challenging volunteer work also impresses future employers.
- Consider taking temporary jobs until a job you like comes along. Personnel agencies can help or you can pursue temporary assignments on your own, using your list of professional contacts as a starting point.
- If continuing full-time studies (such as for an additional degree) would enhance your career, consider settling for a part-time position for a while.

Career planning never ends. These days, most jobs change quickly. New technologies, changes in the economy, shifts in government policy, the rise of unforeseen specialty areas, and the decline of traditional ones—all these factors require legal professionals to be more flexible than ever before.

Nobody can insulate himself or herself completely against unforeseen changes. But you can do a lot to help ensure continued survival and growth in the face of unpredictable change. The key is to do three things. Continually enhance your professional reputation throughout your career. Maintain a broad network of relationships in as many different work areas as possible. And try to keep abreast of new legal and technological developments in your field. Try implementing these survival strategies in some of the following ways:

- Socialize often with colleagues from other offices; find out what their work is like and what new developments they are seeing.
- Be someone who helps out when help is needed. The favor is almost always returned, sometimes in wonderful ways.
- Become active in your local paralegal or legal assistant association.
- Consider taking on responsibilities in your regional or national association as well.
- Consider pursuing voluntary, professional certification either as a Certified Legal Assistant (CLA) or as a Registered Paralegal (RP).
- Sign up for continuing legal education seminars regularly—at least two or three a year.
- Look for opportunities to learn more about emerging technologies, both inside and outside of your office.
- Take advantage of opportunities for paralegal involvement in your state or local bar association—in a paralegal section or through associate bar membership (if available in your state), working on a bar association committee (if permitted locally), or volunteering to work in the bar association's *pro bono* program.
- Welcome the chance to experiment with something new from time to time—a new practice area, a new technology, or new responsibilities. You never know when this might lead to an exciting new career path.

Paralegals who are known and respected among a large number of professionals can usually survive any upheaval and often manage to create positive changes on their own. Alert paralegals with an eye on the horizon for upcoming developments are probably in the best position of all. They are the ones who—like you—will seize opportunities as they arise and, in time, make their career dreams come true.

THE STUDENT'S PERSPECTIVE 16.2: JAN, MARYBETH, AND BRIAN

Turning Dreams into Reality

With their internships over and graduation only a week away, the three former interns agreed to share one last lunch at Mike's Pizza—the "going away lunch," Jan called it. As they waited for their orders, Marybeth posed the question that was on each of their minds. "So what are everyone's plans after graduation?"

Jan was the first to respond. "I've always dreamed of working for myself. I think it would be great to be my own boss, set my own hours, decide for myself what work I'll accept and what work I'll send elsewhere. That sounds like heaven to me."

Marybeth wanted to know more. "So you're going to freelance?"

"Not right away," Jan answered. "I've never run my own business. From what I hear, it can be expensive to set up your own office. And, frankly, I'm not sure I have enough experience yet to work completely on my own. Besides, I need a regular income for a while! So I plan to work for an attorney for a year or two. A general practice law firm might be a good place to start. I'm also going to talk to Bert Friande, who has a successful freelance paralegal practice in town. Maybe he can send an occasional assignment my way so I can get a feel for how freelancing works. I think I could learn a lot from him."

"Good plan," Marybeth concluded. "I, on the other hand, have always wanted to work in Washington, D.C. Anything connected to the House or the Senate would be fantastic. Unfortunately, that's a thousand miles from here. So, as a start, I'm going to work at the State House, doing legislative research. I figure it's a step in the right direction. Once I get some experience and maybe some connections, I'll try for something on the federal level. With luck, maybe that will be my ticket to Washington. What about you, Brian?"

"Remember how tired I was of interrogatories, interrogatories, interrogatories? Well, asking for something different was the best thing I ever did. They put me on a criminal defense case that had me more excited than any work I've ever done. I haven't told anyone else this, but my dream now is to become a criminal defense attorney. I want to go to law school some day. Not right away, though. Like you, Jan, I need to get on my feet financially, first. I also want more paralegal experience in the criminal law area so I can be really sure about this. So, I'm interviewing tomorrow for a job as investigator at the Public Defender's Office."

"Hey, that's great! Good luck to you," Jan beamed. Then he raised his glass high. "Here's to a wonderful future for all of us."

EXERCISES

1. Following the instructions in "Where Do I Go from Here?," review your Job Skills file and identify your professional strengths. Also identify tasks you enjoyed. Then, look to see whether your strengths are compatible with the tasks you like doing. If so, then your immediate career choice is clear and you may skip Exercise 2.

2. If your professional strengths are not entirely compatible with the internship tasks you enjoyed, begin exploring alternative career options in which your skills would be useful. Follow the instructions on this point in "Where Do I Go from Here?" Make a list of possible options and

research them. Schedule an informational interview with a professional in one of the fields you have targeted.

3. Regularly check the classified ads in the weekly publication of your state bar association and also in your local newspaper. Find one or more ads for paralegal positions. (If there are no paralegal ads on the first try, ads for lawyers may also be used for this exercise.) Identify any buzzwords these ads contain. Find a definition for these words by consulting instructors at your school, colleagues at your internship office, or the office running the ad. Review your Job Skills file to see whether you can find examples of the skills these buzzwords call for.

4. Reviewing your list of professional contacts, consider whom you would prefer to use as professional references. Let your consideration include, but go beyond, your internship supervisor and your director at school. Discuss this matter with each of the people you choose, as instructed in "How Do I Use My Professional Contacts?"

5. Reviewing your list of professional contacts, decide if any of them might also be able to help you with your job search in the following ways:
   a. Provide an informational interview
   b. Advise you on your professional strengths and weaknesses
   c. Advise you on your résumé
   d. Give you early notice about the availability of job openings in their office or in nearby offices
   e. Provide news about the availability of part-time or temporary, free-lance assignments
   f. Notify you about the availability of volunteer work
   g. Provide information about upcoming seminars on new developments in their field

6. Draft an all-purpose thank-you note for a professional colleague who has helped you in some way with your job search. Keep this draft on hand. Modify it for actual situations as they arise.

7. Conduct a detailed review of your Job Skills file. Based on what it contains, draft two or three pages of short descriptions (one to two lines each) of skills and accomplishments for possible use in résumés. See the additional instructions on this process in "Build a Better Résumé."

8. Beginning with the résumé you originally created for your internship search, and adding (or substituting) appropriate descriptions selected from the sheets written for Exercise 7, practice creating at least two new résumés—each one for a different office in which you would like to work.

9. Using the three-point list near the beginning of "Prepare for Powerful Interviews," describe, on paper, what you learned from interviewing for your internship. After you have done this, compare your description with those of other interns. Are there important similarities? Important differences? Are there tips you can learn from the experience of other interns?

10. Following the instructions in the five-point list in "Prepare for Powerful Interviews," prepare for a mock job interview. Have another intern play the role of employer/interviewer. Before the mock interview, you and the other intern need to agree on a job description that is somewhat familiar to you both. When you are done, reverse roles and interview your colleague.

11. Think about where you would like to be, professionally, four to six years from now. Describe it in writing. Now, try to answer the following questions:

a. What kinds of jobs might help you reach that goal? Try to identify at least four kinds of positions that might work as a stepping-stone to your dream job.

b. Are there skills, which you do not currently possess, that might be needed for the future job of your dreams? Try to identify those skills. This list of skills could become a subject of inquiry for you during your job search—now, and also in the future.

c. Are there courses, workshops, a degree, or certificate that will help qualify you for your future dream job? Investigate this possibility by contacting paralegal organizations, your local bar association office, local colleges, your program director, your placement advisor, and experienced people on your list of contacts.

ENDNOTE

1. See Chapter 4, "How to Find Internship Offices."

Appendix 1

Practice Exercise: What Is Your Type?

The most effective way to determine your type is to take the Myers-Briggs Type Indicator. The material in this exercise will give you a good working framework that will enable you to obtain an informal determination of your own and other people's preferences. As you read the statements below, you will find that you agree with some strongly, some a little, and some not at all. You will also find that you may agree strongly with some of the statements attributed to, say, Extraverts, as well as some of those attributed to Introverts. This is quite natural. Each of us has some Extraversion and some Introversion, as well as some of each of the other six characteristics. What "typing" is all about is determining which alternatives you *prefer* to use.

This exercise looks at four pairs of preference alternatives. They are

1. Extraversion vs. Introversion
2. Sensing vs. Intuition
3. Thinking vs. Feeling
4. Judging vs. Perceiving

Mark each statement that is true for you.

Extraversion vs. Introversion

If you are an Extravert (E), you probably

___ Tend to talk first, think later, and do not know what you will say until you hear yourself say it; it is not uncommon for you to berate yourself with something like, "Will I *ever* learn to keep my mouth shut?"

___ Know a lot of people and count many of them as among your "close friends"; you like to include as many people as possible in your activities.

___ Do not mind reading or having a conversation while there is other activity going on (including conversation or television or radio) in the background; in fact, you may well be oblivious to this distraction.

___ Are approachable and easily engaged by friends, coworkers, and strangers, though perhaps somewhat dominating in a conversation.

___ Find telephone calls to be welcome interruptions; you do not hesitate to pick up the phone (or drop in on someone) whenever you have something to say.

___ Enjoy going to meetings and tend to let your opinion be heard; in fact, you feel frustrated if not given the opportunity to state your point of view.

___ Prefer generating ideas with a group than by yourself; you become drained if you spend too much time in reflective thinking without being able to bounce your thoughts off others.

___ Find listening more difficult than talking; you do not like to give up the limelight and often get bored when you cannot participate actively in a conversation.

___ "Look" with your mouth instead of your eyes—"I lost my glasses. Has anyone seen my glasses? They were here a minute ago"—and when you lose your train of thought, verbally "find" your way back—"Now what was I saying? I think it had something to do with this morning's meeting. Oh, yes, it was about what Harriet said."

___ Need affirmation from colleagues, superiors, and subordinates about who you are, what you do, how you look, and just about everything else; you may think you are doing a good job, but until you hear someone tell you, you do not truly believe it.

If you are an Introvert (I), you probably

____ Rehearse things before saying them and prefer that others would do the same; you often respond with "I'll have to think about that" or "Let me tell you later."

____ Enjoy the peace and quiet of having time to yourself; you find your private time too easily invaded and tend to adapt by developing a high power of concentration that can shut out nearby conversations, ringing telephones, and the like.

____ Are perceived as a "great listener" but feel that others take advantage of and run over you.

____ Have been called "shy" from time to time; whether or not you agree, you may come across to others as somewhat reserved and reflective.

____ Wish that you could get your ideas out more forcefully; you resent those who blurt out things you were just about to say.

____ Like stating your thoughts or feelings without interruption; you allow others to do the same in the hope that they will reciprocate when it comes time for you to speak.

____ Need to "recharge" alone after you have spent time in meetings, on the phone, or socializing; the more intense the encounter, the greater the chance you will feel drained afterward.

____ Were told by your parents to "go outside and play with your friends" when you were a child; your parents probably worried about you because you liked to be by yourself.

____ Believe that "talk is cheap"; you get suspicious if people are too complimentary or irritated if they repeat something that has already been said by someone else. The phrase "reinventing the wheel" may occur to you as you hear others chattering away.

Did you agree with more of the Extraverted statements than the Introverted ones? If so, enter "E" on the first line, below. If you agreed with more Introverted statements, enter "I."

E or I: _____

Sensor vs. Intuitive

If you are a Sensor (S), you probably

____ Prefer specific answers to specific questions; when you ask someone the time, you prefer "three fifty-two" and get irritated if the answer is "little before four" or "almost time to go."

____ Like to concentrate on what you are doing at the moment and generally do not wonder about what is next; moreover you would rather *do* something than think about it.

____ Find most satisfying those jobs that yield some tangible result; as much as you hate doing housekeeping, you would rather clean your desk than think about where your career is headed.

____ Believe that "if it ain't broke, don't fix it"; you do not understand why some people have to try to improve *everything*.

____ Would rather work with facts and figures than ideas and theories; you like to hear things sequentially instead of randomly.

____ Think that *fantasy* is a dirty word; you wonder about people who seem to spend too much time indulging their imagination.

____ Read magazines and reports from front to back; you do not understand why some people prefer to dive into them anywhere they please.

____ Get frustrated when people do not give you clear instructions or when someone says, "Here's the overall plan—we'll take care of the details later"; or worse, when you have heard clear instructions and others treat them as vague guidelines.

____ Are very literal in your use of words; you also take things literally and often find yourself asking, and being asked, "Are you serious or is that a joke?"

____ Find it easier to see the individual trees than the forest; at work you are happy to focus in on your own job or department and are not as concerned about how it fits into the larger scheme of things.

____ Subscribe to the notion that "seeing is believing"; if someone tells you "the mail is here," you know it really is not "here" until it lands on your desk.

If you are an Intuitive (N), you probably

____ Tend to think about several things at once; you are often accused by friends and colleagues of being absentminded.

____ Find the future and its possibilities more intriguing than frightening; you are usually more excited about where you are going than where you are.

____ Believe that "boring details" is a redundancy.

____ Believe that time is relative; no matter what the hour, you are not late unless the meeting/meal/event has started without you.

____ Like figuring out how things work just for the sheer pleasure of doing so.

____ Are prone to puns and word games (you may even do these things standing up).

___ Find yourself seeking the connections and interrelatedness behind most things rather than accepting them at face value; you are always asking "What does that *mean*?"

Did you agree with more of the Sensor statements than the Intuitive ones? If so, enter "S" on the line below. If you agreed with more Intuitive statements, enter "N."

S or N: _____

Thinking vs. Feeling

If you are a Thinker (T), you probably

___ Are able to stay cool, calm, and objective in situations when everyone else is upset.

___ Would rather settle a dispute based on what is fair and truthful than on what will make people happy.

___ Enjoy proving a point for the sake of clarity; it is not beyond you to argue both sides in a discussion simply to expand your intellectual horizons.

___ Are more firm-minded than gentle-hearted; if you disagree with people, you would rather tell them than say nothing and let them think they are right.

___ Pride yourself on your objectivity despite the fact that some people accuse you of being cold and uncaring; you know this could not be further from the truth.

___ Do not mind making difficult decisions and cannot understand why so many people get upset about things that are not relevant to the issue at hand.

___ Think it is more important to be right than liked; you do not believe it is necessary to like people in order to be able to work with them and do a good job.

___ Are impressed with and lend more credence to things that are logical and scientific; until you receive more information to justify MBTI's "typing" benefits, for example, you are skeptical about what it can do.

___ Remember numbers and figures more readily than faces and names.

If you are a Feeler (F), you probably

___ Consider a "good decision" one that takes others' feelings into account.

___ Feel that "love" cannot be defined; you take great offense at those who try to do so.

___ Will overextend yourself meeting other people's needs; you will do almost anything to accommodate others, even at the expense of your own comfort.

___ Put yourself in other people's moccasins; you are likely to be the one in a meeting who asks, "How will this affect the people involved?"

___ Enjoy providing needed services to people although you find that some people take advantage of you.

___ Find yourself wondering, "Doesn't anyone care about what *I* want" although you may have difficulty actually saying this to anyone.

___ Will not hesitate to take back something you have said that you perceive has offended someone; as a result you are accused of being wishy-washy.

___ Prefer harmony over clarity; you are embarrassed by conflict and will try either to avoid it ("Let's change the subject") or smother it ("Let's all shake hands and be friends").

Did you agree with more of the Thinking statements than the Feeling ones? If so, enter "T" on the line below. If you agreed with more Feeling statements, enter "F."

T or F: _____

Judging vs. Perceiving

If you are a Judger (J), you probably

___ Are always waiting for others, who never seem to be on time.

___ Have a place for everything and are not satisfied until everything is in its place. .

___ "Know" that if everyone would simply do what they are supposed to do (and when they are supposed to do it), the world would be a better place.

___ Wake up in the morning and know fairly well what your day is going to be like; you have a schedule and follow it and can become unraveled if things do not go as planned.

___ Do not like surprises, and make this well known to everyone.

___ Keep lists and use them; if you do something that is not on your list, you may even add it to the list just so you can cross it off.

___ Thrive on order; you have a special system for keeping things on your desk, in your files, and on your walls.

___ Are accused of being angry when you are not; you are only stating your opinion.

___ Like to work things through to completion and get them out of the way, even if you know you are going to have to do it over again later to get it right.

If you are a Perceiver (P), you probably

___ Are easily distracted; you can get "lost" between the front door and the car.

___ Love to explore the unknown, even if it is something as simple as a new route home from work.

___ Do not plan a task but wait and see what it demands; people accuse you of being disorganized, although you know better.

___ Have to depend on last-minute spurts of energy to meet your deadlines; you usually make the deadline, although you may drive everyone else crazy in the process.

___ Do not believe that "neatness counts," even though you would prefer to have things in order; what is important is creativity, spontaneity, and responsiveness.

___ Turn most work into play; if it cannot be made into fun, it probably is not worth doing.

___ Change the subject often in conversations; the new topic can be anything that enters your mind or walks into the room.

___ Do not like to be pinned down about most things; you would rather keep your options open.

___ Tend usually to make things less than definite from time to time, but not always—it depends.

Did you agree with more of the Judging statements than the Perceiving ones? If so, enter a "J" on the line below. If you agreed with more Perceiving statements, enter "P."

J or P: _____

Putting It Together

Now write the letter for each of your preferences in each of the spaces below as indicated:

E or I   S or N   T or F   J or P

_____   _____   _____   _____

You now have your four-letter profile. There are sixteen possible profiles. "ISTJ," for example, stands for an Introvert/Sensor/Thinker/Judger, whereas "ENFP" stands for "Extravert/Intuitive/Feeler/Perceiver. For a more detailed discussion on the implications of each MBTI type, see *Type Talk at Work* by Otto Kroeger and Janet M. Thuesen (Dell Publishing, 1992).

Appendix 2

Answers to
Selected Exercises

Suggested Responses to Exercises in Chapter 7

1. Declining an invitation is fair enough if it is really necessary, but you will not create an impression of warmth by doing so. Attending for nearly an hour shows you are making an effort to be friendly in spite of other plans; this compromise might work fine. But the answer that really builds alliances is b.

2. A busy supervising attorney may forget to mention this arrangement to the secretary. The secretary may already be having trouble keeping up with the workload. By giving the secretary several days warning as described in c, you are creating a new ally in the office.

3. It is the attorney's job—not yours—to address the judge in court. It is also the attorney's responsibility to answer for your presence at counsel table. Do not say anything to the judge unless the judge addresses you directly. Answer c is the best answer.

4. A senior managing partner expects a degree of formality and respect, but also a friendly greeting. Answer c balances these perfectly and further personalizes the greeting by addressing the partner by name.

5. Ending the awkward silence does everyone a favor and shows you are confident among your peers. But showing interest in the other person is the best way to form a new alliance, so answer b is the best answer. Discuss your own pursuits after the other person has had a chance to talk about his or hers.

6. Once again, a compromise is possible here. What you know about the case should be freely conveyed to Scott, but it should be done in a way that promotes a cooperative approach. Answer c is by far the best.

7. Never telephone a judge for advice. Calling an attorney from another office is permissible if he or she has already offered to help you and if you know this attorney fairly well, but taking the time of a lawyer you hardly know is presumptuous and it will probably be resented. Checking with the secretary is always a good idea, but court procedures change over time and so do the court's forms. Even if the secretary has a suggestion for you, it will need to be double-checked.

   The best answer is c: call the court clerk's office first. If you have established a good relationship with that office, this will be easy to do. If you have not established a relationship with that office, now is the time to begin doing so. By researching local statutes and court rules, you will eventually find the answer but, with no leads, research can take hours. Instead, use the books simply to confirm the clerk's advice, if necessary.

8. This scenario describes extremely inflammatory office politics—the kind that literally tears an office apart. Becoming personally involved is never a good idea unless it is necessary to defend your own work or career. Answer c is the best. Privately voicing support for Linda is tempting, but even this involves some risk to your reputation in the office. What if Linda inadvertently mentions your supportiveness to the wrong person?

9. Lawyers like paralegals who have the confidence to speak up when there is a problem the lawyer should know about. Lawyers also like paralegals who respect a lawyer's time. Answer 3 recognizes both factors. It alerts the lawyer to the fact that something has been missed and allows the lawyer to decide when the details should be discussed.

Answers to Question 1 in Chapter 8

	One-tenths	One-sixths
a.	.10	.10 (or .05 if rounding down)
b.	1.70	1.40
c.	.10	.10
d.	2.20	2.10
e.	.50	.30
f.	.70	.40
g.	.20	.10
h.	.40	.30
i.	1.30	1.20
j.	2.40	2.20
k.	.90	.50
l.	.30	.20
m.	.60	.40
n.	2.50	2.30
o.	.90	.50
p.	.60	.40 (or .30 if rounding down)

Appendix 3

Paralegal Codes of Ethics

CODE OF ETHICS AND PROFESSIONAL RESPONSIBILITY OF THE NATIONAL ASSOCIATION OF LEGAL ASSISTANTS, INC.

Preamble. A legal assistant must adhere strictly to the accepted standards of legal ethics and to the general principles of proper conduct. The performance of the duties of the legal assistant shall be governed by specific canons as defined herein so that justice will be served and goals of the profession attained. (See Model Standards and Guidelines for Utilization of Legal Assistants, Section II.)

The canons of ethics set forth hereafter are adopted by the National Association of Legal Assistants, Inc. as a general guide intended to aid legal assistants and attorneys. The enumeration of these rules does not mean there are not others of equal importance although not specifically mentioned. Court rules, agency rules and statutes must be taken into consideration when interpreting the canons.

Definition. Legal assistants, also known as paralegals, are a distinguishable group of persons who assist attorneys in the delivery of legal services. Through formal education, training and experience, legal assistants have knowledge and expertise regarding the legal system and substantive and procedural law which qualify them to do work of a legal nature under the supervision of an attorney.

Canon 1. A legal assistant must not perform any of the duties that attorneys only may perform nor take any actions that attorneys may not take.

Canon 2. A legal assistant may perform any task which is properly delegated and supervised by an attorney, as long as the attorney is ultimately responsible to the client, maintains a direct relationship with the client, and assumes professional responsibility

for the work product. (See NALA Model Standards and Guidelines, Section IV, Guideline 5.)

Canon 3. A legal assistant must not: (See NALA Model Standards and Guidelines, Section IV, Guideline 2.)

(a) engage in, encourage, or contribute to any act which could constitute the unauthorized practice of law; and

(b) establish attorney-client relationships, set fees, give legal opinions or advice, or represent a client before a court or agency unless so authorized by that court or agency; and

(c) engage in conduct or take any action which would assist or involve the attorney in a violation of professional ethics or give the appearance of professional impropriety.

Canon 4. A legal assistant must use discretion and professional judgment commensurate with knowledge and experience but must not render independent legal judgment in place of an attorney. The services of an attorney are essential in the public interest whenever such legal judgment is required. (See NALA Model Standards and Guidelines, Section IV, Guideline 3.)

Canon 5. A legal assistant must disclose his or her status as a legal assistant at the outset of any professional relationship with a client, attorney, a court or administrative agency or personnel thereof, or a member of the general public. A legal assistant must act prudently in determining the extent to which a client may be assisted without the presence of an attorney. (See NALA Model Standards and Guidelines, Section IV, Guideline 1.)

Canon 6. A legal assistant must strive to maintain integrity and a high degree of competency through education and training with respect to professional responsibility, local rules and practice, and through continuing education in substantive areas of law to better assist the legal profession in fulfilling its duty to provide legal service.

Canon 7. A legal assistant must protect the confidences of a client and must not violate any rule or statute now in effect or hereafter enacted controlling the doctrine of privileged communications between a client and an attorney. (See NALA Model Standards and Guidelines, Section IV, Guideline 1.)

Canon 8. A legal assistant must do all other things incidental, necessary, or expedient for the attainment of the ethics and responsibilities as defined by statute or rule of court.

Canon 9. A legal assistant's conduct is guided by bar associations' codes of professional responsibility and rules of professional conduct.

NATIONAL FEDERATION OF PARALEGAL ASSOCIATIONS, INC., MODEL CODE OF ETHICS AND PROFESSIONAL RESPONSIBILITY AND GUIDELINES FOR ENFORCEMENT

Preamble

The National Federation of Paralegal Associations, Inc. ("NFPA") is a professional organization comprised of paralegal associations and individual paralegals throughout the United States and Canada. Members of NFPA have varying backgrounds, experiences, education and job responsibilities that reflect the diversity of the paralegal professional. NFPA promotes the growth, development and recognition of the paralegal profession as an integral partner in the delivery of legal services.

In May 1993 NFPA adopted its Model Code of Ethics and Professional Responsibility ("Model Code") to delineate the principles for ethics and conduct to which every paralegal should aspire.

Many paralegal associations throughout the United States have endorsed the concept and content of NFPA's Model Code through the adoption of their own ethical codes. In doing so, paralegals have confirmed the profession's commitment to increase the quality and efficiency of legal services, as well as recognized its responsibilities to the public, the legal community, and colleagues.

Paralegals have recognized, and will continue to recognize, that the profession must continue to evolve to enhance their roles in the delivery of legal services. With increased levels of responsibility comes the need to define and enforce mandatory rules of professional conduct. Enforcement of codes of paralegal conduct is a logical and necessary step to enhance and ensure the confidence of the legal community and the public in the integrity and professional responsibility of paralegals.

In April 1997 NFPA adopted the Model Disciplinary Rules ("Model Rules") to make possible the enforcement of the Canons and Ethical Considerations contained in the NFPA Model Code. A concurrent determination was made that the Model Code of Ethics and Professional Responsibility, formerly aspirational in nature, should be recognized as setting forth the enforceable obligations of all paralegals.

The Model Code and Model Rules offer a framework for professional discipline, either voluntarily or through formal regulatory programs.

§1. NFPA MODEL DISCIPLINARY RULES AND ETHICAL CONSIDERATIONS

1.1 A paralegal shall achieve and maintain a high level of competence.

Ethical Considerations

EC-1.1(a)   A paralegal shall achieve competency through education, training, and work experience.

EC-1.1(b)   A paralegal shall participate in continuing education in order to keep informed of current legal, technical and general developments.

EC-1.1(c)   A paralegal shall perform all assignments promptly and efficiently.

1.2 A paralegal shall maintain a high level of personal and professional integrity.

Ethical Considerations

EC-1.2(a)   A paralegal shall not engage in any ex parte communications involving the courts or any other adjudicatory body in an attempt to exert undue influence or to obtain advantage or the benefit of only one party.

EC-1.2(b)   A paralegal shall not communicate, or cause another to communicate, with a party the paralegal knows to be represented by a lawyer in a pending matter without the prior consent of the lawyer representing such other party.

EC-1.2(c)   A paralegal shall ensure that all time-keeping and billing records prepared by the paralegal are thorough, accurate, honest, and complete.

EC-1.2(d)   A paralegal shall not knowingly engage in fraudulent billing practices. Such practices may include, but are not limited to: inflation of hours billed to a client or employer; misrepresentation of the nature of tasks performed; and/or submission of fraudulent expense and disbursement documentation.

EC-1.2(e) A paralegal shall be scrupulous, thorough and honest in the identification and maintenance of all funds, securities, and other assets of a client and shall provide accurate accounting as appropriate.

EC-1.2(f) A paralegal shall advise the proper authority of non-confidential knowledge of any dishonest or fraudulent acts by any person pertaining to the handling of the funds, securities or other assets of a client. The authority to whom the report is made shall depend on the nature and circumstances of the possible misconduct, (e.g., ethics committees of law firms, corporations and/or paralegal associations, local or state bar associations, local prosecutors, administrative agencies, etc.). Failure to report such knowledge is in itself misconduct and shall be treated as such under these rules.

1.3 A paralegal shall maintain a high standard of professional conduct.

Ethical Considerations

EC-1.3(a) A paralegal shall refrain from engaging in any conduct that offends the dignity and decorum of proceedings before a court or other adjudicatory body and shall be respectful of all rules and procedures.

EC-1.3(b) A paralegal shall avoid impropriety and the appearance of impropriety and shall not engage in any conduct that would adversely affect his/her fitness to practice. Such conduct may include, but is not limited to: violence, dishonesty, interference with the administration of justice, and/or abuse of a professional position or public office.

EC-1.3(c) Should a paralegal's fitness to practice be compromised by physical or mental illness, causing that paralegal to commit an act that is in direct violation of the Model Code/Model Rules and/or the rules and/or laws governing the jurisdiction in which the paralegal practices, that paralegal may be protected from sanction upon review of the nature and circumstances of that illness.

EC-1.3(d) A paralegal shall advise the proper authority of non-confidential knowledge of any action of another legal professional that clearly demonstrates fraud, deceit, dishonesty, or misrepresentation. The authority to whom the report is made shall depend on the nature and circumstances of the possible misconduct, (e.g., ethics committees of law firms, corporations and/or paralegal associations, local or state bar associations, local prosecutors, administrative agencies, etc.). Failure to report such knowledge is in itself misconduct and shall be treated as such under these rules.

EC-1.3(e) A paralegal shall not knowingly assist any individual with the commission of an act that is in direct violation of the Model Code/Model Rules and/or the rules and/or laws governing the jurisdiction in which the paralegal practices.

EC-1.3(f) If a paralegal possesses knowledge of future criminal activity, that knowledge must be reported to the appropriate authority immediately.

1.4 A paralegal shall serve the public interest by contributing to the delivery of quality legal services and the improvement of the legal system.

Ethical Considerations

EC-1.4(a) A paralegal shall be sensitive to the legal needs of the public and shall promote the development and implementation of programs that address those needs.

EC-1.4(b) A paralegal shall support bona fide efforts to meet the need for legal services by those unable to pay reasonable or customary fees for example, participation in pro bono projects and volunteer work.

EC-1.4(c) A paralegal shall support efforts to improve the legal system and access thereto and shall assist in making changes.

1.5 A paralegal shall preserve all confidential information provided by the client or acquired from other sources before, during, and after the course of the professional relationship.

Ethical Considerations

EC-1.5(a) A paralegal shall be aware of and abide by all legal authority governing confidential information in the jurisdiction in which the paralegal practices.

EC-1.5(b) A paralegal shall not use confidential information to the disadvantage of the client.

EC-1.5(c) A paralegal shall not use confidential information to the advantage of the paralegal or of a third person.

EC-1.5(d) A paralegal may reveal confidential information only after full disclosure and with the client's written consent; or, when required by law or court order; or, when necessary to prevent the client from committing an act that could result in death or serious bodily harm.

EC-1.5(e) A paralegal shall keep those individuals responsible for the legal representation of a client fully informed of any confidential information the paralegal may have pertaining to that client.

EC-1.5(f) A paralegal shall not engage in any indiscreet communications concerning clients.

1.6 A paralegal shall avoid conflicts of interest and shall disclose any possible conflict to the employer or client, as well as to the prospective employers or clients.

Ethical Considerations

EC-1.6(a) A paralegal shall act within the bounds of the law, solely for the benefit of the client, and shall be free of compromising influences and loyalties. Neither the paralegal's personal or business interest, nor those of other clients or third persons, should compromise the paralegal's professional judgment and loyalty to the client.

EC-1.6(b) A paralegal shall avoid conflicts of interest that may arise from previous assignments, whether for a present or past employer or client.

EC-1.6(c) A paralegal shall avoid conflict of interest that may arise from family relationships and from personal and business interests.

EC-1.6(d) In order to be able to determine whether an actual or potential conflict of interest exists a paralegal shall create and maintain an effective recordkeeping system that identifies clients, matters, and parties with which the paralegal has worked.

EC-1.6(e) A paralegal shall reveal sufficient non-confidential information about a client or former client to reasonably ascertain if an actual or potential conflict of interest exists.

EC-1.6(f) A paralegal shall not participate in or conduct work on any matter where a conflict of interest has been identified.

EC-1.6(g) In matters where a conflict of interest has been identified and the client consents to continued representation, a paralegal shall comply fully with the implementation and maintenance of an Ethical Wall.

1.7 A paralegal's title shall be fully disclosed.

Ethical Considerations

EC-1.7(a) A paralegal's title shall clearly indicate the individual's status and shall be disclosed in all business and professional communications to avoid misunderstanding and misconceptions about the paralegal's role and responsibilities.

EC-1.7(b) A paralegal's title shall be included if the paralegal's name appears on business cards, letterhead, brochures, directories, and advertisements.

EC-1.7(c) A paralegal shall not use letterhead, business cards or other promotional materials to create a fraudulent impression of his/her status or ability to practice in the jurisdiction in which the paralegal practices.

EC-1.7(d) A paralegal shall not practice under color of any record, diploma, or certificate that has been illegally or fraudulently obtained or issued or which is misrepresentative in any way.

EC-1.7(e) A paralegal shall not participate in the creation, issurance, or dissemination of fraudulent records, diplomas, or certificates.

1.8 A paralegal shall not engage in the unauthorized practice of law.

Ethical Considerations

EC-1.8(a) A paralegal shall comply with the applicable legal authority governing the unauthorized practice of law in the jurisdiction in which the paralegal practices.

§2 NFPA GUIDELINES FOR THE ENFORCEMENT OF THE MODEL CODE OF ETHICS AND PROFESSIONAL RESPONSIBILITY

2.1 Basis for discipline

2.1(a) Disciplinary investigations and proceedings brought under the authority of the Rules shall be conducted in accord with obligations imposed on the paralegal professional by the Model Code of Ethics and Professional Responsibility.

2.2 Structure of disciplinary committee

2.2(a) The Disciplinary Committee ("Committee") shall be made up of nine (9) members including the Chair.

2.2(b) Each member of the Committee, including any temporary replacement members, shall have demonstrated working knowledge of ethics/professional responsibility-related issues and activities.

2.2(c) The Committee shall represent a cross-section of practice areas and work experience. The following recommendations are made regarding the members of the Committee.

1) At least one paralegal with one to three years of law-related work experience.
2) At least one paralegal with five to seven years of law-related work experience.
3) At least one paralegal with over ten years of law-related work experience.
4) One paralegal educator with five to seven years of work experience; preferably in the area of ethics/professional responsibility.
5) One paralegal manager.
6) One lawyer with five to seven years of law-related work experience.
7) One law member.

2.2(d) The Chair of the Committee shall be appointed within thirty (30) days of its members' induction. The Chair shall have no fewer than ten (10) years of law-related work experience.

2.2(e) The terms of all members of the Committee shall be staggered. Of those members initially appointed, a simple majority plus one shall be appointed to a term of one year, and the remaining members shall be appointed to a term of two years. Thereafter, all members of the Committee shall be appointed to terms of two years.

2.2(f) If for any reason the terms of a majority of the Committee will expire at the same time, members may be appointed to terms of one year to maintain continuity of the Committee.

2.2(g) The Committee shall organize from its members a three-tiered structure to investigate, prosecute and/or adjudicate charges of misconduct. The members shall be rotated among the tiers.

2.3 Operation of Committee

2.3(a) The Committee shall meet on an as-needed basis to discuss, investigate, and/or adjudicate alleged violations of the Model Code/Model Rules.

2.3(b) A majority of the members of the Committee present at a meeting shall constitute a quorum.

2.3(c) A Recording Secretary shall be designated to maintain complete and accurate minutes of all Committee meetings. All such minutes shall be kept confidential until a decision has been made that the matter will be set for hearing as set forth in Section 6.1 below.

2.3(d) If any member of the Committee has a conflict of interest with the Charging Party, the Responding Party, or the allegations of misconduct, that member shall not take part in any hearing or deliberations concerning those allegations. If the absence of that member creates a lack of a quorum for the Committee, then a temporary replacement for that member shall be appointed.

2.3(e) Either the Charging Party or the Responding Party may request that, for good cause shown, any member of the Committee not participate in a hearing or deliberation. All such requests shall be honored. If the absence of a Committee member under those circumstances creates a lack of a quorum for the Committee, then a temporary replacement for that member shall be appointed.

2.3(f) All discussions and correspondence of the Committee shall be kept confidential until a decision has been made that the matter will be set for hearing as set forth in Section 6.1 below.

2.3(g) All correspondence from the Committee to the Responding Party regarding any charge of misconduct and any decisions made regarding the charge shall be mailed certified mail, return receipt requested, to the Responding Party's last known address and shall be clearly marked with a "Confidential" designation.

2.4 Procedure for the reporting of alleged violations of the Model Code/Disciplinary Rules

2.4(a) An individual or entity in possession of non-confidential knowledge or information concerning possible instances of misconduct shall make a confidential written report to the Committee within thirty (30) days of obtaining same. This report shall include all details of the alleged misconduct.

2.4(b) The Committee so notified shall inform the Responding Party of the allegation(s) of misconduct no later than ten (10) business days after receiving the confidential written report from the Charging Party.

2.4(c)   Notification to the Responding Party shall include the identity of the Charging Party, unless, for good cause shown, the Charging Party requests anonymity.

2.4(d)   The Responding Party shall reply to the allegations within ten (10) business days of notification.

2.5   Procedure for the Investigation of a Charge of Misconduct

2.5(a)   Upon receipt of a Charge of Misconduct ("Charge"), or on its own initiative, the Committee shall initiate an investigation.

2.5(b)   If, upon initial or preliminary review, the Committee makes a determination that the charges are either without basis in fact or, if proven, would not constitute professional misconduct, the Committee shall dismiss the allegations of misconduct. If such determination of dismissal cannot be made, a formal investigation shall be initiated.

2.5(c)   Upon the decision to conduct a formal investigation, the Committee shall:

1) mail to the Charging and Responding Parties within three (3) business days of that decision notice of the commencement of a formal investigation. That notification shall be in writing and shall contain a complete explanation of all Charge(s), as well as the reasons for a formal investigation and shall cite the applicable codes and rules;

2) allow the Responding Party thirty (30) days to prepare and submit a confidential response to the Committee, which response shall address each charge specifically and shall be in writing; and

3) upon receipt of the response to the notification, have thirty (30) days to investigate the Charge(s). If an extension of time is deemed necessary, that extension shall not exceed ninety (90) days.

2.5(d)   Upon conclusion of the investigation, the Committee may:

1) dismiss the Charge upon the finding that it has no basis in fact;

2) dismiss the Charge upon the finding that, if proven, the Charge would not constitute Misconduct;

3) refer the matter for hearing by the Tribunal; or

4) in the case of criminal activity, refer the Charge(s) and all investigation results to the appropriate authority.

2.6   Procedure for a Misconduct Hearing Before a Tribunal

2.6(a)   Upon the decision by the Committee that a matter should be heard, all parties shall be notified and a hearing date shall be set. The hearing shall take place no more than thirty (30) days from the conclusion of the formal investigation.

2.6(b)   The Responding Party shall have the right to counsel. The parties and the Tribunal shall have the right to call any witnesses and introduce any documentation that they believe will lead to the fair and reasonable resolution of the matter.

2.6(c)   Upon completion of the hearing, the Tribunal shall deliberate and present a written decision to the parties in accordance with procedures as set forth by the Tribunal.

2.6(d)   Notice of the decision of the Tribunal shall be appropriately published.

2.7   Sanctions

2.7(a)   Upon a finding of the Tribunal that misconduct has occurred, any of the following sanctions, or others as may be deemed appropriate, may be imposed upon the Responding Party, either singularly or in combination:

1) letter of reprimand to the Responding Party; counseling;

2) attendance at an ethics course approved by the Tribunal; probation;

3) suspension of license/authority to practice; revocation of license/authority to practice;

4) imposition of a fine; assessment of costs; or

5) in the instance of criminal activity, referral to the appropriate authority.

2.7(b)   Upon the expiration of any period of probation, suspension, or revocation, the Responding Party may make application for reinstatement. With the application for reinstatement, the Responding Party must show proof of having complied with all aspects of the sanctions imposed by the Tribunal.

2.8   Appellate Procedures

2.8(a)   The parties shall have the right to appeal the decision of the Tribunal in accordance with the procedure as set forth by the Tribunal.

Definitions

Appellate Body means a body established to adjudicate an appeal to any decision made by a Tribunal or other decision-making body with respect to formally-heard Charges of Misconduct.

Charge of Misconduct means a written submission by any individual or entity to an ethics committee, paralegal association, bar association, law enforcement agency, judicial body, government agency, or other appropriate body or entity, that sets forth non-confidential information regarding any instance of alleged misconduct by an individual paralegal or paralegal entity.

Charging Party means any individual or entity who submits a Charge of Misconduct against an individual paralegal or paralegal entity.

Competency means the demonstration of: diligence, education, skill, and mental, emotional, and physical fitness reasonably necessary for the performance of paralegal services.

Confidential Information means information relating to a client, whatever its source, that is not public knowledge nor available to the public. (**Non-Confidential Information** would generally include the name of the client and the identity of the matter for which the paralegal provided services.)

Disciplinary Committee means any committee that has been established by an entity such as a paralegal association, bar association, judicial body, or government agency to: (a) identify, define and investigate general ethical considerations and concerns with respect to paralegal practice; (b) administer and enforce the Model Code and Model Rules and; (c) discipline any individual paralegal or paralegal entity found to be in violation of same.

Disciplinary Hearing means the confidential proceeding conducted by a committee or other designated body or entity concerning any instance of alleged misconduct by an individual paralegal or paralegal entity.

Disclose means communication of information reasonably sufficient to permit identification of the significance of the matter in question.

Ethical Wall means the screening method implemented in order to protect a client from a conflict of interest. An Ethical Wall generally includes, but is not limited to, the following elements: (1) prohibit the paralegal from having any connection with the matter; (2) ban discussions with or the transfer of documents to or from the parale-gal; (3) restrict access to files; and (4) educate all members of the firm, corporation, or entity as to the separation of the paralegal (both organizationally and physically) from the pending matter. For more information regarding the Ethical Wall, see the NFPA publication entitled "The Ethical Wall—Its Application to Paralegals."

Ex parte means actions or communications conducted at the instance and for the benefit of one party only, and without notice to, or contestation by, any person adversely interested.

Investigation means the investigation of any charge(s) of misconduct filed against an individual paralegal or paralegal entity by a Committee.

Letter of Reprimand means a written notice of formal censure or severe reproof administered to an individual paralegal or paralegal entity for unethical or improper conduct.

Misconduct means the knowing or unknowing commission of an act that is in direct violation of those Canons and Ethical Considerations of any and all applicable codes and/or rules of conduct.

Paralegal is synonymous with **Legal Assistant** and is defined as a person qualified through education, training, or work experience to perform substantive legal work that requires knowledge of legal concepts and is customarily, but not exclusively performed by a lawyer. This person may be retained or employed by a lawyer, law office, governmental agency, or other entity or may be authorized by administrative, statutory, or court authority to perform this work.

Proper Authority means the local paralegal association, the local or state bar association, Committee(s) of the local paralegal or bar association(s), local prosecutor, administrative agency, or other tribunal empowered to investigate or act upon an instance of alleged misconduct.

Responding Party means an individual paralegal or paralegal entity against whom a Charge of Misconduct has been submitted.

Revocation means the recision of the license, certificate or other authority to practice of an individual paralegal or paralegal entity found in violation of those Canons and Ethical Considerations of any and all applicable codes and/or rules of conduct.

Suspension means the suspension of the license, certificate or other authority to practice of an individual paralegal or paralegal entity found in violation of those Canons and Ethical Considerations of any and all applicable codes and/or rules of conduct.

Tribunal means the body designated to adjudicate allegations of misconduct.

Index